MILL AND MANSION

Lowell ca. 1833, as Seen from across the Merrimack

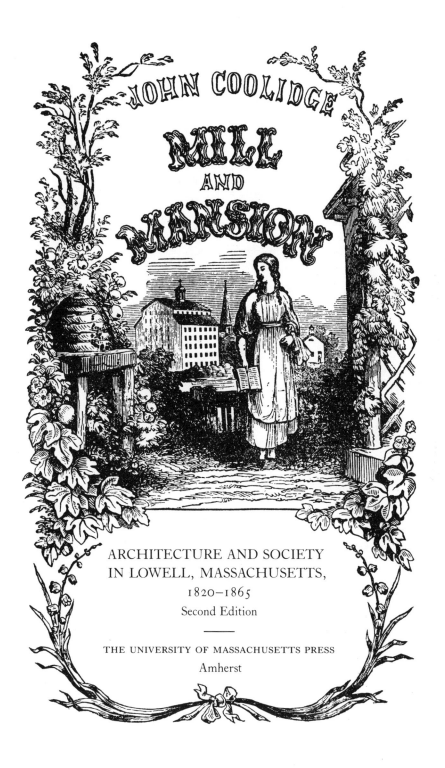

JOHN COOLIDGE

MILL AND MANSION

ARCHITECTURE AND SOCIETY
IN LOWELL, MASSACHUSETTS,
1820–1865

Second Edition

—

THE UNIVERSITY OF MASSACHUSETTS PRESS

Amherst

Copyright © 1942 by Columbia University Press
This edition is published by arrangement with Columbia University Press
Preface to the Second Edition, copyright © 1993 by
The University of Massachusetts Press
Printed in the United States of America
LC 92–14978
ISBN 0–87023–819-1

Library of Congress Cataloging-in-Publication Data

Coolidge, John, 1913–
    Mill and mansion : a study of architecture and society in Lowell,
  Massachusetts, 1820–1865 / John Coolidge. — 2nd ed.
    p.   cm.
Originally published: New York : Columbia University Press, c1942.
Includes bibliographical references and index.
ISBN 0–87023–819-1 (pbk. : alk. paper)
  1. Architecture—Massachusetts—Lowell. 2. Architecture,
Modern—19th century—Massachusetts—Lowell. 3. Lowell, Mass.—
Buildings, structures, etc. 4. Lowell, Mass.—History, I. Title.
NA735.L9C6   1992
720'.9744'4—dc20   92–14978
                                                        CIP

British Library Cataloguing in Publication data are available.

This book is published with the support and cooperation of the University
of Massachusetts at Boston.

To

M. W. C. *and* M. E. C.

PREFACE TO THE
SECOND EDITION

WHEN THIS book appeared originally, Lowell was the shell of a nine-teenth-century industrial city.[1] It had been created for the manufacture of textiles, but by the late 1930's this activity had largely moved south and nothing had fully replaced it. Forty percent of the population was dependent on government relief, in one way or another.[2] The factories were largely empty, but the city was architecturally intact.

Since then many important buildings have been torn down, but Lowell is lively again. It has been resurrected by the city's development as a somewhat unstable center of high technology and by the creation here of both a state and federal urban park,[3] which together attract some 850,000 visitors to the city every year.[4] The population, which declined from 112,759 in 1920 to 91,177 in 1975, has increased to 103,493, according to the census of 1990.[5] Meanwhile, many of the structures that accounted for national interest in the city are gone. This combination of dramatic economic revival and architectural loss justify the republication of this book.

Lowell did not start as an up-country mill village. It was conceived, if not fully planned, as a city with enough controlled space near the factories to accommodate bourgeois houses, shops, churches, schools, at least one hotel, and, soon, one of the earliest railroad terminals in the country. The settlement quickly became a town and, shortly thereafter, a city. Thus, however important they were economically, the mill complexes were never meant to exist in isolation although that is how—and admirably so—the National Park Service presents them.

I hope this republished book will recall the important buildings that

have been destroyed, central as they were both historically and phys-
ically. Thereby it will complement the image presented today. In addition, this preface will take notice of a few of the most important
structures built in the center of the city since the Civil War. These will
inevitably pique the curiosity of some tourists and students. The structures are unavoidable; they do merit attention. The way they and the
mills together constitute the core of a late nineteenth-century industrial
city needs to be pointed out. The remainder of this preface will,
therefore, be an overview of Lowell's social, economic, and architectural history since the Civil War.

In retrospect, it seems curious that the founders of the Merrimack
Manufacturing Company, who planned so carefully for the welfare of
the employees in their mills, gave little thought to the day laborers who
would dig the canals and erect those mills. Perhaps they imagined that
unskilled and semi-skilled workers would turn up as needed to dig the
canals and lay the bricks and then conveniently move on when those jobs
were accomplished.

Turn up they did, and so opportunely that one wonders if the event
was as fortuitous as Lowell's history books would have it. On April 6,
1822, an Irish immigrant, Hugh Cummiskey, led a score or more of
his compatriots from Boston to Lowell—thirty miles along the Middlesex Canal towpath. They were met by Kirk Boott. He provided the
means for them to refresh themselves and then hired them to widen and
deepen the Merrimack Canal.[6]

Move on they did not, or not right away. Further digging and
building were required as new mills were started. Chapter IV notes how
the Irish settled themselves on a limited site ceded to them by the Locks
& Canals Company. The community was at first known as "Paddy
Camps," then "New Dublin," and, finally, "The Acre."[7]

Such was Lowell's success that by the 1840's, rival entrepreneurs had
established large mills in several other cities. Competition began to
reduce everyone's profits. Management decided to lower wages rather
than the dividends it paid. Labor conditions deteriorated and Yankee
farm girls lost interest in working in the mills. The jobs they abandoned

were quickly taken over by Irish women.[8] Irish men found it more difficult to obtain employment in the mills and moved from their initial unskilled jobs into other activities such as retailing and, after the middle of the century, politics.[9] In 1882, John Donovan became the first Irish mayor of Lowell; in the same year, the notorious Benjamin F. Butler was the first Lowell resident to be elected governor of the state.

The first French-Canadian family to settle in Lowell arrived in 1841. It was followed by others, especially after the Civil War.[10] Then came Greeks, Portuguese, Jews, and a diversity of foreign groups, including Hispanics and Southeast Asians in recent years.[11] Whereas the population of Lowell in the 1820's consisted of Yankees and a few English or Scottish engineers, by the end of the century 72 percent of the population was made up of immigrants and the children of immigrants. This made Lowell fourth among American cities in its proportion of foreign-born residents, less than a percentage point behind New York.[12]

The change in the nature of the population proved decisive for the city as we know it today. As Peter Blewett has written: "Lowell is more of a product of the immigrants than it is of the city's enshrined heroes, Kirk Boott, Nathan Appleton, Theodore Edson, or the famous mill girls."[13]

All historians recognize there have been shifts in the ethnic composition of Lowell's population. But no one has examined in detail how they took place. Not every immigrant liked Lowell and remained. Even Hugh Cummiskey left, but after a few years he returned and settled permanently. In general we know something of arrivals, but almost nothing of departures. For example, in 1985 the population of Lowell included 600 Asians and some 4,600 Hispanics. In 1990, the estimates were some 11,600 Asians and 10,500 Hispanics, a total gain of 17,000.[14] But according to the Census Bureau, the population of Lowell increased by only about 12,000 during those five years. Does this discrepancy mean that 5,000 former residents of Lowell departed? If so, who were they? Or does it mean that the total population was grossly miscounted in one or both censuses?

Immigrants were attracted to Lowell by the prospect of higher earnings. Most of them wished to transplant their inherited culture. A large proportion learned but little English. At the end of the nineteenth century, when the administrators of a mill wished to give a written announcement to their employees, the document had to be written in eleven languages.[15] Today that is no longer necessary. Although the number of ethnic groups has increased, there is greater, more thorough knowledge of English. The Lowell school system must have played an important part in this impressive achievement.[16]

Because the desire to transport one's own culture was virtually universal, the behavior of newly arrived groups seems fairly predictable. Each wave sought to live in its own distinct area, and Lowell became a patchwork of ethnically defined districts. Each sought its own diet, so specialized grocery stores and restaurants were soon established. Saloons, or their counterpart, came next. Almost immediately the group sought its own church, though buying or erecting a building so that services could be held in any given language took time and sometimes involved contention. Separate public schools were often set up. Also important were ethnically individual charitable organizations. These provided welcome to new arrivals, succor to those in need, and a suitable opportunity for the successful to make others aware of their achievements.[17]

Early American and European accounts of Lowell emphasized its success as an ideal industrial community. Revising that picture, recent research has brought to light recurrent friction between labor and management from the 1830's onward. There are, in addition, records of occasional ugly battles between the Yankees and the Irish, between rival factions within a single national group, and between diverse ethnic groups.[18] The degree to which each of these communities has maintained its coherence is remarkable. Marriages between members of different groups were rare before World War II and are not yet common.[19]

But "a new appreciation of the vitality that diverse cultural groups bring to a city" has been achieved.[20] Ethnic identities are a source of pride. The annual summer festival offers an opportunity for competing musical and culinary folk celebrations. Every year the occasion attracts tens of thousands of visitors. In these respects, Lowell is in no way unique among our cities. Yet domestic peace is often taken far too much for granted. One has but to consider the contemporary scene to realize how remarkable it has been for varied and often jealous ethnic groups to live for a great many years in such freedom and harmony within one small locality.

The effects of discharging the skilled employees during the Civil War and the success of cotton mills in New England seaports such as Fall River and New Bedford reduced Lowell's national standing in the manufacture of textiles.[21] Competition from mills in the south beginning in the 1890's was to destroy Lowell's textile base altogether.[22]

But the dismantling of Lowell's textile corporations proved long and complex. It began during the teens with the disappearance of fringe operations, such as the production of carpets and of cotton manufacturing machinery.[23] Nineteen twenty-three was a prosperous year; all the mills that had been established a hundred years earlier were still running.[24] The following year was a disaster. In effect, the Great Depression began in Lowell five years before the stock market crashed.[25] In 1919, 18,000 people worked at cotton manufacturing in Lowell. In 1936, the number was less than 3,000. By the later 1930's, only three of the original textile corporations remained in operation.[26]

World War II interrupted the recession temporarily. War industries built new factories and when war contracts expired, the factories were occupied, at least for a few years, by other industries. But soon these too departed. Nothing fundamental had changed the process of decline that had begun in the 1920's. The textile industry was still the largest employer, with 4,000 workers in 1974. In March 1976, Lowell had an unemployment rate of 10.1 percent, which was two points higher than the national rate, and this despite the fact that the city's population had declined by one-fifth in the preceding two decades.[27]

The three survivors of the original textile mills closed down during the 1940's and 1950's. The failure of the Merrimack Manufacturing Company, first chartered in 1822, was particularly drawn out. The firm did not cease production completely until January 1, 1954, and the mill yard was destroyed between 1958 and 1962.[28] It is tragic that its entire plant, complete with its original housing, was torn down.[29] This left thirty acres of empty land between the city hall and the river. In the course of a few years, half the core of the city had become a wasteland.

"When she wrote her portrait of Lowell in 1940 Margaret Terrell Parker concluded that . . . barring change from outside, Lowell was doomed."[30] Ironically the source of that change might have been surmised during the years when Parker and I were gathering the information for our books. Effectively, the federal government entered Lowell's history with the establishment of the Lowell Housing Authority (LHA) in January 1937.[31] The remarkable individuals who have represented Lowell in Congress deserve primary credit for the varied grants that Lowell has received from the federal government.[32]

"The history of the Lowell Housing Authority, in all honesty, has been a stormy one." Among the first to be started, in the fifty-five years of its existence, the LHA has replaced or remodeled more than 10 percent of the city's dwellings.[33] Its achievement has suffered from one curious limitation. Federal building grants must be awarded to the lowest bidder. Although Lowell firms competed, it is puzzling, especially during the earlier years of the LHA, how rarely they won contracts, either to supply material or to construct the buildings.[34] It is easy to imagine how counterproductive the whole procedure appeared: "outsiders" from Washington were telling Lowell's citizens how they should be housed, expropriating their land, hiring other outsiders to tear down and disrupt at least part of one of the communities, and then bringing in yet more strangers to design and build the kind of house they liked.

Julie Leney notes: "After the passage of the Housing Act, the main hindrance to a three-million-dollar project for Lowell was the need for enabling legislation in the state of Massachusetts." By a special effort this was passed and signed before the federal deadline of July 1, 1938. The site selected for the first low-cost housing project was unquestionably congested and one of the city's worst fire hazards; it was also the heart of the Greek-American district. Opposition was intense. The two Greek archbishops concerned took opposing sides. The president of the

Massachusetts Real Estate Association characterized the project as a "Spawn of Moscow."[35] Nonetheless, the LHA won their case and by 1941 the prevailing wooden three-deckers had been replaced by thirty-five carefully landscaped brick buildings. There was no shortage of potential tenants.

The war intervened, but when work resumed the project included two new features. In the late 1950's, the needs of the elderly began to be addressed. But as projects for them were completed, some people came to feel that the idea of an "old people's home" implied unfortunate discrimination. Moreover, building new dwellings in large groups was likely to damage or destroy existing communities and there was no assurance that they would be replaced with another coherent social entity. In view of this criticism, the practices of the LHA have changed. Emphasis has shifted to the rehabilitation of single dwellings scattered throughout the city.[36] This remains the dominant strategy at present.

Nonetheless, five projects, each involving more than a hundred dwellings, have been completed since the war. Some former mills have been converted to housing; for example, the Francis Gatehouse Mill was adapted in 1977 and the Arthur E. Kenfield Manor, in 1980.

The improvement of Lowell's low-cost housing was an early sign of what was to become the city's general revival. The total achievement was the result of an extraordinary change in morale. Countless people were responsible for effecting the change.[37] Enough time may not have elapsed to evaluate objectively their individual contributions. Nevertheless, despite the risk of involuntary unfairness to individuals, I must attempt to tell the story.

Patrick Mogan was one prominent player.[38] He grew up in a close-knit, Gaelic-speaking neighborhood in Norwood, Massachusetts. That community gradually disintegrated and by the time Mogan reached early manhood, it had disappeared, to the disappointment of many who had known it. Mogan graduated from Boston College, completed military service, and then decided to become a school teacher. After serving in several smaller communities, he joined the Lowell school system in 1951. Eventually he rose to be its superintendent. In the course of his work he became appalled at the city's pervasive depression and, recalling Norwood, feared for the fate of Lowell's ethnic communities. He became convinced that the city's future lay in an awareness of its past and in the creation of an Urban Park Program. Lowell's association with the textile industry could bring its past into focus. An Urban National Cultural Park would provide a comprehensive vehicle for community development.[39]

According to the National Park Service, "the initiative to establish the park began in the early 1960's when a Model Cities community group proposed the revitalization of Lowell through the rediscovery of its heritage."[40] By the early 1970's the city's upcoming sesquicentennial and the approaching national bicentennial made it appropriate to act soon. In 1972 both the City Council and the Greater Lowell Chamber of Commerce passed strong enabling resolutions.

These events happily coincided with Massachusetts' concern with the smaller cities of the Commonwealth. Governor Michael Dukakis proposed eight urban parks and in 1974, Lowell became the first in the series.[41] This status was to bring the city millions of dollars in state funds, which were used to restore the waterway system, as both a means of recreation and a historic monument. Included in the effort was a small museum dedicated to water power. This was set up by the state, though it is now being operated by the National Park Service.[42]

In 1972 Representative F. Bradford Morse introduced a bill to make Lowell a national park. The bill was furthered by his successors, especially Paul Tsongas. They claimed that "for a state and a nation about to rediscover its identity through the Bicentennial of the political revolution, Lowell is the most important illustration of the industrial revolution—in its canal system, mills and ethnic cultural heritage."[43] Congress acted favorably on June 5, 1978, and Lowell embodied the first Urban National Park.[44]

Meanwhile, a bewildering succession of committees and commissions (some chaired by Patrick Mogan) worked to obtain other grants of public money and saw to it that all moved toward a single end: the rehabilitation of the center of the city.[45] From the beginning there was a widespread awareness of how much collaboration this would involve: "The concept adopted at Lowell provides for a historical/cultural park in an urban environment, with a unique partnership between federal, state and local governments and the private sector."[46] Arthur Robbins, the experienced developer who built Lowell's new Hilton Hotel, gave a most impressive testimony to the city's success: "I have never seen a place that has as successful a combination of public and private effort as you."[47]

Concurrently, Lowell began to develop as a center of high technology. In 1976 Wang Laboratories, which already had a plant for manufacturing computers in Tewkesbury, was looking for additional space. An Wang, founder and chief executive officer, was attracted by a handsome building in Lowell that had been designed by Minoru Yamasaki for CBS Electronics. This was surrounded by sixteen acres of land on which his company could expand. He decided to move the headquarters to Lowell and maintain the manufacturing in Tewkesbury. He writes in his autobiography:

Our move to Lowell coincided with our most explosive period of growth. Before we moved in, the unemployment rate [in Lowell] was about 15 percent at a time when the rate in the state was 9 percent. . . . The figure is now [1986] about 3 percent which is lower than the figures for Massachusetts and the nation. We are the largest employer in the community; moreover, a good percent of the increase in employment came from businesses that sprang up to service the large influx of people and money that accompanied our expansion. . . .

The city realized it needed a major hotel in the downtown area if Lowell was to attract national and international corporations. Because the area was still run-down, however, there was difficulty finding the financing for the Hilton which the town wanted to bring in. . . . I decided to move our training center from leased space in Burlington, Massachusetts, to a new building we would build in downtown Lowell. Because people would be coming from all over the country to use our center they would need a hotel to stay in while in Lowell. With this commitment, the group was able to obtain financing, and our building of the training center provided further impetus for the revitalization of the downtown area.[48]

Good times lasted until July 1985 when Wang Laboratories announced its first loss in a dozen years. This was but the beginning of misfortune. An Wang died in 1990. Under new management the laboratories cut Wang's worldwide employment by more than 50 percent. In 1991 they became associated with International Business Machines and changed direction.[49] The Wang Training Center was taken over by Middlesex Community College in 1992. Nonetheless Lowell remains committed to high technology.[50]

Since the end of the nineteenth century, Lowell has been fostering higher education. In 1897 two specialized state-supported schools opened their doors. The Lowell Textile School was founded to solve "the textile industry's problems by applying new technology and trained skilled workers to provide more highly finished and higher priced goods." Its aim was to offer superior instruction in textile manufacture and, with this in mind, it sought to put together the finest collection of textile machinery anywhere.[51]

Its partner, the Lowell Normal School, was a teacher-training institution. The opening class consisted of 107 women and 1 man. At its inception, the school was "run by a Yankee Protestant faculty for a primarily Yankee Protestant student body." However, in 1911 Hugh J. Molloy became the first Irish superintendent of Lowell's schools and the normal school "opened the way for a new generation of young women of Catholic background to seek employment in the Lowell public schools."[52]

In recent years these two institutions have merged to form what is now the University of Massachusetts at Lowell.[53] The two campuses remain distinct. The former normal school offers education in the humanities and the textile school campus provides instruction in the sciences.

* * *

Although the founding families of Lowell differed somewhat in their backgrounds, all had moved to Boston and were sympathetic to the oligarchic mercantile outlook of the Boston Federalists. This involved, first, living in a place near or like the place where one sold, but apart from the place where one bought or manufactured, and second, delegating the immediate control of purchase or manufacture to an expert, generally a man of less broad experience or less social status.

A leading Boston merchant of that period might travel a great deal, but he lived in the metropolis. Directly or through a representative, he might buy anywhere, conspicuously; for example, in China. He owned his ships but delegated the sailing of them to his captains. The captain hired and controlled the crew. A crew member with no connections could rise through the ranks, but seldom, if ever, did he have the capital to make the jump from captain to merchant.

Lowell differed from most earlier textile enterprises in that it was founded not by an individual but by a group. The founders did not expect to live in their settlement. The mills were controlled on their behalf by a resident agent, a man whose powers were analogous to those of a ship's captain. Thus Lowell established a balance of power between a group of owners and a single dominant administrator that has proved basic in the American economy. As for the remaining employees, seniors, engineers for example, might be recruited from Britain. The operatives and farmers' daughters came and went.

Right from the start, these social relationships implied that Lowell's would be a stratified, immobile society. As emigrés replaced natives in the work force, it became far more so. Opportunities for promotion were slight. The ambitious citizen of Lowell might work for, condemn, or take over a mill. Rarely did he rise to the very top working within one.[54]

The owners of the Lowell mills proved generous. The list of their charities is impressive, but their charity remained where it began—at home. They made few if any gifts to Lowell. If there was a single institution that benefited especially from their largesse, it was Harvard University. Witness, for example, the university's Lowell House and Lowell Lecture Hall, Lawrence Scientific School, and Appleton Chapel. The consequence of these facts is the relative scarcity and modesty of private charitable institutions in Lowell.

There are, however, a large number of churches—God's plenty. But the diversity of Lowell's ethnic history can be seen in the profusion of small churches. Roman Catholic congregations are a partial exception;

not all their churches are small, but, nonetheless, there are more parishes than might seem necessary. This unexpected proliferation is evidence of the diverse Catholic communities. The church names suggest the particular ethnic groups served: for example, St. Patrick's, St. Jean Baptiste's, St. Casimir's. The city's most conspicuous Catholic church was designed by Patrick C. Keeley of Brooklyn. (Figure 79.) That astonishing architect was reputedly responsible for the design of some 600 churches, and, although unfortunate, it is no surprise that some lack inspiration.[55] More significantly, an ecumenical plaza unites St. Patrick's to the equally monumental Eastern Orthodox Holy Trinity.[56] The juxtaposition is a vivid and appropriate symbol of Lowell's profound and long-standing tolerance in matters of faith.

The dominant images that Lowell presents are high brick walls—"a mile of mills" as the city used to boast. But the walls are of remodeled mills. The monotonous dormitorylike structures along the Merrimack illustrated in the frontispiece have now been altered beyond recognition.

Chapter VI points out that one early change was to fill the intervals between the mills belonging to a single corporation, as is illustrated by the Hamilton Company. (Figure 46.) Next, all the mills were rebuilt, following the example set by the Merrimack Company during the Civil War. This involved using the original foundations and, where possible, heightening the buildings by one or two stories, sometimes added in succession after an interval. (Figure 91.) In every case, a flat roof terminated the whole. If possible, additional blocks might be built within the mill yards. Contemporaries were impressed by the grim uniformity. (Figure 92.) Now that so much has been torn down, the surviving structures make an imposing backdrop to the omnipresent parking lots.[57]

Little variety exists because the process of manufacturing was so similar throughout much of the city and because the specific design of later building was, in large part, governed by requirements imposed by insurance companies. The occasional belfries, which were added to towers of some of the earlier mills in the romantic period, provide attractive accents. (Figure 86.) Interior spaces are even more uniform, though views directly up the stair towers are grotesque. What gives the mills interest is the admirable presentation by the National Park Service of the human activities that formerly took place there.

A water-powered mill did not require complex spaces. (Figure 47.) As will be explained in Chapter III, the river, a mill canal, and the main street ran parallel. The areas they aligned were allotted to industry, housing, and the bourgeoisie. But the topography of Lowell requires it to be somewhat exceptional. (Figure 1.) The Merrimack makes a right-angle turn just below the falls and the Pawtucket canal swings south and east in a large curve to avoid some high land. Every inch of space beside the waterways was used for manufacturing. Thus the total area of the mills described a recumbent *F*. (Figure 1.) The city evolved in and around this *F* as best it could.

The map shows a short road running almost directly east and west in the area enclosed by the top of the *F*. This is the central stretch of Merrimack Street, the heart of the city. National Park's Visitor Center is in the top serif of the F, two short blocks south of that central stretch. West of the central stretch, Merrimack Street bends slightly to the north, creating, as it were, a "square," a western focus for downtown. To the east of this, the Merrimack Canal runs at right angles to the river. This forms a park, flanked on either side by generous spaces lined with trees (Figure 8), with St. Anne's Church and the high school on its eastern side. (Figure 16.) A block or so beyond the Merrimack Canal, a major street comes in from the south, crosses Merrimack Street, and continues to a bridge over the river. The section south of Merrimack Street is Center Street, an important business street adjoining the center of town. Further to the east, just after Merrimack Street crosses the Concord River, there is a major triangular open space constituting an eastern focus. (Figure 90.)

*   *   *

Many visitors arrive in Lowell at the National Park's Visitor Center. Buses stop here and parking is free. This starting point of the excellent official tours is in an admirably reconditioned mill.

Walking the two blocks just mentioned will lead to the center of town and will best demonstrate how Lowell's revival has transformed an ordinary business street. As one leaves the center, the four-story Mack building is immediately on the left.[58] This has been remodeled to accommodate a small museum devoted to water power. It is flanked by two appropriate outdoor exhibits, a statue honoring women and a major mill wheel.

The remainder of the street is lined with good nineteenth-century commercial buildings from various periods, each one admirably reconditioned and in use. Great attention has been devoted to all signs, as well as to street lights and other urban "furniture." The overall effect is tasteful, but quiet, so one is hardly aware that it was planned. Creating such an effect must have involved innumerable small artistic decisions. Most were centrally determined, but the total impression is of such harmony that one could believe that all had been reached by consensus.[59]

By contrast, the central stretch of Merrimack Street is a disappointment. This is too narrow an artery to be the heart of Lowell's downtown. Compare it, for instance, with the broad expanse of Elm Street, Manchester, New Hampshire, a functionally similar thoroughfare in a historically and economically similar city. But in Lowell there was not much space between the mill properties around the Concord River and those of the bank of the Merrimack, as a glance at Figure 1 shows. When Lowell was laid out, it was thought it might become a city of 30,000 inhabitants. Merrimack Street now seems inadequate for a population of 100,000.

Some original three-story commercial buildings (Figure 28) still survive, interspersed with six-story Victorian Gothic and Queen Anne structures and a couple of slick modernistic remodelings. The street may ultimately reflect the fact that the topography of Lowell encouraged the relatively early creation of prosperous residential suburbs, and that the dispersed shops that served these districts limited the development of a normally prosperous downtown.

Until recently, Lowell has been fortunate in its government buildings. Mention will be made on page 97 and following of the exceptionally fine 1852 courthouse, and recently this has been admirably restored. (Figures 84 and 85.) Starting in 1882, under Mayor Donovan's administration, Lowell enlarged the city's poor farm, built schools as well as bridges, and made the public library free to all.[60]

This impetus led to the creation of a remarkable series of public buildings in the then-fashionable Richardsonian Romanesque style. The earliest of these is probably the central fire station of 1889, a modest structure on Palmer Street. Its three round-arched portals proclaim its function. The mandatory hose-drying tower is inconspicuous in the background. The building's style, scale, and material are repeated almost next door, in what is perhaps Lowell's finest commercial building, at the corner of Palmer and Merrimack streets. It has a ground floor of shops and above that, three floors of offices. The windows in the lower two of these are paired and crowned with round arches, and the topmost series are treated as an attic beneath a handsome classic cornice. The building reflects the simple grandeur of Richardson's last commercial structures, but includes some of the classical detail made popular by McKim, Mead and White.

The most conspicuous Romanesque structure in Lowell is City Hall, a monumental building of 1890–1893 in light gray granite. The design is a much reduced version of Richardson's Allegheny County Courthouse in Pittsburgh. The building, and especially its tower, has been slenderized. This emphasizes the tower's corner turrets, which are repeated on the dormers. Perhaps to compensate for the loss in impression of mass, the wall is gently rusticated, which only produces the effect of a decorative surface.

So much for the close-up view. Merrimack Street is laid out in such a way that the facade of City Hall closes a main axis. Thus it does establish a civic center; it stands for and vividly represents Lowell.

Immediately behind City Hall, and part of the same project, is the public library. Here, in contrast, asymmetry governs. The building suggests an expensive country house. It has a huge dark entrance off axis, a wayward turret, and an exceptionally deep roof. The building may not be very convenient for readers and librarians, but as a stage set, the Lowell Public Library is a distinct success.

The finest of the Richardsonian group of public buildings is the former federal post office, now the administrative headquarters of the city's school system. The federal government acquired the property in 1888 and the building, begun in 1891, was designed by the Supervising Architect of the Treasury. The site is slightly angled at the crossing of two major streets. A simple tower rises at the angle so each of the streets faces an asymmetrical facade with the tower defining one side. The two faces differ markedly; neither is a repetition of a known design by Richardson, yet each is satisfactory as an example of his style. The compositions are original but his vocabulary is handled with quiet distinction throughout. This is one of the finest among the Richardsonian buildings.

A contemporary is the high school of 1892. This is a friendly mongrel. (Figure 28, partially visible at far left.) The material is yellow brick. A large hip-roofed block, it has the proportions, the heavy cornice, and the large round-arched windows of the Boston Public Library. It is located directly behind St. Anne's Church, which it somewhat reluctantly overshadows. Despite its classic mass and entablature, its large arched windows are filled with simple tracery, acknowledging those of the church.

Thirty years after the high school was built, Lowell experienced another outburst of monumental public construction. At the eastern focus of Merrimack Street a new federal building was erected, from 1932 to 1938. Designed by the Supervising Architect of the Treasury, this is a limited but flawless monument of Beaux Arts classicism in Indiana limestone. Immediately adjoining it is Lowell's largest public building, Memorial Auditorium, designed by Blackall, Clapp and Whitemore and built in 1921. Again, the exterior is a perfectly schooled classic in Indiana limestone. The vaulted entrance and lobby are equally assured examples of the same style; and the concert hall, handsome by any standard, is probably the most beautiful interior in Lowell. As part of its revival, the city undertook the refurbishing of this building.

A third fine building of this type is Masonic Hall (1928) near the intersection of Merrimack Street and the Merrimack Canal. Here the facade consists of a handsome row of engaged Ionic columns. Again, and perhaps most seriously, a problem lies in the siting. This conventionally handsome building seems to bear no relation to anything around it.

Up to this point, insensitivity to urban design had merely resulted in failures to take full advantage of opportunities. In public construction since World War II, lack of overall planning damaged existing assets. In the mid-1950's, after the Merrimack Manufacturing Company had been leveled, there was no successful attempt to replace the plant with a visually coherent development.[61]

To be sure, from 1945 onwards, various committees, commissions, and graduate seminars identified a list of desiderata. The improvement of highways both within and outside the city was mentioned. Several parking garages have been built, as well as one conspicuous office and apartment block on the site of a Merrimack mill. A sprawl of one-story sheds now satisfactorily accommodates the functions of the post office—so satisfactorily in fact that the distinguished Richardsonian and classic structures that had previously served the federal government are now threatened with demolition. The visually least unsatisfactory among the new structures has been the low quadrangle of offices adjacent to City Hall, a decent if undistinguished example of the International style. These were designed by Victor Gruen and built in 1968.

New buildings created as a result of Lowell's revival are scattered, conventional, and not very conspicuous. Near the "Lowell Connector" to the Boston super highway, a close-knit group of mini-skyscrapers constitutes the Wang Laboratories headquarters. They announce the entrance to Lowell as once the Bastille announced the entrance to Paris. The skyscrapers are less forbidding only because the group appears to be immersed in trees. The university sponsored one conventional high rise, and private developers another, the latter in the 1970's on a small part of the site of Merrimack's mills. The inspiring and focal campanile at the end of the Merrimack Canal has been replaced by the doll's house of an international style bank.

Red brick came back into fashion with the postmodern movement. The worthiest building is a huge, shapeless addition to the high school in dark brick. It required a covered bridge over the Merrimack Canal which, however useful, seriously injures the appearance of Lowell's loveliest park. The Hilton Hotel is an eight-story horizontal prism with a slender vertical stair-tower at one end. The former Wang Training Center, now home of Middlesex Community College, disfigures a prominent downtown site. Not quite a pure cube of seven stories, it is wrapped in two distinct but thin layers of red brick, the outer a series of wide-spaced piers carrying segmental arches. At once overblown and undernourished, the structure reminds one how handsome are the best of Lowell's Richardsonian public and commercial buildings.

Clearly the results of Lowell's revival have not yet fully penetrated the downtown community. An astonishing achievement of preservation and restoration, as presented in a tour led by superbly trained guides, Lowell offers the visitor much. The same cannot yet be said of what private business offers either to tourists or to Lowell's increasing population. A search downtown for book stores or antique shops, for an adequate department store, or for distinctive shops and restaurants is all but in vain. Yet innumerable changes, large and small—things such as vastly improved parking facilities, concern with the look of the streets, new small parks, and the existence of outdoor sculpture—all clearly reflect a profound change in morale. Matching changes in the quality of Lowell's architecture must come soon.

ACKNOWLEDGMENTS

I wish to express my profound gratitude to Mr. Ed Harley of the National Park Service, who introduced me to the later history of Lowell and with considerable trouble found and photocopied for me obscure and most valuable published information. I wish to thank Mr. Patrick Mogan, Mr. Jack Tavaris, and Mr. Michael Sand, who granted me fruitful interviews, as well as Ms. Martha Mayo, Mr. Andrew Cunningham, and Mr. Peter Alexis, who made especially available to me the resources of the libraries with which they are associated. I particularly appreciate the labors of Ms. Amelia Henderson on the repeated retyping of my manuscript. Uniquely valuable was the work of Ms. Karin Alexis of the National Gallery in Washington. She read the manuscript of this preface and contributed many helpful suggestions. I am deeply grateful to Ms. Pam Wilkinson of the University of Massachusetts Press, whose zeal in maintaining scholarly standards was equaled only by her patience with a dilatory author.

John Coolidge

April 1992

NOTES

1. Most of the essays in Robert Weible, ed., *The Continuing Revolution: A History of Lowell, Massachusetts* (Lowell: Lowell Historical Society, 1991), were not available to me at the time I prepared this preface.

    Margaret Terrell Parker, *Lowell: A Study of Industrial Development* (New York: Macmillan, 1940), was the first book on the city by someone who was not a native. Since that time, a great deal has appeared in print. Outstanding is the only new general history, Arthur L. Eno, Jr., ed., *Cotton Was King: A History of Lowell, Massachusetts* (Somersworth, N.H.: New Hampshire Publishing, 1976). Special attention has been paid to the working people of Lowell, civil engineering, especially as it concerned the mills, and the Lowell National Historical Park. Noteworthy studies are Thomas Dublin, *Women at Work: The Transformation of Work and Community in Lowell, Massachusetts, 1826–1860* (New York: Columbia University Press, 1979); Mary Blewett, *Surviving Hard Times: The Working People of Lowell* (Lowell: Lowell Museum, 1983); Brian C. Mitchell, *The Paddy Camps: The Irish of Lowell, 1821–1862* (Urbana: University of Illinois Press, 1982); Mary Blewett, *The Last Generation: Work and Life in the Textile Mills of Lowell, Massachusetts, 1910–1950* (Amherst: University of Massachusetts Press, 1988), as well as Lowell Historic District Commission, *Report to the Ninety-fifth Congress of the United States of America* (Washington, D.C.: Government Printing Office, 1977), hereafter, "The Brown Book."

2. Parker, *op. cit.*, p. 4. The situation is well summarized in two quotations: "In sum, Lowell before the onset of World War II had all the makeup of a dying city. The government, inefficient at best and corrupt at worst, served few of the needs of a depression-ridden city"; and "The cotton industry, Lowell's lifeblood and birthright, was simply closing down"

(Marc Scott Miller, *The Irony of Victory: World War II and Lowell, Massachusetts* [Urbana: University of Illinois Press, 1988], p. 12).

3. C. Chandler Bryan, Jr., "The Remaking of a Mill Town: Hi-Tech, Public-Private Partnership and Economic Redevelopment in Lowell, Massachusetts" (Honors Thesis, Department of Social Studies, Harvard, 1986). This comprehensive and excellent study of the rebirth of Lowell is fully worthy of the Hooper Prize it received. It should be published. Meanwhile it may be consulted at the Harvard University Archives.

4. According to the information desk at the Visitors' Center, Lowell National Park.

5. U.S. Bureau of the Census, and Eno, *op. cit.,* "Appendix A, Population of Lowell." This excellent book has been indispensable in writing this preface. Particularly useful have been chapters by Mary H. Blewett, "The Mills and the Multitudes, a Political History," and Peter F. Blewett, "The New People: An Introduction to the Ethnic History of Lowell." For a century and a half, Lowell has benefited from the distinguished efforts of citizens who have written its history. Eno and his colleagues have surpassed their predecessors not only by including local material hitherto ignored, but also by incorporating into their writings the understanding of Lowell developed by scholars who were not citizens. As this preface will demonstrate, Lowell's revival is largely dependent upon the widespread appreciation of its achievement, which these historians have established together.

6. Peter Blewett, *op. cit.,* p. 190.

7. Ibid.

8. "In 1845 the average length of time for a [Yankee] operative at the mills was four and a half years. By 1850, after repeated speed-ups, the influx of Irish mill workers, and the failure of the Ten-Hour movement, it was nine months" (Nancy Zaroulis, "Daughters of Freeman," in Eno, *op. cit.,* p. 122).

9. Mary Blewett, in Eno, *op. cit.,* pp. 168 ff.

   "By 1900, as the third wave of immigrants flowed into Lowell, the Irish enjoyed the economic dominance of retail business formerly held by Yankees" (Peter Blewett, *op. cit.,* p. 214).

10. All ethnic groups faced the same problems and met them in similar ways, but there were always some differences. The Greeks developed coffee houses, whereas the Irish preferred saloons. The French-Canadians found it easiest to return home and some did so rather then strike in 1903.

Cumulatively, these and similar small variations determined the social history of the city. The writing about Lowell has—quite naturally—taken up single topics; for example, the essays edited by Eno. Similarly, Lowell's population has been described in terms of single ethnic groups. Now the city deserves a single comprehensive and comparative study.

11. Since the story of immigration to Lowell has not been studied completely and in detail, the sequence of arrival of the principal ethnic groups can only be suggested: Irish, 1822; French-Canadians, 1841; Portuguese, 1874; German Jews, Poles, and Greeks, in the 1880's; Swedes and Russian Jews in the 1890's; Lithuanians and Armenians in the 1900's; Syrian-Lebanese, in the 1910's; and, in the last twenty years, Hispanics and Southeast Asians.

12. Parker, *op. cit.*, pp. 18–20. In Lowell, at present, "40 percent of the residents have a mother tongue other than English. Approximately 9 percent of the population is foreign-born and 25 percent are first generation Americans. . . . The three largest groups are French (20.4 percent), Greek (10.1 percent), and Polish (2.8 percent)" (National Park Service Cooperative Research Unit, The Environmental Institute, University of Massachusetts at Amherst, "Economic Impact Analysis: Lowell" [1980], pp. 1, 18).

13. Peter Blewett, *op. cit.*, p. 215.

14. *Boston Sunday Globe*, March 10, 1991, *Northeast Weekly*, pp. 1 f.

15. From a conversation (ca. 1938) with A. Lawrence Lowell, president emeritus of Harvard. He told me he had worked for the mills in Lowell during the 1890's.

16. Mary H. Blewett has provided this insight into one aspect of the assimilation process at the turn of the century: "Miss Devereux was from Marblehead and had become supervisor of kindergartens in Lowell in 1893. She liked to place them in neighborhoods where children came from foreign language homes: 'We can do much to Americanize the parents through their children,' she said" (*Focus* [University of Lowell Magazine] 1 [1986]).

17. Eno, *op. cit.*, especially essay by Peter Blewett.

18. "1831, Battle of Stone Bridge, Yankee vs. Irish" and "1849, Battle of Suffolk Bridge, between Irish from Cork and Connaught and those from the north," in Andrew Cunningham, "Captions for Exhibition in Mogan Center, Lowell, 1991," pp. 7, 14. "Ca. 1915 Battle of the Knives, Irish, and Greeks," in Peter Blewett, *op. cit.*, p. 213.

19. Peter Blewett, *op. cit.*, p. 215.

20. Human Services Corporation, *Lowell Urban Park Development Program* (Lowell: Lowell Corporation, 1974?), p. 48.

21. Parker, *op. cit.*, pp. 172 ff.

22. *Ibid.*, p. 163.

23. Shepley, Bulfinch, Richardson and Abbott, *Report, Lowell National Historical Park and Preservation District, Cultural Resources Inventory* (Offset printed for the Northeast Regional Office, National Park Service, 1980). (The firm's policy is to attribute anything they produce to the firm.)

24. Parker, *op. cit.*, p. 105.

25. Miller, *op. cit.*, p. 5.

26. Bryan, *op. cit.*, pp. 24, 17.

27. Miller, *op. cit.*, pp. 116 ff., 208.

28. *Boston Herald*, December 11, 1957. Some say it was the New York office of the Merrimack Manufacturing Company that announced that production would cease January 1, 1958. The date varies from source to source. This was the most precise I encountered.

29. The Merrimack Company sold its housing just before the war. Merrimack Manufacturing Company "Papers," Baker Library, Harvard Business School, *Textile Labor*, 2, no. 9, 11, 201. In 1966 there was a strong effort to prevent the destruction of the housing. This effort failed, despite much supportive local newspaper publicity. See Loretta A. Ryan, "The Re-Making of Lowell and Its Histories," in Robert Weible, ed., *The Perception of Industrial History* (Local History Library, 1989), pp. 80–84. Ryan cites thirty-three letters to or articles in the *Lowell Sun* between September 29, 1965, and August 8, 1966.

30. Miller, *op. cit.*, p. 213.

31. Julie M. Leney, *Lowell as a Laboratory: An Experiment in Public Housing* (Lowell: Lowell Housing Authority, 1987), p. 2.

32. The members of Congress during the most important period were Edith Nourse Rogers (1925–1960), F. Bradford Morse (1961–1972), Paul Cronin (1973–1975), and Paul Tsongas (1975–1979). Tsongas became junior senator from Massachusetts (1979–1985).

33. Leney, *op. cit.*, p. i. The statistics are computed from figures cited on p. 84.

34. *Ibid.*, p. 8 and elsewhere. The problem continues and is not confined to housing. Recently water power from the canals has been used to produce electricity. Not only was the project's designer an outsider, all materials

that were used were bought outside Lowell and the electricity that will be produced will be used in Rhode Island!

35. *Ibid.*, pp. 4, 9.

36. *Ibid.*, p. 82.

37. It seems likely that there was no single point of origin for Lowell's revival. Different sources make different statements. On one hand, the origin is sometimes imprecisely attributed to a Model Cities Program of 1949. On the other hand: "The first phase of the Lowell Urban National Cultural Park Program is traceable to the converging [early in the 1970's] of a number of separate forces, each trying to treat an aspect of the urban malady" (Human Services Corporation, *op. cit.*, p. 23). The city manager, Paul Tully, and Paul Tsongas, Representative from the Massachusetts Fifth District, appear to have been exceptionally energetic and resourceful in promoting the revival of Lowell. See Bryan, *op. cit.* Under their leadership, the Lowell Plan was formed in 1979. Its original objective suggests both Tully's and Tsongas's priorities and the scale of their ambitions. These were to "foster and develop the concept that, through cooperative effort of the municipal government and by investment from private firms and private funds, the City of Lowell shall continue its return to preeminence as the foremost middle-size city in the United States" (Lowell Historic Preservation Commission and the Lowell Development and Financial Corporation, *Revitalization through Partnership, Public and Private Investment in Lowell Massachusetts* [1984], p. 1; cited hereafter as *Revitalization*).

38. Mogan's importance, acknowledged by all, is symbolized by the fact that in the midst of the restored Boott Mills there is a special library named in his honor, which is devoted to the history of Lowell. Much of the material in this paragraph was derived from an interview with him in late 1991.

39. Human Services Corporation, *op. cit.*, p. 26.

40. U.S. Department of the Interior, National Park Service, *Lowell National Historical Park, General Management Plan*, p. 1.

41. Bryan, *op. cit.*, p. 50.

42. It was reopened to the public in 1991. The Commonwealth's contributions were particularly important because they were most timely. The state granted $12,600,000 to the Lowell Heritage State Park and made $41,000,000 available in industrial loan commitments.

43. Human Services Corporation, *op. cit.*, p. 20.

44. U.S. Department of the Interior, *op. cit.*, p. 1.

45. Bryan gives the largest list of these groups, but he does not include the Human Services Corporation and the Model Cities Education Program under the chairmanship of Patrick Mogan, both of which were important in the early years. Perhaps the most remarkable of the organizations is the Lowell Historical Commission, an independent federal agency within the Department of the Interior which develops properties as well as makes loans and grants within the central district. It has fifteen members appointed by various interested parties, such as the secretary of the interior and the mayor of Lowell. In contrast to Bryan, Loretta A. Ryan, in "The Remaking of Lowell and Its Historians 1965–83," in Robert Weible, ed. *The Popular Perception of Industrial History* (American Association of State and Local History, 1984), fascinatingly tells much the same story in terms of broad ideas and local politics but with little mention of individuals and organized groups.

46. U.S. Department of the Interior, *op. cit.,* p. 1.

47. Bryan, *op. cit.,* p. 46.

48. An Wang with Eugene Linden, *Lessons: An Autobiography* (Reading, Mass.: Addison-Wesley, 1986), pp. 231, 232–33. His story gained little in the telling. "Lowell's unemployment has decreased steadily from a high of 12.6 percent in 1975 to 3.7 percent in May 1984" (*Revitalization,* p. 4). In August 1984, the unemployment rate in Lowell was 3.8 percent compared to a national rate of 7.4 percent. Wang employed about 14,000 people locally.

49. In the later 1980's, Wang fell victim to the worldwide competition and stagnation in the computer industry. (Miller, *op. cit.,* pp. 214 ff). "In May 1991, Lowell's unemployment rate was 12.5 percent compared with a statewide figure of 9.2 percent and a national one of 6.9 percent" (*The Economist,* August 3, 1991, p. 20).

50. The money involved in the revitalization of Lowell has been substantial. During the decade of 1974–1984, $200,000,000 was invested in the revitalization of Lowell. "$141,000,000 of this represents public-private investment in the city's central business district alone. . . . Over $50,000,000 has been committed to the construction of the Lowell Hilton Inn, the Wang Corporation Training Center and the Smith Lot Parking Garage" (*Revitalization,* p. 4). This source also lists individual contributions by various governmental agencies to specific projects.

51. "James T. Smith Uncovered," *Focus* [University of Lowell Magazine], 1, no. 1 (1985), n.p.; see also George Kenngott, *The Record of a City: A*

Social Survey of Lowell, Massachusetts (New York: Macmillan, 1912), p. 170.

52. *Focus* 1, no. 1 (1985), p. 17. I am deeply grateful to Mary H. Blewett for this and the preceding reference.

53. Beware! These institutions have had different names in the course of their existence. One school was formerly Lowell Technological Institute, or Lowell Tech; the other, Lowell State College. In 1975 the pair became the University of Lowell (ULowell) and today they constitute the University of Massachusetts at Lowell.

54. I know of no example of an employee's rising through the ranks in Lowell. The most conspicuous examples elsewhere were Frederick Dumaine, the last chief executive of the Amoskeag Mill in Manchester, New Hampshire, and William Wood, chief executive of the Lawrence Manufacturing Company in Lawrence during the early years of the twentieth century. Both Dumaine and Wood came up through the business offices of their companies. Wood was Portuguese and changed his name.

55. *Macmillan Encyclopedia of Architects,* s.v., "Keeley, Patrick C."

56. Lowell Historic Canal District Commission, *Report* (1977), p. 45. Holy Trinity Church is thought to be the first Greek Orthodox church built in this country.

57. "The Boott Mill is probably the single most important historic structure remaining in the city. The original buildings (1835) and all subsequent additions remain intact and clearly show how the mill form evolved" ("Brown Book," p. 38).

58. "This Queen Anne style commercial building was constructed in 1866. . . . The fourth story was probably added between 1890 and 1900" (U.S. Department of the Interior, *op. cit.,* pp. 27, 43).

59. The city has contributed funds to the rehabilitation of more than 50 downtown buildings through Facade Grants. Paul Tsongas appears to have been exceptionally energetic and resourceful in promoting the revival of Lowell; see Bryan, *op. cit.*

60. Mary Blewett, in Eno, *op. cit.,* p. 174.

61. Plans there were, and some were comprehensive, but while successful opponents can achieve their common purpose in a variety of ways, successful support is likely to involve more agreement than can be easily mustered in a city as diverse as Lowell.

FOREWORD AND
ACKNOWLEDGMENTS

A STUDY of the architecture of a city inevitably touches upon a great deal of material that is not strictly speaking the history of art. This material is essential, but it is hard to know just how it should be introduced. I believe that the first desideratum in a book such as this is that it should read easily as a whole. This will be true only if there is a certain continuity in the text. Accordingly, I have severely limited the range of the material which is discussed in the body of the book. As a result, much of the most important, much of the most interesting, and much of the most amusing data has had to be relegated to the appendices and footnotes.

I am greatly indebted to Mr. Alfred Barr of the Museum of Modern Art and to Professor Robert Keen Lamb, late of Williams College, thanks to whose initial suggestions I embarked upon this topic; to various members of the city government of Lowell; to Mr. William Goodwin of the Lowell Historical Society; and to Mr. Arthur Safford of the Locks and Canals Company, without whose coöperation I should not have had access to the documents on which this study is based. I am deeply obliged to Miss Margaret Noyes, who has taken most of the photographs used for the illustrations; to Mr. Willard Starks, who has assisted me with the others; and to Mr. Edward Moulthrop, who has made the drawings.

I am indebted to the following publishers for courtesy in permitting quotation: Houghton Mifflin Company, Boston—*The Early New England Cotton Manufacture* by C. F. Ware, *The Industrial Worker: 1840-1860* by N. Ware, *A New England Girlhood* by L. Larcom; to Penguin Books, Ltd., Harmondsworth, England—*An Introduction to Modern Architecture* by J. M. Richards, *Town Planning* by Thomas Sharp; to the Thomas Y. Crowell Company, New York—*Loom and Spindle* by H. H. Robinson; to the Macmillan Company, New York—*The Record of a City* by G. F. Kenngott; to the University of Chicago Press, Chicago—*Household Manufactures in the United States, 1640-1860* by R. M. Tryon; to the Royal Institute of British Architects, London—"The Great Landowners' Contribution to Architecture," by J. Summerson, in the *Journal of the Royal Institute of British Architects*; to the Waltham Watch Company, Waltham, Mass.—*A Model Factory in a Model City* by J. Swinton; to the Museum of Modern Art, New York—*The Architecture of H. H. Richardson and His Times* by H. R. Hitchcock; to Harcourt, Brace and Company, New York—*Modern Building* by W. C. Behrendt; to *Time*, Inc., New York —*The Architectural Forum*; to the McGraw-Hill Book Company, New York—*The Metropolitan Community* by R. D. McKenzie; to the National Association of Cotton Manufacturers, Boston—*Lowell, an Industrial Dream Come True* by H. C. Meserve; to the Lewis Historical Publishing Company, New York—*History of Lowell and Its People* by F. W. Coburn; to the Adelphi Company, New York—*Jacob Fugger the Rich* by J. Strieder. I am obligated to the editors of the *New England Quarterly*, who have permitted me to include in this book material which I originally published in their magazine; to Professor Edward Gordon Keith for allowing me to include material from his unpublished doctoral dissertation, "The Financial History of Two Textile Cities," Harvard University, 1937; to the Courier-Citizen Company of Lowell for permitting me to use one of the illustrations in the *Illustrated History of Lowell and Vicinity, Massachusetts*; and to the New York Public Library for permitting me to make a reproduction from a photograph of their copy of the 1834 Pendleton Lithograph of Lowell.

I wish to take this opportunity to thank Professors Carl Feiss of Columbia University, Karl Lehmann-Hartleben of New York University, Richard Krautheimer of Vassar College, and Mr. Lewis

Mumford, who were kind enough to read this book in manuscript, and whose suggestions have been included in the final text. I am most anxious to express my gratitude to Mr. Talbot Hamlin of Columbia University, and Professors Henry-Russell Hitchcock of Wesleyan University and Dmitri Tselos of New York University. Their books and courses have provided the background for this study, and they have given me suggestions, information and encouraging criticism at every stage in the preparation of it.

Finally I wish particularly to thank the directors of the Grants-in-Aid of the American Council of Learned Societies and General Butler Ames of Lowell, whose generosity has made the publication of this book possible.

J. C.

Princeton, New Jersey
January, 1942

CONTENTS

MILL AND MANSION

I

INTRODUCTION

THERE ARE few historical subjects about which so much is known as nineteenth-century American architecture. Most of the important buildings are intact, and the essential facts can be found out easily, for there is a wealth of documents to work with. Nor has the field been neglected by scholars. Several books have treated the subject as a whole, and a considerable number of monographs has appeared covering various of its aspects. The writing of yet another study on this limited and comparatively unimportant material demands some justification therefore.

Despite all the monuments which have survived, and despite all the attention which they have been given, it is nearly impossible to visualize nineteenth-century American architecture except as a confusion of building types and style phases. Basically, it is not the complex character of the period which makes it so puzzling. It is the fact that, at least among the younger generation, the attitude towards the Victorian age and its buildings is changing.

The older generation, the men who established modern architecture, have a simple and clear-cut conception.[1] As they see it, the nineteenth century produced two kinds of buildings. These are generically bad and good. There is orthodox architecture, a wearisome pageant of revivals that represents the fraying away of the great Renaissance heritage. Opposed to this there is a handful of works which run counter to the dominant trends of that age. The typical Victorians did not even admit that the Crystal Palace and the Salle des Machines were architecture, much less great architecture.[2] It was the older generation who first recognized them as masterpieces. They continue to glorify heterodox buildings such as these. Are they not the initiators of a revolution in which "pure" and "functional" forms have freed themselves from the toils of a "literary" tradition?[3]

The younger generation has not rejected this thesis. Its positive implications are accepted in full, and those isolated figures and monuments which foreshadow the modern creative attitude are wholly respected. But we can no longer dismiss conventional Victorian buildings with the phrase, "sentimental architecture." They fascinate us. Scholars, responding to this interest, have produced a whole series of studies dealing with the designers and edifices great-grandfather admired.

This new appreciation is the source of our present confusion. Even the orthodox architecture of the nineteenth century cannot be thought of as a unity any more. Under the impact of research that bugaboo has dissolved into a bewildering succession of revivals and dogmas. What is more important, it is no longer possible to visualize nineteenth-century building as a dualism—bad architecture versus good engineering. The younger generation recognizes that the Victorians were creative in many phases of both these fields.[4] Our problem is to evolve a coherent picture of an age which has to its credit such a diversity of achievement.

The responsibility for constructing this picture falls largely on the scholars, for it is primarily they who brought about the present state of affairs. It was they who discredited the dualistic view of Victorian architecture by pointing out its gross over-simplifications. Now it is up to them to work out an alternative concept. That cannot be done to order. First, the fundamental resemblances between the various types of nineteenth-century buildings must be recognized. Unfortunately, the only means of discovering affinities between distinct groups of structures is to make a close analysis both of their origins and of their characters. Since this is the sort of detailed work which no general history can undertake, there is need of a whole series of preliminary studies, before any grand synthesis can be attempted.

That need is the justification for this book. It aims to be just such a preliminary study. It will examine thoroughly a few buildings which constitute a single complex. Thereby it hopes to suggest a basis on which a comprehensive and consistent image of nineteenth-century American architecture could some day be built. Necessarily, the material discussed will not be uniform in character and, necessarily, more emphasis will be placed upon the relationships between the diverse structures than upon their superficial differences. For its value as groundwork depends upon the success with which it can establish those relationships and upon the extent to which they can be applied to Victorian building as a whole. But the character of the relationships depends on the nature of the material which is studied. If they prove to have a wide significance, then the complex of buildings where they are to be found must be in some sense a microcosm of nineteenth-century American architecture. The next step, therefore, is to discover a suitable microcosm for the preliminary study to investigate.

Hitherto, particular discussions of American nineteenth-century architecture have been of three kinds: monographs dealing with a series of buildings all in the same style or all devoted to the same purpose, biographies of architects, and surveys of the architecture of a single geographical region. Neither the group of similar buildings, nor the works of an individual designer, nor the monuments of one area are satisfactory as microcosms.

The single group of buildings is not sufficiently comprehensive. To investigate it reinforces rather than destroys our shallow conception of Victorian architecture as a succession of style phases, some sweet, some stodgy. The creations of one man are not adequately representative. For until one has a complete understanding of building in the last century, how is one to select a typical architect? The alternatives are to pick out an artist whose extreme views made him notorious among his contemporaries or to fall back on one of

those seeming geniuses who appear to have played a decisive part
in the formation of modern architecture. In both cases one almost
inevitably loses touch with the background, and the biography becomes a study of an individual in isolation. Such a study may resur-
rect distinguished achievements which have been forgotten; it may
even make comprehensible some bizarre aspect of the past. But,
whatever its intrinsic merits, it begs the question which is fundamental now. For the basic problem is not the prophet but his public.
What is of first importance is not the discovery of new and unsus-
pected excellences, but the establishment of the unity and meaning
of the commonplace.

There remains the regional survey. This certainly provides a
limited amount of material that is both comprehensive and typical.
But the unit so far chosen has been arbitrary. The most popular
subject has been the state. During the nineteenth century the single American states were organisms only in a political sense. Geo-
graphically, socially, and culturally they were not entities. Their
architecture had no coherence. Collectively, the structures of Ken-
tucky or of western Pennsylvania present a panorama of nineteenth-century building. They indicate vividly the sequence and
the relative importance of the diverse movements and types. But
they do not make clear the reason for all the tendencies, nor the
dynamic relationships of one to another. Clear though it is, the
picture they offer of nineteenth-century American architecture lacks
an essential element, the element of vitality.

The multiplicity of Victorian building is not the result of an accumulation of isolated movements. It is the expression of a continuing clash of ideals that sprang up and met within one narrow
theater. A meaning can be found in the confusion only if nineteenth-century American architecture is visualized as the product of
this conflict. The significance of its separate tendencies can be understood only if they are recognized as the symbols of these contrasting ideals. The vitality and turbulence of its opposing conceptions
can be appreciated only if they are studied in that theater where
they originated and came into conflict. That theater was the Vic-

torian city. Comprehensive, representative, and alive, there is the microcosm to study.

The most striking social development of nineteenth-century America was the change from a rural to a predominantly urban mode of life. That change was the result of a great migration from country to town. But there was another factor at least as important in establishing the ascendancy of the urban point of view, namely, the concentration of the ruling elite in the cities. This was the movement which centralized control over social activities.[5] The eighteenth-century seaports were merely the habitat of a minority of the population, a minority that was influential rather than dominant. The Victorian cities were not only the dwelling places of a great number of people, they were the ganglia from which the whole country was run. Small wonder that the meaning of nineteenth-century architecture can only be grasped if that art is understood as an expression of urban life, for the buildings of the cities are the record of the way the masses lived; they are the monuments of the intelligentsia; taken as a whole, they are the mirror of communal ideals.[6]

If a preliminary study of American nineteenth-century architecture should concentrate on the buildings of a single city, then there is still the problem of choosing the specific city. The number of possibilities is large. A century ago there were many communities big enough to be representative. Plenty of them have survived sufficiently intact to merit investigation. According to what criteria shall one of these be selected?

Obviously, the study must attempt to unify the maximum number and diversity of trends and building types into which nineteenth-century architecture is now subdivided. It is not necessary that the book should deal with the whole range of time between 1800 and 1900. It has only to cover enough so that the relation between a succession of attitudes and movements becomes evident. Even more important, the city should include a great variety of architectural types within the period considered. It must be a city rich in orthodox Victorian buildings, but it must also include heterodox structures. Therefore, it must be a city stamped by the impact of those problems which arose from the Industrial Revolution. Ideally, it should be a city which met at least one of these new challenges with distinction.[7]

In central New England there is a group of textile manufacturing communities which fulfill all these conditions. They are nothing if not characteristically Victorian, for the single-industry manufacturing town, common in the nineteenth century, is peculiar to that period.[8] Immensely prosperous a hundred years ago, such towns can boast a splendid array of solid bourgeois buildings. Yet, certainly, they illustrate the impact of new problems. Novel techniques of construction there are none, but every city centers around a new architectural species, the mill, and in each case the founding fathers were conscious of the need for city planning, however inadequately they satisfied it. Finally, the settlements illustrate a most original attempt to solve the problem of low-cost housing.

To be sure there must be other Victorian cities which exemplify these same traits. But among them all it is the cotton manufacturing centers of mid New England which display the greatest span and variety of nineteenth-century architecture. The first industrial cities to be founded, they were the first to be abandoned.[9] Consequently they have suffered little alteration in recent times. Started in the twenties, the thirties, and the forties, outmoded by the time of the Civil War, and definitely obsolete at the turn of the century, almost all their architecture is of the Victorian period.

One of this group must serve as the focus for this book. It is not difficult to choose which. Lowell, Massachusetts, was always the senior member of the galaxy. Built before the others, it was to a great extent the model of all the rest. The largest and wealthiest, it developed the most splendid architecture. Among the first to suffer sharply from the shift of the cotton industry to the South, it has not undergone much modern rebuilding. Finally, being the best known, it is the one about which the most has been written. It is the one which can be the most thoroughly investigated.[10]

II

THE BACKGROUND OF
LOWELL

THE OUTSTANDING achievements of Lowell are its housing and
its city planning. They are not the result of exceptional philanthropy on the part of the men who founded the town. Rather,
they are the direct outcome of the unique social and economic situation in which those promoters found themselves.

In America, as in England, textile manufacturing was the first
trade group to develop into a modern mass-production industry.
In England, the soil had been prepared by centuries of a special
economic evolution. When the invention of the steam engine and
of various special machines made factory manufacturing possible, it
was speedily able to replace household manufacturing. Indeed, the
new method of production soon surpassed the old. Expanding to
supply foreign markets, the textile industry grew like a weed.

But in America manufacturing was from the start a hothouse
plant, raised in the artificial atmosphere of war.[1] It was the English Civil War that sowed the seed. It was the series of crises that
started with the American Revolution and ended with the War of
1812 that raised the sprout and brought it to maturity. Then, suddenly, the crises being over, this cultivated flower was obliged to
adjust itself to an unfostered existence in a peaceful world. Moreover, to make matters more difficult, it was just at this time that

machinery was introduced. Thus the American textile industry was obliged to transform itself simultaneously in two fundamental ways. All at once it had to change from wartime to peacetime conditions, and from home to factory production. Small wonder, therefore, that it was faced with problems which were unknown to its English counterpart; problems which it must solve if it were to survive and develop.

Survive and develop the American textile industry did, but only at the cost of introducing several startling innovations. Of these, the most significant today is the type of manufacturing settlement that was produced. These factory towns provided model housing for the employees; also, for the first and only time in America, they aimed to solve at the start all the problems of shelter and city planning that would be likely to occur. Naturally, such a remarkable scheme was not perfected overnight. It evolved, and its evolution can be divided into distinct stages, corresponding to the growth of textile manufacturing itself.

As early as the 17th century small fulling mills had been established in America, wherever there was a little stream and a population large enough to support them.[2] But modern textile manufacturing really began only in 1790. Then an English immigrant named Samuel Slater set up the first efficient spinning machinery in America for the firm of Almy & Brown.[3] That achievement transformed what had been a handicraft into a small business. It led at once to the building of mills specifically designed for spinning.[4]

These new enterprises turned raw cotton into yarn. At first this yarn was sold directly; later it was put out among weavers who turned it into cloth that the factory owner disposed of.[5] In either case the size of the business was limited. It was difficult to sell yarn; it was not economical to have it woven at a distance.[6] There was therefore no point in producing more than local looms could handle, so that when business was good, one was obliged to start another small concern elsewhere, instead of expanding the original plant. As a result, by 1810 there were almost two hundred and fifty little cotton mills in the United States.[7] Most of them were scattered about the New England hinterland. All of them were imitations of Slater's establishment, whose primary importance was as a training school.[8]

In the long run few of these concerns were financially successful.[9] The risks were always great. With most of the capital invested in the plant, little was left for operating, and the business was at the mercy of the market. A small change made the difference between relative prosperity and bankruptcy. There were no facilities for disposing of the products, so the manufacturers themselves were completely responsible for all sales. They were obliged to carry a great many small accounts over a wide area, an arrangement that proved both unsure and costly.[10] At best the returns were small.[11] Almy & Brown were merchants and enjoyed the finest marketing facilities available. Slater, their overseer, knew more about machinery than anyone else in the country, and he ran their mills well. But even so, the profit was modest: $18,000 in the ten good years between 1793 and 1803.[12]

But the early spinning mills have to their credit one great architectural accomplishment. Around them arose a series of attractive mill settlements. At this time water provided the cheapest form of industrial power, and factories had to be located near a waterfall.[13] This meant that generally they were so far off the beaten track that there was no place for the employees to live. Almost from the start the entrepreneurs were obliged to provide housing for the staff. The scheme adopted was straightforward. A single mill stood beside the stream. As most of the work was done by children, the manufacturers hired prolific families, and housed them in snug, individual cottages.[14] These they placed in rows behind white picket fences, beside the street.[15]

The first mill hamlets with their ample, regular planning, their broad, well-shaded roads, their simple, but finely proportioned houses seem today like the realization of some utopian dream. Actually, the settlements were neither visionary nor strikingly novel. The handful of houses, the company store, the lone church constituted little more than an up-to-date example of manorial paternalism. So far from breaking with tradition, in architecture they were conservative, and as a social conception they represented an extension of the recognized scheme of things, rather than the first step in the creation of a new order.

The textile industry passed out of this adolescent phase in 1814 when Francis Cabot Lowell set up the first successful American power loom in Waltham, Massachusetts.[16] Stringent British regulations had prevented Lowell from importing English machinery or obtaining drawings of it. But he had visited the mills in Manchester, and on his return to America he was able to "re-invent" the mechanical loom and other devices.[17] These revolutionized the organization of all the technical processes by which cloth was made.[18]

Now, the manufacturer could use unskilled labor throughout his plant. Now, the individual concern might be indefinitely extended.[19] Every stage in the transformation of raw fiber into cloth could be performed under one roof, and for the first time the mass production of finished goods became possible. Just as spinning machinery had turned a craft into a business, so the power loom turned this business into "big business." But before large manufacturing organizations could commence operations, there were three new problems that had to be solved, a problem of labor supply, a problem of public relations and a problem of capital.[20]

Scarcity of labor had been a characteristic of America since the first settlement. "It was bound to be a permanent obstacle so long as western lands were open on easy terms to discontented easterners."[21] The small spinning mills had managed to side-step this problem. They offered little. Wages were low, payments were only made quarterly, and then they were not in cash, but in yarn, or in script, good only at the company stores.[22] Few workmen came out consistently ahead.[23] Still, by vigorous advertising, the spinning mills managed to attract the ne'er-do-wells, and these with their numerous progeny provided a barely sufficient labor force.[24]

But the new, large-scale plants were obliged to face the issue squarely and overcome it. Occasionally, they imported foreigners who worked under contract, but this solution was so expensive that it was only used as a means of obtaining skilled labor. For the bulk of their employees, the manufacturers turned to the unmarried young women of the farms, who, hitherto, had busied themselves spinning and weaving clothing for the family (hence the term "spinster"). Now the very progress of industrialism left them with time on their hands. These girls had the further advantage of being the least mobile element in the population. But they were a class who could not be exploited. Unlike the English operatives, who in the early days had been recruited from the poorhouses, they would not be driven to the mills by the need to earn their living.[25] They would have to be attracted there. They would have to be offered good cash wages, paid monthly or fortnightly.

Almost everybody in America was opposed to the development of industry on a large scale. People of property felt that it would compete with agriculture and shipping, attracting workers away from the farms and the sea. Far more lasting and important, however, was the fear that industry would disrupt the American social structure and deprave the working man. The general public was all too familiar with the standard of living to which machinery had reduced the English proletariat. As Nathan Appleton soberly wrote, "the operatives in the manufacturing cities of Europe were notoriously of the lowest character, for intelligence and morals. The question therefore arose, and was deeply considered, whether this degradation was the result of the peculiar occupation or of other and distinct causes."[26] There were plenty of people who replied that manufacturing itself was a tainted pursuit. They resolved, "it shall not happen here."

The earliest mills had escaped notoriety because, individually, they were small in size, and nowhere was there a sufficient concentration of them to blight a whole neighborhood and to create a proletarian problem. The new mills, however, were too conspicuous to avoid censure. They had to exorcize the prejudice. In order to make life in the factories respectable enough to attract the daughters of Puritan Yankee farmers, the manufacturers had to guarantee that working in the mills would neither corrupt the girls, nor debase them socially. At all costs they must prevent the creation of a permanent proletariat. The labor must be transient. The girls would be encouraged to come and work for a few years only, and then to return to their homes.[27] During this brief period, of course, the manufacturers would have to assume the responsibility for the whole daily life of their employees.[28] Consequently, they must not only provide model low cost housing, but they must even develop and control a whole settlement dependent upon the factory.[29]

This they undertook to do. A minimum twelve-hour working day and a six-day week went a long way toward keeping their charges out of mischief.[30] For the rest the girls were quartered in boarding houses, kept by seemly widows in straitened circumstances. Every provision was made for religious worship (compulsory), and a moral tone was maintained that amazed the statesmen of France and inspired the churchmen of England.[31]

As for capital, spinning mills were built on a very small amount of it. The financial backing was rarely adequate, and the early factories were constantly in trouble because of their shortage of liquid funds. Right from the start Francis Cabot Lowell made up his mind to avoid any difficulties arising from such a cause. He launched the Boston Manufacturing Company at Waltham with a capital of $400,000[32] and this amount was doubled shortly afterwards. Of the initial sum only three-eighths was invested in the plant, in contrast to the seven-eighths that was not unusual among the earlier mills.[33]

The capital of a spinning mill was generally contributed by one or two farmers and professional men of the locality.[34] But it was obvious that no such group could raise the great sum which Lowell was seeking. Mass production would be possible only if another and wealthier class could be interested in manufacturing. American wealth at this time was in two forms, the wealth of the planter and the wealth of the merchant. The wealth of the planter was securely vested in his land. The wealth of the merchant during the halcyon days of Federalist commerce had been completely absorbed in shipping, which offered fantastic opportunities for profit and loss.[35] Fortunately for the textile industry the embargo ruined American commerce. By 1812 there were many traders who were on the lookout for other fields where they might profitably invest their energies and capital. It was they who financed the new type of textile mills.[36]

The attitude of the group of men who now took over the direction of the industry was completely different from that of the earlier entrepreneurs. The old mills "were one and all controlled by men intent upon the process of production, spinners and mechanics at heart, whose business was the making of cotton thread and cloth."[37] Lowell and the associates he was able to persuade to join him were successful traders, "men with the best business imagination in the land, unhampered by . . . traditions, concerned with making fortunes and building states, not with manufacturing cotton cloth."[38] "These men relied not on their technical knowledge of production, but on business organization, executive capacity, and their ability to lure the best talent in every field. This fact in itself was one reason for their success, for it left them unconcerned with detail and free to organize and plan, to finance their companies, market their product, and consider the social as well as the productive problem involved in their hiring of labor."[39]

But even the resources of this class of backers were not enough to finance the new mills. So much money was needed that no one man, not even a small group of rich merchants could afford to risk investing it. The whole capital structure had to be changed. The old, personal form of ownership was given up.[40] In its place the modern limited liability corporation was gradually evolved.[41]

The solution of the problems of labor supply, public relations, and capital had two important results. In the first place it concentrated the textile industry for many years. Only in New England were there rich and enterprising merchants who were unable to invest their money profitably in other local ventures.[42] Only in New England was there the combination of adequate water power and a highly developed transportation system.[43] Only in New England, where the soil was exhausted and the population dense, was there the beginning of a labor supply. The section had other advantages. The climate was sufficiently humid for spinning; the water was pure enough for bleaching. Finally, once started in New England, the supply of skilled labor tended to keep industry there for a long time.[44]

Far more important was the second result. The relationship of millworker to millowner was profoundly altered, and both of them assumed a new status with regard to society as a whole. Corporate ownership involved the reallocation of those rights, responsibilities, and powers which in earlier enterprises had been vested in the single person of the owner. The executives took over the duties of ownership and wielded the power; the stockholders acquired the rights. But the executives were just hirelings; they could not act independently; they were only agents of the stockholders. While the stockholders, by sacrificing their power of immediate control, became *rentiers*. They, too, were dependents upon, rather than rulers of, the business. There was a similar development at the opposite end of the scale. Mass production involved so many workers, that each one was no longer personally engaged by a specific owner. All were the employees of a corporation; all became members of a proletarian class.

At every level the independence of the individual was subordinated to the requirements of the collective, creative process. Earlier, the needs of national warfare had transformed the captain of mercenaries into a general, and changed his men-at-arms into soldiers. Now, the requirements of modern industry turned owner, manager, and worker into cogs and levers that operated a superpersonal, a national manufacturing organization.[45]

Thus it was necessary to create a new type of industrial settlement. The old mill hamlet was obsolete; it was too small. Communities are organisms; they grow complex in geometric ratio to their expanding size. Accordingly, an increase in the number of the employees and of the bourgeois population dependent on them meant a complete change in the character of the mill settlement. Where one general store and a single church had sufficed before, now a whole quarter would be needed just to satisfy the incidental demands of the workers. A hamlet would no longer be adequate. The new settlements must be towns, even cities.[46]

Moreover, the scale and the impersonal character of the activities were bound to give these new communities a self-sufficiency which old ones strikingly lacked. The villages had been wholly dependent upon the single figure of the owner, reflecting him in every building. The cities would be self-dependent[47] organisms—a creative nucleus ringed by groups of people in various sorts and degrees of relationship. If the former had represented the last version of the manor village, the latter were to be new examples of an even older urban type, the *purveyor town*.[48] Like Oxford, like papal Rome, like Washington, the new cities would owe their existence to the presence of an institution of national, even of international importance, and this existence would be completely focused on the problem of running and supplying that institution.

III

THE FOUNDING OF
LOWELL

FRANCIS CABOT LOWELL seems to have recognized most of these things even before he set up his first power loom.[1] He must have hoped to create ultimately a community which would satisfy all the requirements. But Mr. Lowell was a man no less remarkable for his caution than for his inventiveness.[2] He was no mere designer of utopias. He was well aware that the entire conception could not be realized until various aspects of it had proved themselves feasible individually.

Waltham was conceived as a testing ground. Purposely, he bought a site which had already been developed and which was convenient to Boston, instead of seeking out a location which had great possibilities for the future. The need, at the moment, was to make sure that the machinery ran properly, and to find out if there was a market for American machine-woven goods. Once he had entirely satisfied himself on these points, then he would embark on a large-scale venture. Then, and only then, would he carry all his schemes to completion.

The Boston Manufacturing Company in Waltham was an immediate and an immense success. In striking contrast to the paltry gains from Almy & Brown, the new concern earned as much as its initial capital within the first seven years.[3] In 1815 it disposed of only $412 worth of goods. Five years later it was selling $260,000 worth annually,[4] and all despite bad times.[5]

Before long business conditions improved, and the prospects of the textile industry grew even brighter. Capital became more and more interested in manufacturing as commerce failed to revive after the War of 1812. The labor supply increased daily as the progress of industrialism released additional women from the necessity of spinning and weaving at home.[6] The domestic market grew by leaps and bounds, with the growth of the population and the migration westwards.[7]

By 1820 expansion was obviously in order. But expansion at Waltham was impossible. The Boston Manufacturing Company already had more machinery in operation than was efficient on the sluggish Charles River.[8] It was necessary to seek out a new site and to start afresh. This, then was the occasion to carry out the great plans to the full.

It was to be a considerable undertaking. In those days the founding of a new manufacturing concern involved the digging of canals, the damming of rivers, the building of machine shops, and of dwellings for executives and employees, as well as putting up the mills themselves. All had to be done by the parent company, since there was no one else to do it. In the present case the greatest textile manufacturing establishment in the country was intended. Furthermore, it was planned to go into the production of calicoes, and there was a Print Works with its numerous dependencies to be built.[9] But first, a place must be found where there was water power enough to run all the projected factories and a surplus which would permit unlimited future development.

Francis Cabot Lowell himself had died unexpectedly in 1817, and the initiative in the enterprise passed to two of his early collaborators, his friend Nathan Appleton and his brother-in-law, Patrick Tracy Jackson. Appleton was an importer and did not wish to become involved in the administration of mills. Jackson was the treasurer and agent of the Boston Manufacturing Company, and he found that he had his hands full.[10] The two of them therefore decided to associate themselves with someone else who would actively direct the new enterprise. They picked on a certain Kirk Boott, who had been a Boston merchant until the evil days of the embargo.[11] It was these three then who set out to find a site on which to begin the new venture.[12]

After one or two false starts, they heard of a suitable location in the autumn of 1821. This is Appleton's account. "I was at Waltham one day when I was informed that Mr. Moody[13] had been lately at Salisbury, when Mr. Ezra Worthen, his former partner said to him, 'I hear Messrs. Jackson and Appleton are looking out for water power. Why don't they buy up the Pawtucket Canal? That would give them the whole power of the Merrimack, with a fall of over thirty feet.' On the strength of this, Mr. Moody had returned to Waltham by that route, and was satisfied to the extent of the power which might thus be obtained, and that Mr. Jackson was making inquiries on the subject."[14]

That was an excellent suggestion. The Merrimack is one of the largest rivers in New England. It had suitable rapids in what was then the town of Chelmsford.[15] Around them ran a small canal which, with some rebuilding, could be used to operate the mills. Finally, a second waterway, the Middlesex Canal, connected the river just at this point with Boston Harbor, twenty-six miles away. (Frontispiece.)

The smaller passage, or Pawtucket Canal, was intended for river traffic. It was owned by the Proprietors of the Locks and Canals on Merrimack River, a group of Newburyport merchants. They had dug it late in the eighteenth century in order to make their town the logical port for backwoods New England. Unfortunately, the Middlesex Canal was completed a few years later, and diverted most of the trade.[16] Over a period of twenty-five years the Pawtucket Canal hardly managed to pay 3½ percent interest annually,[17] and Mr. Lowell's associates were able to buy it up for some $30,000. They then acquired a few farms, aggregating some four hundred acres for about $40,000.[18] This gave them sufficient land and the water power rights along the Merrimack.[19]

Having purchased the property, Appleton, Jackson, and Boott incorporated themselves. On February 6, 1822, they received a Charter for the Merrimack Manufacturing Company.[20] The land was turned over to the new concern, and Boott was put in complete executive control, being appointed treasurer and agent.[21] All was now in readiness. Boott prepared to create the town of Lowell, Massachusetts.[22]

Before analyzing in detail the settlement that Boott started, it is important to determine how much he was guided by conceptions inherited from Francis Cabot Lowell. Certainly the latter looked forward to founding a complete industrial organization. But, before 1817, the Boston Manufacturing Company did not produce any considerable urban development at Waltham, and there is no positive proof that Mr. Lowell ever visualized specifically the form the community should take.[23] On the other hand the story of the creation of the new town is told in great detail by Mr. Lowell's associates. Although they take full credit for any minor features they contributed, they never suggest that in founding and laying out the community they were making any departure from or extension of Mr. Lowell's schemes. They were merely carrying to completion a plan already thought through, a plan whose execution only awaited a reasonable assurance of success. This the profits at Waltham provided.

Thus Lowell, Massachusetts, as actually built was something more than one man's notion of the perfect town executed at full scale. Behind the community Boott realized lay Francis Cabot Lowell's ideal project. This project must be considered under two distinct aspects, the relation of the settlement to the rest of the country and the internal organization of the town itself. Then it will be necessary to discuss the modifications of the utopia which Boott was forced to make.

Mr. Lowell intended to create an independent industrial city which would be to Boston "what Manchester, Leeds, Birmingham and Sheffield are to their respective seaports."[24] This was not a new idea. Tench Coxe had proposed just that program in the late eighteenth century. Lowell took it over partly because it was at that time such a natural conception. In 1814 men never thought of manufacturing as a secondary function of a commercial town. With the spinning-mill tradition behind them and the English development in mind, they always visualized it as taking place in cities especially devoted to that particular purpose. But an even stronger reason in favor of this idea was its appropriateness to the undeveloped state of the country at that time. In America manufacturing depended upon water power. Large-scale manufacturing, such as Francis Cabot Lowell intended, demanded the considerable fall of a great body of water. As this was a requirement which was not apt to be satisfied near any existing commercial town, it necessitated that industry create new towns for itself, and it practically insured that these towns would be located in the wilderness.

The new element which Mr. Lowell introduced was the vision of a manufacturing town as an ideal community and the desire to organize it as such. In one sense his project was but the first of all those attempts to build a new abode of sweetness and light according to a preconceived plan for the ideal society which were characteristic of Transcendentalist New England.[25] But, unlike most visionaries, for Mr. Lowell the object of the community was not to establish a new and peculiar type of social organization. For him it was the work to be performed in the community that was central. The social organization was merely a technique which made it possible to keep the work going. Hence, he conceived of the town as made up of two distinct groups, the employees and the citizenry. Their ways of life would be quite different, the one wholly controlled by the corporation, the other free, at least up to a point.

This idea in itself greatly simplified the formulation of architectural objectives. As Mr. Lowell did not conceive of a city as

a choate community, he was not obliged to design the framework
for a complete civic organism. All that had to be done was to
designate two zones, one for the corporation, and one for the
bourgeoisie, and to lay out the former in accordance with a strictly
functional technique of planning.

That was the problem. The most straightforward solution was
a scheme of ribbon development.[26] A great road would be built
following the course of the river about a quarter of a mile away.
This road was to serve two functions: it would be the backbone
of the community, with shops, public buildings and parks clustered around;[27] it would also divide the property into two distinct portions. The land between it and the river would be reserved for industry. The land away from the river would be
given over to the bourgeoisie.

With regard to developing the industrial section, the procedure was almost as mechanical. The first necessity was to obtain
the water power from the rapids, which might be at some little
distance. This would be done by means of a canal which would
be dug parallel to the bank of the river, perhaps a hundred yards
away.[28] This would make an island between the canal and the
river, and it was here that the factories would be placed. Behind
them, the section between the canals and the high road was to
be devoted to industrial housing. If the company owned any land
across the highroad, it would be laid out in streets, divided into
lots, and then auctioned off to the bourgeoisie. This ideal scheme
was exemplified countless times in the many imitations of Lowell,
which were built during the first half of the nineteenth century.[29]
But when Boott set out to plan the original city itself, he found
that topography forced him to make certain major alterations.
The ideal scheme presupposed several things, that the course of
the river should be straight, below the rapids, and that the canals
and the highway should run parallel to the stream. At Lowell,
none of these conditions prevailed. The river made a right angle
turn and the canal, so far from following the stream, actually

curved away. (Frontispiece.) Roughly, it formed the arc of a quadrant, whose center was a great bend in the Merrimack.[30] Finally, when the highroad was built it had to abide by the locations of existing bridges. These gave it a course that diverged from both the river and the canal. It became a third factor in forcing a compromise with the ideal scheme.

It was inevitable that this compromise should be at the expense of the town, rather than of the factories. In the ideal scheme the two elements were conceived together. They balanced about the central axis of the main street. But when geography made such a balance impossible, it was the town which was sacrificed.

At Lowell the factories were conceived first. They were planned as normally as possible, and when they were finished, the town was arranged to fit into the area left over. Boott's initial problem in laying out the city was to fix the location of the Merrimack Manufacturing Company and then to decide where other plants might advantageously be placed. He wished to give the Merrimack Company the benefit of the full thirty-foot drop in the river level.[31] This meant that its factories would have to be situated on the bank of the stream, and fed from a point above the uppermost of the four sets of locks in the Pawtucket Canal.[32] That was impractical. Instead, the first two sets were abolished, water was carried through to what had been the third set at the highest level. Then a new canal was built, the Merrimack Canal. It ran in a straight line from the third, or Swamp Locks, to meet the bank of the Merrimack River at right angles. This junction was set aside as the site of the new concern. (Frontispiece.)

A logical location for later mills was on either side of the Merrimack Company. They would be provided with power by a series of canals, radiating fan-fashion from the Swamp Locks. Accordingly, the Merrimack River bank was saved for manufacturing for about three quarters of a mile above the mouth of its tributary, the Concord. Another obvious site for factories was on either side of the Pawtucket Canal, below the Swamp Locks.

They would get their power directly from the old canal. This area, likewise, was reserved.

The next consideration was the location of the housing. The best place for it was right behind the mills, and that is where it was put in the ideal scheme.[33] At Lowell likewise land was earmarked for housing in back of the band of property held for plants. In general, the additional areas ran parallel to the waterways, but there were two exceptions. As the Merrimack Manufacturing Company and its Print Works were the only concerns which would enjoy the full drop of water, they would presumably be larger than the other establishments and they would need more room for housing. They were allotted a great tongue of property running inland. As the hinterland of the mills on the north bank of the Pawtucket Canal was cut up by canals radiating from the Swamp Locks, they had to be given some extra land for housing off to the west.

There remained the matter of laying out the streets. The undeveloped site of the town was crossed by two winding roads.[34] These were "through" ways, and would have to be retained in the final organization. Accordingly, Boott accepted them as axes, and decided to develop the pattern of secondary communications around them. His first task was to "rationalize" these crooked highways, and turn them into major city streets.[35] In tackling this problem his hands were by no means free. The ends of the roads were fixed, for they had to connect with various bridges and a ferry, which it would have been too expensive to move. In addition the streets had to avoid as far as possible the areas reserved for manufacturing and housing. Between these two necessities there was very little room for choice, and a street plan that was really suitable for the city was out of the question. The land set aside for the Corporation constituted a great F-shaped area.[36] The highways were related to this area in the most unfortunate way imaginable. The main traffic arteries converged upon the one space surrounded on three sides by Corporation property.

The logical place for the center of the town was the spot of free land in the head of the F.

Such then, was the plan of Lowell; a series of mills arranged on various waterways, a hinterland of housing, and a gridiron of streets fitted into the space left over. It had many faults, particularly in the organization of the roads. In addition Boott made one serious error when he failed to line up the main north-south highway with the ferry across the Merrimack.[37]

These initial mistakes and inconveniences were aggravated by the manner in which the real estate was handled.[38] After the mill areas had been reserved, the rest of the property was awkward enough in shape. It would have been a hard task for the town just to squeeze its way into, and to grow up freely around, these great tracts of land. But to make matters worse, the Merrimack Company owned many of the choicest parts of the residue. For more than twenty years it held two thirds of this additional land off the market, thus warping yet further the evolution of the town. Then, all the real estate was sold in one great auction, but only because the immediate prospects of industrial expansion were even more attractive than the hope of future real estate profits.[39]

These shortcomings in conception and faults in administration were not the result of a lack of foresight. Neither were they entirely the product of a consuming will to exploit. They were largely the outcome of ignorance.

The founders of Lowell certainly expected a city to grow up around their factories.[40] They were resolved that it should be an ideal city. But they failed to appreciate the important part which planning and real estate management would play in the layout and gradual evolution of the perfect town. They did not conceive of a city as a coherent community which could and should develop around a determined three-dimensional framework. A city was merely an aggregate of individuals. Architecturally speaking, it was a good city if it was made up of substantial buildings. Planning had nothing to do with its quality, for planning was not recognized as a controlling activity. Planning was merely a technique of arranging neatly certain given things. Accordingly they did not feel any need to visualize specifically and completely the skeleton about which their city would grow. Still less did they feel any responsibility to mold the form that the community assumed as it developed. For them the growth of a city was merely an opportunity to make a killing in real estate, and they bought property corporately and individually with that object in view.[41]

Appleton, Jackson, Boott, and Lowell can hardly be blamed. Their naïveté was the result of the time and place of their birth. Coming from small New England seaports and market towns, they were men of limited architectural experience and narrow social insight. They genuinely wished to create an architectural utopia; but they could dream only of a group of well-built factories, of a settlement of tidy cottages growing up between them, and of profits resulting from the whole. That dream Boott enabled them to realize in full.[42] (Figure 1.)

IV

THE FIRST BUILDING
CAMPAIGN

APPLETON, Jackson, Boott, et al. were not men to dawdle. Once in control of the property, they immediately set to work. Six months after Worthen had suggested the site to Moody, building was well under way.[1] On September 4, 1823, Boott sat down and made a memorable entry in his diary. It was less than two years since he first set foot in Chelmsford. He wrote, "After breakfast, went to factory and found the wheel moving round his course, majestically and with comparative stillness."[2] Lowell had begun.[3]

The building of the Merrimack Manufacturing Company's factory was but one of several projects that were all proceeding together. The Pawtucket Canal had to be reconstructed to change the system of locks and to quadruple the capacity. The Merrimack Canal had to be dug. There was a Print Works to be created. There were houses to be erected for operatives and executives. In 1825 it was decided to put up a church, and, finally, the founders determined to start a machine shop in the new town.[4] All these operations together constituted the first building campaign. It will be well to treat them separately, taking up the different edifices one after another.

Little need be said with regard to the work on the waterways.[5]

It was a great task to raise the level of the Pawtucket Canal, and to enlarge it so that it was sixty feet wide and eight feet deep.[6] The digging of the Merrimack Canal was difficult also, since much of its bed was rocky. But neither undertaking involved any particular problems, other than that of organizing enough man power to get the jobs done.[7] Nor were the mills of the Merrimack Manufacturing Company unusual, individually. Considered singly (and they were built one by one), the factories were remarkable only for their size.[8] It was the manner in which they were grouped, and the way that the whole mill yard was integrated to the housing, which constituted something new. The single forms were but the end product of a long tradition.

Grist mills, saw mills, and fulling mills had existed in America since the seventeenth century. These small structures were generally made of wood, despite the danger of fire. Except for their location beside a stream, they did not differ in appearance from contemporary houses or barns.[9] This type of mill continued to be built well into the nineteenth century, at least in New England.

The first American mill built to shelter cotton-spinning machinery was put up in Beverly, Massachusetts, in 1787.[10] The only significant feature about this structure was the fact that it was built of brick. This shows that even in the late eighteenth century it was considered desirable that a mill should be a substantial edifice, more substantial than the average house.[11]

Three years later, Samuel Slater installed his imitation English machinery in an old fulling mill.[12] This ran so successfully that in 1793 Slater erected a water mill which was especially designed to accommodate spinning machinery.[13] It was wooden, forty feet long, twenty-six feet wide, and two stories and a half high. It did not differ essentially from a large barn or farmhouse of the same period, except in two minor features. Over one gable there was a very simple wooden cupola containing a bell. In the middle of the roof there was a curious long dormer or monitor. Unlike most later monitors, this did not extend through to the gables.

Instead, it looked like a giant trap-door opening out of the middle of the roof, and held slightly ajar. Inside, there was a single large room, open from end to end.[14]

This mill was entirely satisfactory, and very shortly after its completion it was lengthened, and a wing containing a staircase was thrown out at right angles. The plan of the completed structure was a short-stemmed long-headed T. The height remained the same, and the monitor was continued over the new portions, but the old cupola was removed, and replaced by a far more elaborate one over the wing. In this form, the "Old Slater Mill" survives at the present day. As extended, it was the largest and best-equipped factory in the country, and it remained without an equal for many years.[15]

Once Slater had shown the way, others were not slow to follow. Even before 1800, a few cotton spinning mills were built in and around Pawtucket, and the number went on increasing during the very first years of the nineteenth century. About 1810, however, there was a sudden burst of factory founding. Cotton manufacturing began to boom in southern New England, and it continued to do so for five years.[16]

With the second decade of the century a new type of factory building was evolved. The mills began to lose their domestic character as their size increased and as masonry construction became more and more common. Simple rectangles in plan, they were now frequently five stories high, instead of the two or three that was usual before.[17] They were no longer squat in proportions, like their forerunners, and while they were sometimes as long as Slater's structure, the increased height, and above all the greater breadth, gave them an entirely different appearance. The trap-door monitor was still to be found in some instances.[18] Gradually, even this was replaced by another type, the clerestory monitor, which ran right through the building from gable end to gable end. The cupola remained. It was placed over one gable, as it had been in the Slater mill before its enlargement.[19]

The first mill which was built in Waltham in 1814 was merely a variant of this new form.[20] It was a brick structure, six stories high, including the basement and attic, and covered by a clerestory monitor of slight projection. Unlike contemporary Rhode Island mills, it was placed parallel to the course of the stream, and its cupola stood in the middle of the roof.[21]

A second mill was added to the plan by 1818.[22] Although similar in material, height, and covering to the former, it was somewhat longer, and the stairway was placed in a tower, independent of the main body. In 1820 still a third mill was built at Waltham.[23] This combined the central cupola of the first, with the stair tower of the second. Between them, these three established a new type. Once this form had been stereotyped in Lowell, the renown of the new city tended to make it accepted as standard, at least throughout northern New England.[24] The plant of the Merrimack Manufacturing Company was made up of a series of five such units[25] (Figures 2 and 3.) each about twice the size of the second mill at Waltham, from which individually they did not differ greatly.

An important advance, however, was in the conception of the "establishment" as a unit.[26] The dominant consideration in the arrangement was the need to economize in frontage along the river bank. Every extra foot consumed by the initial concern meant that an additional foot of canal would have to be dug later for the benefit of contiguous companies. Therefore the Merrimack Canal terminated in a hairpin bend. (Figure 3.) Three mills were placed parallel to the river, and the other pair and the long structure of the Print Works were turned at right angles to the stream. Strings of low buildings, serving as storage rooms, were soon put up. The central one towards the town was the "Counting House," or office of the company. On either side of the Merrimack Canal, between the mill and Merrimack Street, land was set aside and planted with elm trees. In addition there were (and still are) trees and shrubs inside the mill yard. Thus, what with the conventional cupola on the central mill, this trim little quadrangle must have shown a marked resemblance to the academic groups of the period.[27]

It is a more difficult task to reconstruct the original appearance of the interiors. Certainly there were always a series of undivided rooms, some ten feet high, and the stairs, usually circular, rose in a turret outside of the building. The floors, instead of being supported by joists (as was the case in England), were carried on large beams. It soon became the practice to fasten these beams to the side walls by means of bolts and plates on the outside of the building. These beams were about five feet apart and were supported in the center by wooden pillars, with a double floor above.[28] In most cases the wooden columns have been replaced by cast iron supports.[29]

In addition to the mills, it was necessary for the Merrimack Manufacturing Company to erect housing and a few public buildings. Francis Cabot Lowell had a conservative social outlook, as was only natural in a member of the New England trading class. He visualized the industrial town in terms of an early republican seaport, with the community organized as a hierarchy of clearly defined groups. In the industrial town, however, the structure would be utterly rigid, the castes immutably fixed.[30]

When the time came, Lowell was organized into five distinct classes. At the top was the tight little oligarchy of corporation executives, under the leadership of "His Imperial High Mightiness," Boott.[31] As the stockholders were for the most part merchants living at some distance (it was a day's trip to Boston), these executives were not immediately responsible to anybody. They formed an isolated and compact group which had complete immediate control over the community. Next to this small aristocracy there was a gentry made up of the skilled employees, that is, everybody from junior executives to mere foremen. Beneath them were the mill hands, the thousands of sturdy farm girls who were actually responsible for production and who formed a yeomanry. Finally there were the day laborers, a proletariat of Irish immigrants, who dug the canals and built the mills. Outside of these four groups there were the settlers who lived on the other side of the main street. They ranged all the way from adventuring gentlemen who thought they saw a chance to make a killing in real estate, to scallawags typical of any booming community. But the vast majority were lawyers, ministers, and tradesmen, busily engaged in becoming substantial citizens by providing country girls with city conveniences.[32]

For three of these five castes the Merrimack Manufacturing Corporation undertook to provide housing. With a working week of six days and a working day of at least twelve hours, the first essential was that the dwellings should be in a compact group near the mills. But the same fact made it unnecessary that the houses should be more than dormitories. Bedrooms and dining rooms were unavoidable, but further facilities were luxuries which could be doled out in proportion to the importance of the recipient and the magnanimity of the Corporation. Finally, the fact that the houses would be next the mills necessarily meant that they must advertise in unmistakable terms the benevolence of the Concern. Hence they must be "a superior class of buildings,"[33] well constructed and well maintained, "finished off in a style much above the common farm houses of the country, more nearly resembling the abodes of respectable mechanics in rural villages."[34] Respectability was the watchword. Respectability at all costs![35]

Within the residential development the various types of accommodation would be strictly segregated. Thus, standing prominently apart, would be the residence of the agent. (Figures 13, 20.) An ample square mansion, severely plain save for a fan light over the door or a little beading at the eaves, it should be patently as solid and conservative in character as the Puritan dictator who lived in it. Preferably it should be near the main street, acting as a sort of buffer between the bourgeoisie and the laboring class. But it must be close to the employees. For the agent should guard his flock from his home by night, just as he watched over them by day from his counting house.

Secondary executives would be provided with more modest residences. The skilled employees would be given double houses, or else "tenements," that is, apartments arranged in long blocks. (Figure 9.) One and all, these would repeat at smaller scale the dwelling of the agent. The only difference would be the absence of even those sparse decorative features with which his mansion was adorned. But however simple, the buildings must be substantial and four square, homes fit for the deacons of the church and the pillars of industrial society.

The boarding houses of the farm girls could be arranged in pairs, or in long strings. (Figures 8, 10-12, 19, 21, 42-44.) Each unit would hold at least thirty girls, and if the units were grouped, eight or more would form a single block. Generally the buildings would be made two and a half or three and a half stories high.[36]

None of these decisions was arbitrary. Individually the mansions of the executives and the homes of the skilled employees were intended to be indistinguishable from normal contemporary houses of similar size. Their design would be controlled entirely by accepted practice in domestic architecture. The appearance of the boarding houses would be determined in the same way. They, too, would follow the dictates of tradition; for both in England and in America there was at this time a well-established tradition of low-cost housing design.

In England the houses of the proletariat were in a wretched state, by the end of the eighteenth century. "It was observed that the habitations of that useful and necessary rank of men, the Labourers, were become for the most part offensive both to decency and humanity."[37] With the rise of great estates some of the more enlightened of the gentry were wont to put up model cottages for their dependents, and the practice had become sufficiently general by the seventeen seventies so that a distinguished architect like John Wood found it worth his while to turn his "thoughts toward an object of such importance to the public as plans for cottages appeared to me to be."[38] It is significant that he found "it necessary not to confine myself to the habitations

of labourers in husbandry only, but to consider those of the workmen in the clothing and other manufacturing counties."[39] The
result was the appearance of *A Series of Plans for Cottages, or
Habitations of the Labourer, Either in Husbandry or the Mechanic
Arts*. (Figure 7.) This book was but one of several such efforts on
the part of British designers. It is outstanding, thanks to the
realism of its approach.[40]

In America somewhat the same situation prevailed, although
the problem here was more the absence of shelter than its degenerate state. As has been mentioned, even small-scale mills, like
those spinning cotton yarn, were obliged to erect houses for
their employees. By a remarkable coincidence one of Wood's
projects was virtually duplicated in some cottages actually built
in Middlesex Village near Lowell several years before the cotton
corporations appeared in the vicinity.[41] (Figures 6, 7.)

Therefore, when Boott set out to design the housing of the
Merrimack Manufacturing Company, he was by no means free.
He had to embody and express a rigid social organization which
Francis Cabot Lowell had conceived and which he, Boott, en-
thusiastically accepted. He was bound to work within the limits of
an architectural tradition that lacked variety. There remained only
one field in which individual accomplishment was possible, group
organization. It was here that Boott distinguished himself, in the
layout of the housing no less than in the organization of the mill
yard. But even here his freedom of creation was strictly cur-
tailed. The locations of the river, the canal, and the highroad
were fixed. The functional requirements he had to satisfy were
stringent.

It was desirable that all the housing should adjoin the mills.
The most economical arrangement was to make all the mill properties rectangular. Accordingly, the land between the Merrimack
River and Merrimack Street was divided into sectors by a series
of lines at right angles to the bank. The width of the individual
sector was determined by the amount of frontage on the stream

which was necessary in each case. Thus the Merrimack Manufacturing Company took over a trapezium of property bounded on two sides by the converging lines of the river and the thoroughfare, and on the other two by parallel property lines which would one day separate the Corporation from its neighbors. (Figure 3.)

At the northern end of this tract the mill buildings occupied a great L-shaped space. The remainder was divided into two parts by the Merrimack Canal. It was decided to devote the smaller of these, a very narrow rectangle east of the canal, to other purposes. The larger, an irregular parallelogram west of the canal, provided ample accommodations for the housing. On this last, then, the contractors set to work, and by 1826 at the latest they had covered it with some thirty dwellings.[42]

Although the buildings in this area have been considerably changed, the original arrangement can be reconstructed. To the south, between Merrimack and Moody Streets, was a triangular piece of property where was placed a house belonging to an executive. The remainder of the land was divided up into blocks by a series of short streets running from Moody Street to the mill yard, and parallel to the canal. Only the two easternmost streets, and the alley between them, had been laid out in 1826.[43] The first of these, facing the canal, had a row of houses along one side, a park along the other; the second was lined with houses on both sides. (Figures 4, 5, 8-11, 74.)

The houses were one and all cubes, crowned with double-pitched roofs although some were built in brick and some in wood. With double doors on the street, and three pairs of windows across the façade, they are splendid late examples of the "colonial" tradition in domestic architecture. Within, all have been rebuilt. None are now used for their original purpose; indeed it is no longer possible to say with certainty what the original purpose was, and which houses were for boarders, which for the skilled laborers. The only indication of the original arrangement in any of them is a ground plan made about 1900 when one of the wooden houses was turned into a mansion for the agent.[44] (Figure 5.)

There is, of course, no way of knowing the age of the disposition there shown, but it is probably close to the original one, as the type of plan is quite typical of row houses of the nineteenth century. Certainly the arrangement varies only slightly from that of boarding houses of the forties, where contemporary ground plans have survived. (Figure 42.) Each of these houses must have accommodated at the very least twenty girls.[45]

It is curious that Boott should have preferred to erect rows of double houses, rather than long strips, each containing several dwellings.[46] It certainly was not the most economical arrangement, and it was not the one generally followed thereafter.[47] Perhaps the reason was functional, for double houses permitted each unit to have three exposures. Yet in private building it was quite customary to string houses together, and we must not impute to the early nineteenth century our own standards of ventilation.[48] (Figures 23, 26.)

It is quite likely that the choice was a deliberate question of taste. If so, it would be a striking indication of that strange transitional character which all the architecture of the first building campaign in Lowell exhibits. The normal late baroque approach to a problem of street design such as was here presented would be to consider the space as a sort of corridor, the façades of the houses forming a continuous wall on either side. The normal nineteenth-century procedure would be to treat each side as a series of individual units, each designed for itself.[49] (Figures 75, 77.) This solution falls somewhere between. That, in itself, is not surprising, because in New England, thanks to the sharp social division between the independent Puritan farmers and the Tory commercial class, the high Georgian style never really took root.[50] Individual monuments of the cities sought to ape the works of Wren and Gibbs, but generally the cubic simplicity of the early Georgian period lingered on and merged into the cubic classicism of the late Georgian period.

It is not the fact that the baroque conception is toned down by being executed with the essentially anti-baroque native units which is unusual. Such a procedure would be normal New England practice. But a tension arises just because Boott was conscious of the conflicting possibilities of both styles. His sense of the simple prismatic beauty of the traditional New England house is obvious. (Figure 10.) Moreover he appreciated the way in which it can become the nucleus of an agglomeration of geometric forms. Towards the street each unit has its pair of wings, like epaulettes, building a pyramidal composition with the main structure. (Figure 10.) To the rear, sheds and outhouses oppose themselves to the bulk of the dwelling. Yet Boott places his units so close together that one is forced to see each, not as a climax of an independent composition, but as a member of a series.

A further indication of the sensitiveness of Boott's planning is the manner in which he varied the materials. Almost all of the units are wooden double houses, but approximately in the middle of the front row, and in line with it on the other two rows, was a quadruple house built of brick. (Figure 9.) Evidently he visualized the area between the front row of houses and the buildings on the opposite side of the canal as a single space, a cul-de-sac, surrounded by buildings. This area he treated as though it were a baroque plaza with a watercourse down the middle, placing a central accent in each closed side—a mill, the brick house, and, as it turned out later, the gable end of the high school opposite. Having established an alternation of brick and wood in his front row, Boott repeated it on the second and third rows, although, thanks to the narrowness of the open space, it can never have had the same meaning.

Time has played hob with this would-be piece of sophistication. The axial cupola has gone. The high school has been torn down, and a successor built, off axis, out of scale, and in a different colored brick, while on both sides of the canal great rows of elm trees have grown up, so that the plaza has become a magnificent *allée*, in the Victorian manner. Finally, one whole wooden series of the front row of housing has been rebuilt as a single brick unit at twice the height. (Figure 44.) Between the front row of the houses and the nearest of the elms the space is now so narrow that it is impossible even to imagine the housing as a flanking façade of any sort. As in the second and third rows one is forced to consider it as a progression of units carrying the eye to the mill at the end of the vista.

The houses of the executives of the Merrimack Manufacturing Company have all been destroyed long since, but the house built for Paul Moody, as agent of the Machine Shop, survives. (Figure 13.) This is almost identical with the boarding houses, being a simple square block with a double pitched roof. Its one distinguishing feature was an elaborate garden in front that culminated in a semicircular pond near the bank of the canal.[51]

It is disillusioning to turn from all these tidy dwellings of the native employees to the huts of the immigrant day laborers. The corporation made no provision for these men; they had not entered into the calculations of those who planned the town. In their destitution they had to content themselves with miserable hovels, clustered about the crude Catholic church on some otherwise useless piece of property. Their shacks have all been destroyed in the later growth of the city, but descriptions of them remain. Here is the situation in 1831.

Within a few rods of the canals there is a settlement called by some New Dublin, which occupies rather more than an acre of ground. It contains a population of not far from five hundred Irish, who dwell in about a hundred cabins, from seven to ten feet high built of slabs and rough boards, a fireplace made of stone in one end, topped out with two or three flour barrels or lime casks. In a central situation is the school house, built in the same style of the dwelling houses, turfed up to the eaves, with a window in one end and small holes in two sides for the admission of air and light. In this room are collected together perhaps 150 children.[52]

At that, this state of wretchedness was the achievement of nine years of hard labor. Conditions the first spring defy imagination.

Dreadful as were these living conditions, in the heyday of

Lowell they only applied to some 5 percent of the population. They were less serious, therefore, as a fact than as a symptom. They were one of the first signs of that social callousness which in a hundred years has allowed rural and urban slums to become the normal habitat of one third of the nation. The tragedy of Lowell lay not so much in the horror of the initial situation, but in the fact that it grew progressively worse. Not only did a constantly increasing proportion of the population live in squalor, but the squalor deepened as the century went on. By 1850 a hut in New Dublin would have seemed like suburban luxury to an Irish immigrant.[53]

The basic dualism of Boott's taste is visible again in the two other important buildings erected during the first campaign. Boott, a gentleman of independent means,[54] designed for himself a porticoed mansion which stood near the center of the town, between Merrimack Street and the river, just below the Merrimack Manufacturing Company.[55] (Figure 14.) It is unfortunately impossible to tell much about the original interior of the house, although the exterior is virtually intact. It consisted originally of a square main block and an ell at the back. Various additions to the main block have been made at later periods, but for the most part towards the rear. The house is crowned with a hip roof which terminates in a railing, and is ornamented in front with a tetrastyle Ionic portico. The entablature of the portico runs all around the main block, and is carried at the corners of the façade by pilasters. The front is five bays wide, and as the blinds on the windows existed in 1841 they are probably original.[56]

It is interesting to contrast the Boott house with a mansion built in the neighboring town of Haverhill.[57] (Figure 15.) Both are approximately the same in date and they are almost identical in size and pretentiousness. The Haverhill building shows up admirably the provincially conservative character of Boott's dwelling. In both a cubic hip-roofed block is the core of the design. In Lowell the main block is merely a nucleus to which a portico, dormers, and an ell are attached. The texture of the different faces is strongly marked, and the contrast between the clapboarding of the sides and the matchboarding of the front tends to emphasize the façade. This is modeled forwards by the portico, and the richness of the design increases towards the center with the increasing plasticity. The proportions of Boott's portico show some of the attenuation that was characteristic of Federalist New England, but it retains its high Georgian pseudo-structural character.[58] It is a self-sufficient trabeated system applied to the block of the house. High Georgian, too, is the way in which, by the use of blinds, the windows are indicated as being on a plane in front of the wall surface. Their square proportions give them something the appearance of medallions pinned against a rich textile.

At Haverhill the whole block is covered with matchboarding, and the façade is cut back to form a great elliptical-headed niche in the center. Thus, the corners are emphasized, and the integrity of the cube is maintained and underlined. The roof is flatter than at Lowell, smooth surfaced, rather than shingled. Instead of the cornice's being gradually modeled forward and uniting the roof and the walls like a richly designed hinge, it projects boldly, emphasizing the mutual independence of the two units, so that the roof looks like a pyramidal lid, slightly too large for the cube on which it is set. Finally, the windows were merely neat rectangles sawn out of the smooth wall, like holes cut deliberately in a sheet of ice. The decoration around them is not plastic, but seems as if it were painted upon the surface. The Haverhill house shows how highly developed was the architect's fascination with the interplay of geometrical forms. His interest in surface treatment and the design of detail is secondary to his insistence upon the clear expression of the prisms. The scheme of two blocks with a hollow between, against which stand two columns, was endlessly repeated in Greek Revival work.

In April, 1824, the directors of the Merrimack Company voted to build a church of stone, at a cost not to exceed nine thousand dollars.[59] (Figure 16.) This was placed on the narrow slice of land remaining at the eastern end of the company's lot. (Figure 3.) Shortly afterwards a rectory was started next to it. The church was built and the rectory almost completed by the fall of 1826. As Kirk Boott was an Episcopalian, the church was naturally of the same persuasion, and as Christianity does not recognize a St. Kirk, the parish was perforce dubbed St. Anne's, in honor of the agent's wife. The board of directors, who were Unitarians, doubted whether an Anglican church would be supported. Boott got around that difficulty neatly by decreeing not only that all the operatives must go to *his* church, but also that they must contribute thirty-seven and one half cents a month towards its upkeep.[60] As the great majority of the employees were members of other sects, this arrangement was not popular, and with the founding of additional Protestant churches, it had to be given up. None the less, St. Anne's survived and even prospered.

The church is a simple structure, built like the adjacent rectory of stone, dug out of the Merrimack Canal. It consists of an almost square auditorium with a gabled roof and a small tower projecting at the west end. It was planned from the start to make the building three bays long, although only two were put up at first. At a later time the third was added, together with a projecting choir. The building is Gothic in style. In every way it is a typical Episcopal church of the period.

Americans had become conscious of the Gothic Revival as early as the nineties of the eighteenth century, and thereafter "pointed" was an admissible alternative style for churches, although classic remained by far the more common.[61] Indeed, few Gothic buildings of any sort were erected until the 1820's. Before the thirties, when a few good English handbooks appeared, it was well-traveled amateurs rather than professional builders who were responsible for romantic designs. The scheme of a square auditorium with a projecting western entrance tower had survived in America from the Middle Ages. However, its use was common in New England only after Bulfinch had designed at Pittsfield the first nonconformist building which adopted this as opposed to the meeting-house plan.[62] In so far as St. Anne's was not merely a compound of tradition and Boott's memories of English parish churches, it was derived from Harrison's Kings Chapel, Boston, the ancestor of a whole flock of stone Gothic churches built in and around Boston in the later twenties and thirties.[63]

The specifically Gothic features of the building are the point-ing of the windows, which are filled with wooden tracery, and the design of the tower. Originally this had four pinnacles at the corners, in addition to the battlements which still survive. But its significance is less in the fact that it was Gothic than in the fact that because it was Gothic it was abreast of advanced architecture of the day, and was the most progressive building of the period in Lowell. This is evident particularly in the fine treatment of the unbroken sheets of masonry, and in the fashion in which the thin prism of the tower is set out against the great shed of the church. Thus, it reflects the same delight in the contrast of elemental geometric forms as was visible in the boarding houses individually and in the Haverhill mansion as well. But, signifi-cantly, as contrasted with the latter, the interplay of the forms here is simpler and harsher, less sophisticated. The interior is of the utmost plainness, a bare, rather ill-proportioned room. Quite characteristically, the only handsome feature, a magnificent timber roof, is carefully hidden by lathe and plaster.[64]

V

A DECADE OF GROWTH
1825–1835

CONSIDERED from almost any angle, the history of Lowell falls into three great periods—the establishment of the city, from 1820 to 1865; expansion, from the end of the Civil War to the turn of the century; boom and depression, bringing one down to the present day. Closer examination reveals that the opening chapter no less than the concluding should be divided into two distinct phases. The first of these was characterized by the rapid growth both of the city itself and of its industry. It was a period of comparatively little internal friction, it represented the heyday of Lowell as a utopia. Already in the late thirties, however, there are signs of change taking place, and these continue during the early forties. There is no distinct break, but thanks to the cumulative effect of all these minor transformations, the town had clearly entered upon a new phase by 1845.

From a strictly architectural point of view it is necessary to subdivide Lowell's early history still further. The period from 1825 to 1835 forms a unit by itself. At this time architecture continued the Georgian tradition, by and large. Next there comes a group of buildings which reveal the influence of the mature Greek Revival. The first examples date from 1830, the last from about 1845. They dominate the architecture of the city during the late thirties and early forties, and can be considered to represent an early stage of romanticism in Lowell. The full impact of that movement only struck in the early forties, however. Its influence lasted undiminished until 1865. Although there was no stylistic change, the last few years of this period were years of depression, when little building was accomplished. Thus, one can divide Lowell's early architectural development into four interlocked stages, the first lasting from 1825 to 1835, the second from 1830 to 1845, the third from 1840 to 1855, and the last from 1855 to 1865.

By 1826 the framework of the city plan had been drawn up, and the model which the later factories of Lowell were to follow so faithfully was visible in bricks and mortar.[1] The next fifteen years saw the filling in of the industrial outline. Company after company was founded, each patterned upon the Merrimack Manufacturing Company. Appleton, Jackson, and their associates had originally put up $600,000 for the new scheme. By 1847 almost twelve million dollars was invested in textile manufacturing in Lowell.[2] The number of spindles had risen from five or six thousand to two hundred and fifty thousand.[3] Meanwhile the hamlet of East Chelmsford with a population of some two hundred in 1820 had grown into the city of Lowell with nearly 30,000 inhabitants in 1845.[4]

The period was one of great building activity, but of slight architectural achievement. Much that was put up was temporary and had to be replaced in the years immediately succeeding.[5] The rest was unadventurous. The mills repeated *ad infinitum* the standard architectural type, and creative energy was focused upon the evolution of suitable structures for the rest of the town. But the bourgeois pioneers took no such interest in architectural subtleties as had the cultivated Boott. They were not restrained by his strong, eighteenth-century sense of planning. Their concern was to shelter themselves and their activities as quickly as possible in substantial buildings.

The Boston Manufacturing Company at Waltham had paid

104½ percent dividends in ten years, and its stock was soon selling above par value.[6] This taught the capitalists a valuable lesson. Obviously, the lucrative thing to do was to promote companies, and as soon as they were running profitably, unload one's stock at the greatest possible increase in prices.

Once the Merrimack Manufacturing Company was well started, Jackson and some of his partners set to work to found a second concern, to be located in Lowell.[7] As a result of their efforts the Hamilton Manufacturing Company was incorporated in 1825. Its mills were in operation before 1830.[8] The Hamilton Company was followed by others. The Appleton Manufacturing Company was incorporated in 1828 and built two mills just above the Hamilton Company. The Lowell Manufacturing Company was formed in the same year and built two mills just below the Machine Shop in the Pawtucket Canal region, and just across from the Hamilton mills. In 1830 three new companies were inaugurated, the Tremont, the Suffolk, and the Lawrence. During the same year the Middlesex Company was incorporated and built two mills on land bought from Thomas Hurd, outside the holdings of the Locks and Canals Company. Finally, in 1835 and 1839 the Boott and the Massachusetts mills were incorporated. Except for the small Prescott Mills, which soon merged with the contiguous Massachusetts, and a few minor concerns like the Lowell Brewery, the roster of the corporations was now complete.[9]

The mill buildings of the new corporations did not differ from their prototype to any great extent. Two changes were made, however. The first process that took place in the mills was picking. In this the cotton, unwrapped from the bales, was cleaned of dust and wound round wooden cylinders.[10] As the machinery moved very fast, there was considerable danger of fire. One of the original Merrimack Mills had burned down in 1829 and thereafter it was common to place the pickers in special little fireproof houses, a few feet from the mills.[11] (Figure 46.) Beginning with the Boott mills, the monitor type of roof was abandoned, being replaced by a simple double-pitched covering.[12] This meant an additional story

in height. It simplified and added greatly to the impressiveness of
the mill buildings. Also, the later companies dispensed with
cupolas, being less interested in display. (Figure 1.)

None of the mill buildings of this period survive unchanged
in Lowell today.[13] To see the effect they must have made, one
must turn to less successful textile centers. There, the number
of these structures is legion, for, as with the monitor roof type,
the rest of northern New England followed the precedent of the
large centers. At Amesbury there is a large brick mill—probably
dating from around 1840—that is a close reproduction of the
structures put up for the Massachusetts Company. The most beautiful of these buildings, however, is one of the mills of the Newmarket Manufacturing Company at Newmarket, New Hampshire.
(Figure 17.) Here a great granite pile rears itself eighty feet
upright out of the water. The increased height and the resulting
slender proportions combine to give an impression of threatening
instability. As with St. Anne's, one is struck by the magnificent
use of the stone, which gains added effectiveness by its juxtaposition
with the wood of the bridge, the slate of the roof, and the red
brick of the stair tower. Noteworthy also is the harshness of the
building, unrelieved by any detail, and the uninterrupted clarity
of the outlines which define the simple forms.

More striking is the change in the design of the housing. Hardly
was the Merrimack Company completed when its housing system was abandoned. The Hamilton built, both for its skilled and
unskilled operatives, a series of long rows facing one another across
the narrow streets. None of these survive, except for a small and
ruinous fragment.[14] However, before 1830 the Merrimack Company itself built similar units for the skilled English workmen
whom they imported to run the print works. These are still standing. (Figure 18.) Originally they were only one and a half stories
high. Presumably they were identical in type with the housing
of the Chelmsford Glass Factory. (Figure 6.) Later, a second
story was added. They differ from the original quadruple house

only in the fact that all are strung together into a single building, and that the dormers which are tentatively used in the early work are regular and bold in the later.

In the thirties, the boarding houses of Lowell were made larger, and the standard height became three and a half, rather than two and a half stories. Elsewhere, notably at Somersworth, New Hampshire, and Chicopee, Massachusetts, this was accomplished without any essential change in the design. At Lowell, and at Manchester, however, there was a slight alteration.

In any row house the simplest plan was to group the doors in pairs adjacent to one party wall. It was desirable that the chimneys should be astride the other party wall. In the quadruple house two doorways had been put at the extreme ends, and two sets of chimneys in the middle. It was better looking to place the doorways in pairs in the center of the building and the chimneys on the end walls. It meant also that the living rooms, rather than the corridors of the end dwellings, had the advantage of the additional exposure. This arrangement, however, tended to make an awkward juncture where the diagonal of the gable met the vertical of the chimneys. This difficulty was solved by filling in the space between the two chimneys up to the ridge of the roof. (Figures 19, 21.) A further change occurred. At first, windows in the end walls tended to be placed near the corners. Later, the almost invariable practice came to be to run them up between the two chimneys. So far from creating a new type of building, however, these changes merely gave to the housing blocks an extraordinary resemblance to such an early eighteenth-century structure as Massachusetts Hall, Harvard University.[15]

At Lowell the definitive solution was reached in the housing for the Lawrence Company. (Figure 19.) Here four great blocks stand side by side. Each one is some 250 feet long and three and a half stories high. As is usual, the blocks are separated by streets and alleys running down to the mill yard. Cross streets mark off the ends of the blocks. Opposite one of the outer units at the end away from the mills is the house of the agent, like a corporal and his squad.[16] (Figure 20.)

Far more important than the mills and mill housing of the period were the buildings of the bourgeoisie. The arrival of the Merrimack Manufacturing Company in East Chelmsford produced, of course, a great increase in the population of the neighborhood. The growth of the settlement was rapid during the first half dozen years, but it seems to have been caused chiefly by the influx of the employees of the initial corporations.[17] Thereafter, a bourgeoisie not directly dependent on the manufacturing concerns appeared, and the town boomed in spectacular fashion for three decades.[18]

Inevitably the expansion fostered great building activity. It is worth while analyzing this activity in terms of the types of building produced and the exact period when each was being erected. Quantitatively, the most striking feature was the enormous number of private houses which were put up continuously throughout the period.[19] Since by the twenties there was already a considerable working population whose purchasing power was independent of the bourgeoisie, and since the town became an important center of communications overnight, a great number of commercial buildings were put up before the mid-thirties. However, once adequate accommodations had been provided, the demand for such structures did not increase proportionately with the population, so that a lull in this type of building followed.[20]

Twenty-six churches were erected in three waves of construction of decreasing intensity. Ten were created in the five years from 1827 to 1832. Twelve were built between 1837 and 1846, and the final quartet rose in the early fifties. Thereafter church building was negligible until after the Civil War.[21]

The location of these buildings was determined largely by the fashion in which the Locks and Canals Company sold off their land. The houses fall into five distinct groups.[22] The first and the least important set, were along the river bank, near the rapids. The founding of Lowell meant increased activity on the Middlesex Canal and increased travel on the highways north and west. This little settlement was strategically placed[23] to take advantage of these factors, as well as being conveniently close to the dam building and the canal deepening. However, at least by 1832, houses inspired by this prosperity ceased to be built in that neighborhood. Thereafter the area lay fallow. Boott moved his house out there when the original site was taken for mills, and it seemed likely that this area would become the fine residential district. But the opening up of Belvidere deferred this movement until after the Civil War.

In general, the Locks and Canals Company was chary about parting with its property, so few of the bourgeoisie were able to settle in the central portion of the town. However, as each mill was completed, a piece of land was sold off in front of it, so that by 1832 there was already a straggling row of buildings across from the Merrimack Corporation and St. Anne's, and by the forties this had become a compact mass of churches, houses and shops, crammed into a narrow tongue of property. (Figure 89.)

The bulk of the town was forced off the company land altogether onto three contiguous areas. The most important of these was the Chapel Hill district that lay between the Locks and Canals Company and the Concord River. This was the first to be settled, the most thickly settled, and it acquired almost at once a petty bourgeois character that it has retained to this day. Across the Concord River lay Belvidere, the nearer portion of which was filled up with small houses. Most of the land here, however, was part of a single great estate which was bought up by real estate developers and was sold off in the forties for expensive residences. Across the Merrimack River lay a similar area, Centralville, which likewise received a scattering of small houses. For some reason this section was sparsely settled until the last decades of the century.

Within these areas the pattern of development was fairly consistent. The settlement would begin as a group of houses at a crossroads on one of the highways leading into the center of town. The process of expansion consisted not in filling in evenly the property on either side of the arterial highway up to the next crossroads, but in jumping to this focal point at once and there forming a second group. These groups expanded, necessitating the creation of minor streets around the crossroads, and eventually they would come to touch one another. Except in the case of the limited property in front of the Merrimack Street mills, the evolution was never that of pure and simple ribbon development. Always it exemplified in embryo the molecular growth of the large city today.[24]

The distribution of the remaining buildings was determined by a variety of factors. The shops naturally lay along the two great highways, Merrimack and Gorham-Central Streets, particularly as in both cases these formed a dividing line between the mill property and the bourgeoisie. As the Chapel Hill district was the most populous and lay beside the main road to Boston, it was the most important commercial center at first. However, it never had the style which the Locks and Canals Company consciously cultivated on Merrimack Street. This was the "main street" of the town. Here or near here were the more important commercial centers, the more important public buildings, and also the churches. Belvidere was wholly residential in character, acquiring at a later time a sprinkling of churches. Centralville and the village near the falls were too unimportant to rate either churches, or shops, although thanks to the beauty of its location, the latter boasted one of the finest of Lowell's hotels.

In and about Lowell before the coming of the Corporations, houses were of two types, both gable roofed. One had four rooms on the ground floor, was almost square in plan, and squat in appearance. This type had a high roof. The other was one room deep, high and narrow in appearance, and capped with a comparatively low roof.

The former was continued in the Moody house and in the

corporation boarding houses. (Figures 4, 10, 13, 74.) It was found frequently in the bourgeois homes of the twenties and thirties, more rarely even in the forties. Many of these buildings, perhaps a majority, were double houses, and they did not differ substantially in ground plan from the wooden boarding houses. (Figure 5.) The others were made up of even more than two dwellings. (Figure 23.) Almost always there was an ell at the back. With space and to spare, generally the ell looked out on an alley or a noxious back yard, but in one instance the ell itself had been developed into a row of houses. (Figure 26.) It is evident from the tax records that much of the domestic architecture of Lowell was built speculatively. A man would put up two or three houses, live in one and rent the others.[25] Thus there are instances of identical double houses placed side by side in a fashion similar to Boott's scheme for the Merrimack Corporation.

The type could easily be glorified. A frequent change was to make the end walls of brick, placing two chimneys there instead of one, and running a diaphragm of brick between them to produce the same H-shaped design that is to be seen in the later boarding-house blocks. (Figure 22.) Not infrequently the rectangular blank space was relieved by a blind arch in the brick, enclosing a lunette window. In one or two cases the architect, taking a hint from the mills, ran his dormers together into a single long monitor. An almost invariable adornment of the houses of the twenties and thirties was a porch consisting of free-standing columns carrying a little entablature before the door. In the usual double house, classical precedents were thrown to the winds and the entrance was graced with three columns.

Conventional in type, yet splendid in size, such a square house lent itself to other uses when tricked out beyond the average. Thus, for the Lawrence Company it made an admirable agent's house, substantial as it was. (Figure 20.) It might also serve as a hotel, as in the case of the "Howard House." But, whatever the function, and however great the elaboration of ornament, one is always struck first by the great cubic solidity of the block, by the just proportioning of the somewhat harsh forms, by the lavishness yet simplicity in the handling of the materials.

Single square houses, like the agents' houses, with all four rooms at the disposal of the owner were all but unknown among the bourgeoisie. The single bourgeois house was generally of the narrow type. This is to be found in Lowell at least as early as the middle of the eighteenth century and remains popular until the forties.[26] Here the doorway in the middle of the façade led into a stair hall. Within, on one side there would be a living room, on the other a dining room, with the kitchen in an ell behind. Above there were two or more bedrooms around a central hall.

Most of the houses near the rapids follow this scheme, as do some in Centralville. (Figure 24.) Indeed, it was apparently *de rigueur*, except in the more crowded central quarters of the town. Despite its slighter form, in no sense was it considered inferior to the square type, rather the reverse. In a less pretentious town than Lowell it was good enough for the agent of the mill, and even Boott himself built just such a house to be the rectory of St. Anne's.[27] (Figure 25.)

The design of these houses was on the whole more stereotyped than that of the other group. The proportions varied little. The chimneys stood at either end, the nine windows of the façade were flanked with blinds, the door was accented by a two-column portico. Indeed, the only manner in which these houses could be differentiated stylistically was by the variations of their entrance treatment. The *retardataire* houses by the rapids showed the spindly delicacy of the Federalist period. (Figure 24.) The rectory boasted a very academic Doric porch.[28] (Figure 25.) The latest examples, avoiding all such heavy plasticity, were content with a shallow lintel or with a hood.

The commercial buildings followed similar conservative traditions. The majority of those built in the twenties were of wood, but by the early thirties many of these structures were already being replaced by brick buildings of a standard type. These were presumably larger than the wooden shops they succeeded, but they themselves were of such a simple pattern that they cannot have differed very much in form from their predecessors. The original wooden shops have all disappeared, but examples survive from the thirties which substantiate this conclusion. (Figure 27.)

The brick norm was three and a half stories high, gable roofed, and of considerable, although varying, length. (Figure 28.) Below would be a row of shops; above, the dwellings of the owners. Except for its larger scale, it was identical with the row type of dwelling houses. Never, however, was it as elaborately decorated as a group of residences of comparable size. One can deduce from examples outside Lowell that the type must have passed through a development essentially similar to that of the boarding house. A row of stores survives in Newmarket, New Hampshire, and another in Somersworth which suggest the manner in which the problem would have been treated in the twenties. (Figure 29.) As with Boott's brick blocks, the form is built up of structural units. The walls are covered with a simple projecting roof, out of which the great chimneys rise in splendid independence. Here and there one's attention is caught by a slight elaboration of detail. The doorways at Somersworth are arched and provided with fan lights, the gable end at Newmarket is enlivened with a sort of Palladian window motif, and the corner is rounded, by way of experiment. One feels that the contractor is designing with a series of autonomous elements, over each of which he has complete control. The building is considered as an individual and slightly whimsical combination of these elements.

Later, however, the point of view changed, and the builder's attention was focused increasingly on the totality of the form. The ordering of minor details ceased to be an opportunity for playful variety, and it was rigidly determined by the desire to emphasize the prismatic block of the whole. The juncture of roof and wall received its cornice, which commonly ran up the gable, thus drawing flank and front into a single composition. The chimneys lost their solidity and importance. The roof was punctured by dormers,

and a formula was evolved for the treatment of the ground floor—
a series of large openings between granite piers and lintels. Even
the rounded corner became regularized, losing something of its
charm, but gaining in frequency of use, just because standardized it
involved no problems in application. (Figure 28.) On the rare occasions where a slightly greater emphasis was demanded, it would
be supplied by some such simple device as the arching of the windows above the shop level, but the basic type remained unchanged.
(Figure 30.) For economic reasons, comparatively few stores were
built during the forties, and there was little incentive to alter the
established formula. A group of stores in Haverhill of 1849, one of
the few such dated buildings of this decade hereabouts, continues
exactly the old arrangement.

Aside from the stores, the only other significant type of commercial buildings were the hotels. Inn-keeping was an important business in early days at Lowell. The first bourgeois building of any
size was the Stone House, put up in Falls Village in 1825, and between 1830 and 1835 Lowell contained thirteen taverns and inns.
These were well patronized, so much so indeed that the landlords
were frequently forced to call upon private people for additional
accommodations.[29] None of these early hotels has survived unchanged. The Stone House exists, but it is now used for an or-
phanage. The Howard House is visible only in a decrepit state.
The Washington House and the Merrimack House, both built
early in the thirties, still survive, drastically remodeled. (Figures
30, 48.) However, old views and unrestored buildings in smaller
towns make it easy to reconstruct the original exterior appearances.

The Stone House was by way of being a family hotel. Prettily
located, during the summer it was crowded with boarders, and it
was here that visiting stockholders stayed. It consisted of two rectangular blocks joined by an ell, and each crowned by a hip roof.
(Figure 32.) Facing the river there were famous long balconies,
whence one could enjoy a view of the rapids. Except for its handsome use of building material, the hotel was almost completely
lacking in architectural character.

The Merrimack House was built by the Locks and Canals Company opposite the railroad station. (Figure 48.) It was the business hotel. In form it was simply an enlarged version of a round-angled store. The Washington House was similar to a large multiple dwelling, with double-storied porches across the front. (Figure 30.) It was almost identical with the Newmarket House, Newmarket, New Hampshire, although twice as large.[30] (Figure 31.)

As a whole, the hotels were possibly the least attractive buildings in town. They lose rather than gain by their great size, for that represents simply the inflation of a small-scale domestic architecture. One contemporary observer called them the only barracks in the town.[31]

Finally there were the churches. In 1831 the Irish Catholics of Lowell built themselves a wooden building in the Gothic style.[32] (Figure 33.) This building, long since destroyed, consisted of a rectangular auditorium with a spire-bearing tower projecting from the center of the front. It was lighted by a series of pointed and circular windows; it was ornamented with battlements and mighty pinnacles. In every respect it appears to have been a typical "carpenter" Gothic structure, similar to, if not so elegant as, the First Unitarian Church in Cambridge, which Isaiah Rogers designed for Harvard University two years later. Like that, it represented essentially a builder's corruption of the type of Gothic church which amateurs had planned during the twenties.

The two most important of the earliest churches were the First Baptist Church and the First Congregational Church. (Figure 34.) Both followed the traditional meetinghouse scheme, being made up of a barn-like auditorium preceded by a porch which carried a staged tower. The First Baptist Church of 1826, with Palladian windows and a lunette in the front of the porch, with two rows of rectangular windows, and with a cupola rising out of an open arched story, might have been copied from an Asher Benjamin plate.[33] It is all but identical with a great number of churches erected after Bulfinch built the meeting house in Pittsfield in the early seventeen nineties.[34]

The brick First Congregational Church of 1827 differs only in decoration.[35] The windows of the auditorium are round headed and enclosed by blind arches. There are panels above the entrance doorways, and the tower, which carries a steeple, is composed of a series of boxes, each a little smaller than the one below. The handling of the detail is quite as traditional as that of the First Baptist Church.

VI

THE IMPACT OF
ROMANTICISM
1835-1845

UNTIL the early eighteen thirties almost all the buildings of Lowell were uniform in style. With a few exceptions they can be classified as the products of a folk art. The architecture vividly illustrates how eighteenth-century traditions persisted in the cultural backwaters. Since it has all the inflexible consistency of a survival, it can be studied as a unit in itself. About that time, however, a great change took place. Lowell became aware of romanticism. Culturally, the city ceased to be a backwater and became provincial. There was a decade of transition; then the architecture of the mill town grew to be directly dependent on the great seaboard cities.

After 1835 the buildings of Lowell no longer constitute an entity which can be studied apart. Considered purely by themselves, they are confusingly diverse, for they were only the reflections of random fragments taken from an orderly sequence. There is only one way to find some meaning in their variety—that is to think of them as part of American architecture as a whole, to see them against the background of the general development.

One of the great contemporary illusions about the nineteenth century is the belief that orthodox building was fundamentally static throughout that period. "For a hundred years architecture lay smothered in a dead eclectic atmosphere."[1] Decade after decade the Victorians devoted themselves to the same "sterile copying" of the past. Not that architecture lacked a superficial variety. Designers were free to choose their models from the whole range of history, and they tried now this, now that. But beneath the restless succession of fads, the escapist ideal and the imitative method remained constant.[2]

This thesis is a direct reversal of the facts. So far from being free to choose whatever style he wished, the number of models available to the Victorian at any moment was limited by fixed principles of selection. So far from being obliged to follow his chosen model in accordance with an immutable method of imitation, the attitude of the designer towards the works of the past was always evolving. So far from being at heart aesthetically stagnant, revivalism, the orthodox architecture of the nineteenth century, developed continuously in a logical fashion.

The existence of this development has been generally ignored or denied because the process was so complex that it defies a simple exposition. The development was, in fact, the resultant of at least three distinct but interlocking types of evolution. A changing repertory of revivals, a changing conception of the role that historical styles should play in contemporary design, and a changing feeling for mass, space, shape, color, and texture, those are three movements which collectively helped determine the nature of orthodox nineteenth-century architecture.

The progress of the art can only be compared to an immense fugue. The various revival manners correspond to so many subjects and counter-subjects. The different attitudes towards the past are the equivalent of different instruments taking up the themes. The sense of architectural form evolving beneath the shifting styles and manners may be likened to the modulation of the whole piece of music from one key to another. Furthermore, just as a fugue can be legitimately divided into sections, so, at least in America, the history of orthodox nineteenth-century architecture can be broken

up into a series of distinct stages. Each has its characteristic pen-
chant for certain styles out of the past, each its particular way of
adapting them creatively, each its peculiar feeling for architectural
form.

In the first or decorative stage details from the past are used to
decorate buildings which in their essentials are still traditional. The
mass is generally simple, and the delicate ornament is often executed in a contrasting material or color. A fine product of this way
of thinking is St. Anne's church in Lowell.[3] In the next, or archaeological, stage the total form of the building is conceived as the accurate duplication of some accepted model. The decorative elements are larger in scale and bolder in handling. Often these
ranges of buttresses or pretentious porticoes seem to swallow up the
whole building, as in the first railroad station in Lowell, for instance.[4] Finally, the attempt to organize the whole structure according to canonical principles is given up. There had been an
eclecticism among the historical styles that produced a great variety
of building types. Now there is an eclecticism of motifs derived individually from the past. These compose a vocabulary. They are
organized according to original principles, so that the multiplicity
of historical forms constitutes but a single style. Detail is more disciplined, and is subordinated to hierarchical compositions of masses.
This mode of design only became common in central New England
after the Civil War.[5]

The citizens of Lowell did not become aware of revivalism until
it had passed out of its initial decorative stage. By the middle thirties architects in the more sophisticated centers were wholly preoccupied with the problems of reproducing Greek temples, Gothic
churches, and Tudor cottages entire. But there was a great dis-
parity between the point of view in the seaports and the point of
view in the up-country towns. Apart from one or two structures
designed by Boott, there had never been any buildings in Lowell
which represented the decorative phase of revivalism, and the majority of inhabitants continued to think architecturally in terms of
the eighteenth-century tradition. They were anything but prepared

to accept the romantic point of view at its advanced contemporary level. Indeed it was ten years before the general public became reconciled to a changed way of building. And so a compromise had to be found between the old attitude and the new. The result was a whole series of buildings in which the Georgian mass was trimmed with a greater or lesser amount of Greek detail.

But while these timidly conceived structures form the bulk of building between 1835 and 1845, edifices were occasionally erected which truly represented the second or archaeological phase of revivalism. Thus the architecture of Lowell at this period is a dichotomy. On the one hand there are a considerable number of buildings which are *retardataire* in tendency, on the other, a few which are progressive in tendency. The difference between the classes does not correspond to any substantial difference in date. Rather, it reflects different levels of sophistication on the part of the men who commissioned and designed the structures in question.

The earliest monuments to show the influence of revivalism were the churches and the public buildings.[6] The first of the latter erected by the new community was the town hall. This was put up in 1830 on a plot of land purchased for this purpose from the Locks and Canals Company.[7] The site was opposite St. Anne's. The building still exists, although no longer used for its original purpose; it was redecorated in the nineties. At first it was a simple, gable-roofed brick barn, two stories high.[8] Below there was a series of doorways and windows leading into small rooms; above, a great hall lighted by five long windows on the flanks and three at either end. By way of adornment there were slender Doric pilasters in brick at the four corners, and these carried a simple entablature, consisting of a friezelike band of brick and a sharply projecting wooden cornice which ran around the building and up the gable. In the gable was a simple semicircular window.

The design of the town hall was repeated at a slightly smaller scale in 1835 for the building of the Middlesex Mechanics Association,[9] and again, in 1837, for the City Market House, which stands on Market Street just off Canal.[10] (Figure 35.) A final example was Barristers' Hall, built in the early forties at the corner of John and Paige Streets.[11] Here the scheme remained the same, except for the brick pilasters between all of the windows and the slightly more elaborate design of the frieze.[12]

The most important series of public buildings in the first two decades of the city's history were the schools. The town of Chelmsford had two small schoolhouses within the district that became Lowell. One of the first acts of the Merrimack Manufacturing Company was to put up a two-story hall, the upper half of which served as a church, the lower as a school. Other corporations followed suit, and by 1826 the town was in possession of five schoolhouses. These doubtless were small affairs; indeed, for many years the majority of the primary schools were wooden buildings valued at $500 and approximately the size of a wooden boarding house.[13] At a later period some of these were replaced by brick schoolhouses of about the same dimensions. A typical one survives on Howard Street which looks like the City Hall in miniature, without the pilasters.

The real architectural activity along this line began in 1833, when, against the wishes of Kirk Boott and the corporations, the town built two large grammar schools.[14] Others followed in close succession. After the opening of the Centralville Grammar School in 1858, the city could point to a series of six grammar schools and a high school, all sturdy buildings of brick.

One of the first pair of grammar schools was standing until recently, a gable-roofed barn two and a half stories high. It differed from other public buildings only in its lack of corner pilasters and frieze. The next stage is represented by a school built in Belvidere in 1840. (Figure 36.) The basic form remains the same, but it has acquired a pronouncedly Greek entablature and broad pilaster strips at the four corners. These slight changes are a significant indication of the invasion of romantic ideals.

The high school, likewise built in 1840, shows one important modification. Previously the long axis of the buildings had been parallel to the street.[15] Here, however, the gable faced the street, and the entrances were in the middle of the short ends.[16] This tendency to accent the façade is carried one step further in a grammar school of 1843. This building was strikingly placed on a triangular plot as a fork in the road, and a cupola was added over the front gable.

The grammar school in Centralville also stands at an intersection, with its cupola-crowned short end forming a façade on the axial street. (Figure 37.) Only in very minor details has the scheme been changed. The old wide strips have been replaced by narrow pilasters with capitals, the cornice has been elaborated, but in its essence it remains the same. This is striking, in view of the fact that the basic arrangement harks back almost a quarter of a century, and that the intervening period had been one of great stylistic changes. It becomes more surprising when one sees that the school committee had proposed a much more up-to-date "Italian style" design when recommending the building. Who shelved this scheme, and why, remains a mystery.[17]

Grimy and ill maintained, these public buildings are singularly dreary as one sees them today. That this was not always the case is evident from such a structure as the Town Hall at Nashua, New Hampshire, resplendent with white paint and black ironwork. (Figure 38.) This building indicates clearly how much the public structures of Lowell have suffered with time, and how much their pristine trimness of effect depended upon appliqué detail. For while no detail could alter the essential rawness and crudity of the forms, it did serve to distract the attention. The two-dimensional character of the ornament is striking. The feeling for the texture of materials has all but disappeared, and the conception of design in terms of color contrasts upon a surface is so dominant that even the elementary relationships of the masses is obscured.[18]

Taken as a whole, the series of public buildings illustrates the degree to which Lowell's citizens tended to think in terms of architectural formulae. One can hardly speak of a tradition here, for a tradition implies a vocabulary of shapes and a grammar of relationships within the limits of which growth and development is possible. But here there is something less flexible than a vocabulary and a grammar. Here there is a complete and fixed arrangement which is repeated to order whenever the occasion demands.

Such a way of thinking is understandable in a field like industrial architecture, where the form of the building is wholly determined by the demands of the manufacturing process. It is a strange attitude to take in monumental architecture. For the primary problem in designing a public building is generally not a functional problem, but a problem of expression. Usually, the essential requirement is to represent the ideal character of the activities that are to be sheltered. The public buildings of Lowell, with their pilasters, entablatures and cupolas, are not primarily functional. They belong to a representational type; but they represent nothing, individually or collectively. All too obviously the city fathers accepted communal activities as humdrum occupations. They did not think of them as pursuits which should be glorified in architecture. They bedecked their public buildings with classic ornaments, not because they wished to express anything through these ornaments, but because such ornaments were the indispensable attributes of a fixed type of structure, which they took over complete. Thus the public buildings of Lowell are a splendid gauge of the profoundness of that social and architectural inertia which the full force of romanticism was so explosively to destroy.[19]

The first series of churches erected in the city fall into three distinct types, Gothic, traditional, and classic.[20] Taking the first half-dozen churches of which there is any pictorial record, it is interesting to notice the distribution of types among the sects. The two most firmly established denominations commissioned the two most conventional buildings. The other four structures were more experimental; three of them were erected by smaller and less prominent sects.[21] Here the stylistic division was just what one would expect. The tradition-conscious Catholics and Episcopalians built the Gothic structures; the classic churches were designed for the Congregationalists and the Unitarians.

Both these last were variants of the shed scheme used for public buildings. The Appleton Street Congregational Church, built in 1831, was a stone structure with one short gabled end facing the street.[22] (Figure 76.) In the middle there was a recessed porch, its roof supported by two stone piers. Decoration there was none, except for a lunette in the gable. Not so the Unitarian Church, built in 1832.[23] This small, socially prominent sect, with its intellectualized creed, provided for itself a brick barn girt about with an order of pilasters carrying a full Doric entablature, all in wood. It is highly significant as the first appearance of any of the historical styles in Lowell, in an approximately academic form. The fact that the agency responsible should be a church, and the church of such a group, is indicative of the architectural trend and the sources of cultural leadership at that day.

The classical type of church is found among the second group built. A striking example is the First Universalist Church, which was moved and given its final form in 1838.[24] This was so correct in taste as to have a tetrastyle prostyle portico. A significant, but far less orthodox, building was the Worthen Street Methodist Episcopal Church, built in 1842.[25] This had two great pilasters at the corners, with recessed panels cut into them, a common treatment in the forties and later. These pilasters carried a great flat arch which sprang clear across the façade. The church was later sold to the Catholics, who dedicated it to St. Peter, and subsequently tore it down.

It is significant that the classical type church soon replaced the traditional meetinghouse. Nothing illustrates better the weakening sensitivity to mass composition than the fashion in which, after the early thirties, the projecting porch was omitted, and the towers were set directly upon the blocks of the auditoriums. Nothing illustrates better the increasing interest in display, and the association of magnificence with the classical orders than the manner in which the later meetinghouses invariably received deep friezes and projecting cornices, supported at least by pilasters at the corners and frequently by a whole series across the façade. The Lowell Street Methodist Episcopal Church of 1838 shows the first stage in the process, for it was a hall, identical with any of the secular halls, crowned by a tall, end-set cupola.[26] The contemporary Worthen Street Baptist Church followed the same scheme, but with pilaster across the front. Moreover, detail of a definitely Greek Revival character has crept into the design of the spire base and window enframements. St. Paul's, the Methodist Church on Hurd Street, built in 1839, is slightly less elaborate in detail, but otherwise it is almost identical.[27] (Figure 39.) The John Street Congregational Church introduced another classical feature, the recessed porch, here supported by Ionic columns.

Lowell had its eclectics too. The First Freewill Baptist Church built in 1837, was similar to St. Paul's except that several of the windows were pointed, and an attempt was made to carry the tower down to the ground by means of double pilasters at the center, and pilaster strips running through the pediment.[28] (Figure 40.) The spire was exceptionally tall, quite the most prominent landmark in Lowell. Moreover, the church was placed on the axis of Central Street, at Merrimack, probably the most expensive, certainly the most dramatic, site in town. Nor did its unorthodoxy end there, for the church was built as a real-estate speculation with savings which a scamp of a minister wheedled from the mill girls.[29] Truly the fabulous forties were near at hand.

Certainly the variations in these buildings are not great; variations, however, are there, as well as marked developments over the design of churches a decade earlier. They show that the builders were intrigued by the combination and re-combination of various traditional and new elements. They were conscious of a problem, and were experimenting with the possible solutions. This gives the buildings a freshness and liveliness lacking in the stereotyped public monuments.

Up to the mid-thirties only the churches and the public buildings had been glorified by the use of a limited vocabulary of decorative details, and frequently by a certain emphasis on their façades. During the last half of this decade, however, these same features begin to appear on other types of structure. About 1835 the standard type of dwelling is modified in some instances. In the double houses, the plan remains essentially the same, but the front is crowned with a gable, so that the ridge of the roof now runs along the short axis. (Figure 41.) There is a suggestion of the emphatic self-assertive temple façade which ten years before had been considered fitting only for churches. This was merely a hint of a vastly more significant change that soon followed—the gradual abandonment of the double house altogether.[30] The two halves are moved apart, as it were, and each becomes a free-standing unit. This is generally three bays wide, with a door and distyle porch in one corner. The whole is covered with a double-pitched roof, the gable facing the street. By this simple change was evolved what was quantitatively the most important house type of the nineteenth century.[31] This scheme, the stock in trade of the jerry builder, occurs practically without interruption over whole districts in the poorer quarters of Lowell. (Figure 75.)

The effect of this shift in the roof axis was to make each building independent of its fellows in appearance, as well as in actuality. As the symbol of the new freedom, both these types, as well as the narrow five-window house, were fitted out with corner pilasters, a frieze and a projecting cornice. The trim was painted a different color from the wall to give it the emphasis which the contrast of wood against brick had supplied in the monumental buildings. All other types of edifice followed suit. Stores, granaries, multiple dwellings, and in those smaller concerns which followed the Boott tradition, boarding houses—all were furnished with these cheap classical trimmings.

Even the brick blocks showed the influence of the movement. At Chicopee the boarding houses sported columned porticoes. At Lowell, about 1845, the Merrimack Manufacturing Company pulled down half of Boott's front row of wooden cottages and erected instead a block which shows slight romantic influences.[32] In plan, the building differed from others of the time only in retaining the ell, which was frequently omitted now, and in making it not one but two and a half stories high. (Figures 42-44.) Boott had tended to place his buildings rather closer together than was most desirable, and this rebuilding intensified the overcrowding.

The "New Block" of the Merrimack Company was the last example of this standard type erected in Lowell.[33] Also its elevation was more advanced than those of any of its predecessors. An analysis of the building presents, therefore, a good opportunity to review the development in housing design. It seems proper to begin with one of Boott's brick blocks. Much of the charm of any one of these buildings derived from the fact that it was effective, not in its totality, but piecemeal, as a composition of parts in clearly structural relationships to one another. (Figure 9.) The wall was an alternation of solids and voids, and thanks to the richness of the brick surface, one felt the thickness of the piers and lintels that run between the windows. The structural relation of the front wall to the roof was likewise visible. The roof was a great sheet of slate, and it ran out beyond the line of the wall in simple eaves, casting a deep shadow. It flapped down and covered the vertical surface. In every case, the dormers were so trivial and the four chimneys were so definite and independent that none of them disturbed the effect of the roof as a surface.

In the thirties there was a definite change. This was partly the result of the increased size of the units, but it was far more fundamental. The interest in surface and in the interrelation of the parts of the building was lost, and, in the housing of the Lawrence corporation, for instance, the concern shifted to the effect of the whole as a geometric form. (Figure 19.) The wall lost its rich texture. It ceased to be a crust and became a membrane. The chimneys were linked to the outer wall and gave up their independence. The roof lost its importance partly because at the greater height it was less visible, partly because it was so punctured by dormers that it no longer existed as a surface.

A further step was taken in the Merrimack block with the desire, so characteristic of the forties, to make the abstract geometrical form more communicative. (Figure 44.) The building was not so much a prism as a series of four great surfaces, arranged at right angles to one another. Each face was carefully designed as a plane. The upper edge, where the roof meets the wall, was particularly marked. During the thirties it received an ornamental brick cornice. To this now was added a deep frieze, a reflection of the Greek Revival. But this feature had no structural character. It was merely an aesthetic emphasis, an upper border to the façade. Beneath it the components of the great sheet of brick lost all individuality. Their mechanical regularity gave the surface a glossy sheen. The whole was as cold and as negative as the front of a boiled shirt. The windows of the quadruple house had been voids, reducing the wall to a grillwork of piers and lintels. Later, the windows with an ample margin all around, lost their character as holes in the surface. Provided with blinds, they became ornaments, centralized in character. Above, the roof disappeared; one saw only a crenelation of dormers. The feeling for the building as a whole disappeared. One perceived only blank faces, punctuated by the staccato accents of window, door, and dormer. In it architecture was conceived as typography, the façade was designed like a title page.

It was an easy matter to adorn with a cornice the great barn factories of the later thirties. (Figures 17, 45.) The results can be seen in the mills and storage buildings of the Middlesex Company at Lowell and in the old Essex Machine Shop at Lawrence, which bears the date 1845. Both these buildings, however, are set down at random in the mill yard. A new point of view towards the ordering of industrial groups first becomes evident with the building of an additional Hamilton mill in 1846.[34] The simplest way for the Lowell concerns to increase the size of their plants was to link up two of the original mills. In the forties many of the corporations went in for this practice.[35] Since at Lowell the linking unit was generally given a double-pitched roof at right angles to the main axis, it formed a sort of pavilion in the middle of what was now a single long façade. In the Hamilton Corporation the whole was crowned with a cupola and it was emphasized by a carefully arranged axial pathway and projecting picker houses. (Figure 46.) In form this represented no great advance over the Merrimack Company, but the effect was different. For the Merrimack yard, like the whole of the establishment was conceived as a series of isolated units around a space. The nearest analogy in composition is the Harvard College Yard in Cambridge.[36] Now, however, the main mill rises like an obstacle across the vista. It does not enclose space; it is an enormous three-dimensional screen, impressive because of its great lateral extension. It blocks the view.

At Lowell, where it was a question of rebuilding old plants, the full possibilities of this conception of mill design could not be worked out. But a project for the construction of the Bay State Mills in Lawrence, dated shortly before 1846, shows the trend of contemporary thought.[37] (Figure 47.) The plant stands on an island, isolated by the river and the canal. The yard consists of three identical mills in a row, surrounded by a quadrangle of smaller industrial buildings arranged in solid lines. There is a break in the enclosure opposite the single entrance bridge, so that one can look through and be suitably awed by the great central mass of the middle mill with its distinguishing cupola. The middle of the range on the river is accented by a raised pavilion, and the center of each of the short sides is emphasized by a tall chimney. Additional chimneys rise from the middle of the open space between the mills. Across the canal lie four enormous blocks of housing, parallel to the river on either side of the axial street. All the components here are traditional, but their organization into such a complex and articulated scheme represents a more sophisticated viewpoint than is exemplified anywhere in Lowell. This fact, together with the rendering of the whole in a drawing, suggests the intervention of an architect.[38]

So much for the buildings which were conservative in tendency.

In addition there were in Lowell three edifices which revealed a complete understanding of the point of view which characterizes the second phase of revivalism. Certainly the most amusing of them was the first railroad station, built shortly before 1836.[39] (Figure 48.) The task of designing such a building was a difficult one. Since the Boston and Lowell Railroad was one of the two oldest in the country, there were few precedents upon which the architect could fall back. The solution was striking. The station was a rectangular building surrounded on at least two sides by a peristyle, like a peripteral temple with the cella pushed off center. The narrow gabled front made an impressive entrance portico on Merrimack Street, while the pillared flank provided a train shed, for the single line of track ran unabashed down the pteroma.

The building was ingenious, even if it lacked Periclean purity. It was amazing at this time in Lowell. It is not surprising that Patrick Tracy Jackson and his fellow capitalists should wish to make their depot an impressive, monumental building. Was not the railroad the marvel of the age? The conception of the Merrimack Corporation with its central cupola, its symmetrical arrangement of houses, and its axial canal lined with elms, that conception was the result of just such a demand for display, prompted by exactly the same motives. But the architecture of the depot reveals the fact that by this time the idea of grandeur had become inextricably associated with the academic use of classical Greek forms.[40]

A second landmark was the dedication in 1838 of the Gothic Second Universalist Church, designed by a certain Dr. Duesbury.[41] (Figure 49.) The basic forms here did not differ from those of the Catholic Church. There is the same rectangular box preceded by a square tower carrying a spire. It is the detail that introduces a new note. It still falls far short of Pugin's idea of archaeological correctness, but it does manifest a greatly increased familiarity with Gothic forms. The pinnacles, instead of perching at the corners of the tower, are the terminations of buttresses. The buttresses, moreover, are not merely octagonal turrets; they are compound clusters, although the artist seems to have confused them with clusters of columns, giving them bases, capitals, and battlements by way of entablature. The tracery remains primitive, but drip mouldings make their appearance, along with a string course around the clock. Finally the doorway is crowned by an ogee arch ending in a finial and equipped with plausibly Gothic jambs.

In the greatly increased height, in the way that the tower is fused with the mass of the church, and in the relative proportions of tower and spire, the design suggests the influence of Richard Upjohn's first church, St. John's, Bangor, Maine.[42] It is difficult to see what other building could have been the model, for most American churches of the thirties follow closely the type of St. Anne's or St. Patrick's. It is hard to believe that working with sources known to all, Duesbury alone should have approximated the work of Upjohn. But if this is a derivative of the latter's building, then one must pay tribute to the Doctor's intellectual spryness. St. John's was drawn in 1835-36 and probably completed in 1837.[43]

The third unusual building of the decade is the house which Zadock Rogers built for himself in 1837-38, and which is now a girls' school.[44] The scheme is basically similar to Paul Moody's house, consisting originally of a rectangular block, five windows wide, with a central door, and presumably with four rooms on the ground floor. It is remarkable, however, in having a free-standing Ionic colonnade clear across the front. The design itself is of little interest, but that any wealthy citizen might glorify his private house with this prime architectural symbol of monumentality, such an idea was new in Lowell. It was a notion which opened up a wealth of possibilities for future development.

VII

FULLY ROMANTIC ARCHITECTURE, 1845-1865: THE PRIVATE HOUSES

AFTER 1845 the civic and industrial development of Lowell changed in character. Kirk Boott died suddenly in 1837, and one by one the other executives and capitalists who had been present at the start passed from the scene during the next few years. New hands took control. The kind puritanical paternalism and the experimental point of view of the original amateurs were replaced by the hard-boiled self-confidence of professionals trained in the business.[1] After the opening of the Massachusetts Mills in the early forties there was no more water power available for new enterprises. Further expansion could come only through more efficient use of existing facilities. Competition was beginning to be a serious factor, and the prosperity of the corporations increasingly came to depend upon the exploitation of the employees. As working conditions deteriorated, immigrant Irish girls with their lower standard of living began to replace the Yankees in the mills.[2]

These changes in turn reacted upon the town. The retirement of the first generation of the bourgeoisie occurred at the same time as the withdrawal of the first generation of executives. The early business leaders had by now reaped enough of their harvest so that they could settle back as capitalists, consolidate their holdings, and concentrate upon the expenditure as well as the accumulation of wealth. Their successors, the new generation of rising young men, returned with interest the "realistic" attitude of the new executives. Moreover, the very size the settlement had now attained made for civic self-consciousness and a growing resentment at subservience to the mills.

As the problems of a pioneer community were solved, the social and economic pattern of the city became crystallized. In addition, people were becoming used to manufacturing, and Lowell ceased to be an amazing novelty. Americans stopped thinking of the industrial utopia as one of the seven wonders of the new republic. Distinguished Europeans no longer felt obliged to visit the community and to marvel in print at its sudden rise, its physical cleanliness, and its high moral tone. With the lessening of such outside admiration, the city lost something of its intense self-absorption. It began to be aware of the religious, social, and political ferment of the nation at large.[3]

Thus both in manufacturing and in civic life there comes a break in the first years of the eighteen forties. The pressing problems of the preceding period had been solved, and it was possible to review, analyze, and revise what had been accomplished. Slowly the realization dawned that the old days of coöperative endeavor were over, and that success in the future would be obtained by struggles, struggles not only between competing concerns, but among the various opposing groups into which industrial settlements were beginning to disintegrate. It was to be mill against mill, town against town, but the bitter conflict would be between mill and town, employer and employee.[4]

There ensued a sudden desire for expression, prompted on the one hand by pride in past accomplishment, and on the other by the need for consolidation in the face of rivalry. There was a demand both for eulogies and for fighting slogans, and this applied to architecture, no less than to literature.[5] The conception of the function of building changed. It ceased to be merely the technique of sheltering a given activity; it became a language. Lowell felt the need for a more specifically expressive architecture.

The consciousness of that need was all that was wanting to ensure the triumph of revivalism in its second or archaeological form.[6] For architecturally, no less than socially, the years from 1835 to 1845 were years of transition. The use of Greek detail became increasingly popular, and the traditional manner of design was rapidly giving way. By 1845 the large majority of structures appeared in would-be Hellenic costumes of greater or less elaboration. But the widespread acceptance of the Greek Revival in a compromise form was not the most important aspect of the transformation in Lowell's architecture during this crucial decade. The really fundamental development was that the public gradually became aware of the implications for building of the mature revivalist point of view. Indeed, by 1845, they were anxious that their buildings should vividly recall the past. To be sure, the provincial citizens of Lowell were not sufficiently cultivated to make sure that their structures were accurate reproductions of European monuments. But if they were not interested in an architecture that was historically correct, they were interested in an architecture that was historically convincing, at least to themselves.

So the simple, comfortable, traditional blocks gave way before the new gods of efficiency, size, and self-assertiveness. Bigger mills were built; old mills were rebuilt, enlarged, strung together. Housing had long since lost its domestic character, but now the great rows of boarding houses became impressive barracks. The files of solid bourgeois dwellings, four square and identical, began to be punctuated by the prettiness of an occasional Gothic cottage, or the parvenu splendor of a two-story portico. Dignified, if dull, uniformity was disrupted, as each institution, each group, each individual sought to create for itself an "appropriate" building.

The architectural history of Lowell in the two decades preceding the Civil War was not lacking in drama. In the early 1840's the future development of the town seemed clearly to lie in Belvidere. Where else, indeed, could the city spread? The Chapel Hill district was already full, the land along Merrimack Street likewise, while Centralville was still part of another township. Belvidere, where the city had annexed 384 acres of land in 1834, was the logical place.[7] Its importance was vividly illustrated by the action of the city with regard to street improvements. In the early forties there was much minor work on the great highways, widening, grading, and sidewalks on Merrimack, Lowell, and Central Streets. Secondary streets were laid out around the newer mills, and additional ones were put through to accommodate the population of Chapel Hill. In Belvidere, however, a whole new network was created.[8] (Figure 90.)

Then, in 1845 the Locks and Canals Company decided to sell off almost all their remaining real estate.[9] The picture immediately changed. The city fathers hastened to acquire two large sites as parks, and were forced to embark upon an extensive program of road building and repair. Up to this time, all the streets running across the property of the Locks and Canals Company had been private. The city now took them over, and its first care was to set them in order. Its next was to complete already existing roads by extending them across the newly opened land. A third and more serious task soon presented itself. Lowell had been forced to develop as a sort of chevron, two great strips meeting at an obtuse angle. The head of the triangle of territory within this angle was all owned by the Locks and Canals Company or the Manufacturing Concerns. The area was not large, but it blocked the development of much property further away from the center of the city. There were comparatively few roads across that land, and the main highways following the old travel routes ran around it rather than through it. Now it was suddenly thrown open to the public, and the city was faced with the problem of linking up the new land with the existing scheme of the town. This problem was never wholly solved, but the effort was made, as is shown by the creation of a number of radial thoroughfares in the fifties, notably Cross Street, Broadway, and Westford Street. These, rather than the old roads, became the basis of the gridiron of streets that was soon platted over the newly opened area. (Figure 89.)

The secondary street pattern followed to a considerable extent the line of building activity. It is interesting to notice that the first section to be built up, and the part which was most thickly populated, lay in front of the Tremont and Suffolk mills on Merrimack Street. A similar situation on a smaller scale occurred further down the street in the triangle of land before the Boott and the Massachusetts Mills. The restricted amount of land available along Merrimack Street before the sale, had necessitated concentrated ribbon development, and the habit persisted after the immediate cause was removed.

A second natural result was the extension of the Chapel Hill area. This worked out less logically, for the street pattern was not in accord with the main thoroughfares but followed the haphazard property lines. Much of the land here, though not owned by the Locks and Canals Company, had been useless as long as their possessions were vacant. When the area was thrown completely open, it was too late to rationalize the system of communications, and the chaos of oblique alleyways became yet more profound.

A third sector that prospered lay along Middlesex Street, a highroad that ran parallel to the Pawtucket Canal just to the south. There had been a settlement here in the thirties, around an important crossroads. This expanded enormously and was linked up to the area behind the Appleton and Hamilton mills by a new group of buildings. At first, at least, the territories lying around the two parks were conspicuous by their emptiness, largely because of the lack of radial roads connecting the districts to the center of town. Granted proximity to such a highway, people were glad to build at some distance, but they resented the need to walk around two sides of a triangle before reaching town.[10]

Another development of the period was the growth of pseudosuburbs. In 1831 the Nesmith brothers had purchased the great Belvidere estate of Judge Livermore, which lay above the rivers along the hill crest. Divided into house sites, this was soon up for sale, and in the forties and fifties a series of great new mansions began to arise here.[11] At the same time Centralville also was filling up, and the settlement here culminated in the annexation of the area by Lowell in 1851.[12] To the west a large but straggling group of houses formed itself along the old Pawtucket-Boston road, now called School Street, while in 1847 a certain Daniel Ayer inaugurated a wild scheme for a whole new residential city, far to the south.

The spreading out of the city was of course merely a reflection of the great amount of building activity that went on during the years between 1835 and 1855. Naturally, the form of all this construction was determined by the type of growth which was taking place in the town. In the period under consideration the character of this growth changed remarkably. The increase in the population of the community gradually became less striking than the increase in its wealth. Between 1835 and 1845 the number of inhabitants rose by 75 percent, but between 1845 and 1855 it rose only by 34 percent, and between 1855, when it reached a peak, and 1865 it declined. At the close of the Civil War Lowell was little larger than it had been twenty years previously.[13] Meanwhile riches continued to pile up apace.

So it came about that few churches were put up during these years, since the existing supply was large and splendid enough to meet the demand. At first there was comparatively little commercial building; later, a few concerns remodeled their establishments on a larger scale. The new public buildings were prominent, but rather from the splendor of the individual examples than from their number. There was little mill housing erected, for, as the exploitation of the workers became increasingly necessary, emphasis was naturally placed on stepping up the productivity of the individual employees rather than on increasing their number.[14] The period closes with a great rebuilding of the mills, however. The corporations took advantage of the war years to modernize their plants.

But the economic and social development being what it was, far and away the most conspicuous group of structures erected between 1845 and 1865 were the private houses. Moreover, they are the only class of buildings of which enough examples remain to suggest the full variety of architecture at the middle of the century. That is why domestic design provides the touchstone for understanding Lowell's architectural development during these years. That is why in the pages to follow the major emphasis must and will be laid on it. The procedure will be to begin with those styles which exemplify the second stage of revivalism, and to continue with those that anticipate the third.

In the design of domestic architecture before the Civil War, it was the men of wealth who led the way. One reason for this was that their particular problem, the large house, was new in this neighborhood. There was no recognized solution within the local tradition. Even more important, however, was the fact that riches generally coincided with sophistication. The one important exception to this statement is the case of the professional men, who as far as domestic architecture is concerned must be associated with the wealthy. These two groups included most of the educated people in the community. It was they who enjoyed the greatest contact with the world outside Lowell. It was they who were best prepared to accept a new architecture, and it was they who were actually responsible for propagating it. The result was that the first outstanding fully romantic houses are to be found among the mansions and dwellings of the new residential suburb in Belvidere.

One handsome new type of house was created by following closely the usual form of public building, although adding more detail. Whereas in the structures discussed in the last chapter the cornice and the pilasters did not substantially alter the basic forms, now the cornice becomes an important feature of the design, and the pilaster strips, instead of being a mere ribbing at the corners, articulate the whole surface.

In a fine house in Belvidere two of the front upper story windows are equipped with handsome ironwork balconies, and the door is enriched by a distyle porch of very spare proportions. (Figure 50.) There is the usual absence of texture in the surfaces, for while the sides are clapboarded, this is effective less as a rich wall treatment than as a means of isolating and emphasizing the smooth cornice and matchboarded façade. The interest of the block of the house has been completely lost in the attention given to the pattern made by the separative decorative elements in relation to one another. Each of these units, cornice, porch, balconies, is flung outwards from the body of the house.

These elements originated as a simplification of Greek forms. The buildings probably derive ultimately from Regency architecture, and it is not surprising, therefore, that in two striking houses of about 1840 there is a direct return to the pure English manner. These are the John Nesmith house and the Lawrence house in Belvidere. (Figures 54-57.) Both are simple rectangular blocks surmounted by a deep cornice beneath a hipped roof. The Nesmith house is entered through a cube of a vestibule, protruding from one side. In front there is a great bow window surrounded by a curved ironwork porch which once had a balustraded terrace before it. The whole surface of the house is divided into two planes, the forward plane of the broad pilaster strips, the recessed plane of the walls and windows. The Lawrence house has two bow windows in front and between them a hemitholos porch. The pilasters between the windows are more slender, and they are ornamented with carved capitals. In both houses the details are of a purity of form and delicacy of execution unmatched anywhere in Lowell.

It is regrettable and significant that these two houses, perhaps the handsomest buildings in Lowell, should stand completely alone. Their designs must have seemed too subtle, too reserved, to the average man of the time. Provincial wealth demanded something more boastful, more tangibly classical, and found it in the temple house. This was an ideal form, grand, yet cheap and adaptable.

A portico, not being part of the body of the house, did not make any demands on the planning and actually provided additional space in the attic. Moreover, the recent change in practice with regard to roof axis, meant that one could be even more Greek than Mr. Rogers.[15]

So Lowell in the forties could boast a number of tetrastyle prostyle mansions. It is not surprising that this, the most obvious type, was the first to spread to the lower middle class. It is the first new species to appear on Chapel Hill, where frequent porticoes adorn the fronts of the usual three bay houses. (Figure 58.)

It was likewise the first to be modified by the ingenuity of local builders. On Chapel Hill it is used to emphasize the *piano nobile* and the bedroom floor, over a ground-floor shop. In Manchester, New Hampshire, the columns support an ample second floor gallery, as well as the pediment, while the roof carries a cupola. In a later house in Lowell the portico is reduced to a row of five pilasters which are interspersed between seven windows and a stepladder of sunken panels. These create an interlocking of varied rhythms which must be the envy of every mannerist.

Considering the importance of the Greek Revival to American architecture as a whole, it is at first sight surprising that there are so few purely classic houses in Lowell and similar towns. The reason for this is the fact that by the time Lowell had accepted the ideology of the second stage of revivalism, the Greek manner had seen its best days. It was the Greek Revival that introduced that ideology and established it in the twenties. By the middle forties people were beginning to tire of the innumerable porticoes.[16] Ideals of living were changing. The cult of grandeur and formality was replaced by the desire for picturesqueness and a more intimate scale in domestic architecture. Moreover, the Greek was the most rigid of the Revivals; it made the fewest concessions to the demands of convenience. The fact that it was given up so early is significant. It foreshadowed the eventual rejection of the entire second phase of orthodox nineteenth-century architecture in favor of a mode of design which should be rooted in contemporary conditions, rather than in the past.[17]

At the opposite pole from these buildings was the Gothic house. In theory, the Gothic house avoided symmetry, emphasizing picturesqueness of form. (Figures 51, 52, 59.) In practice, this had produced buildings that were cruciform in plan. These were crowned by roofs which were so deep they took up half the height of the dwelling. This roof projected on all sides, and the sharp edges were adorned with barge boards of varying elaboration. The blank surfaces were interrupted by projecting members, dormers with their own barge boards in the case of the roof, bow windows and porches for the wall below. The effect was never that of a piling up, an interplay of masses, for the forms were made as open as possible. It was never the solidity of the shapes that was emphasized, but always the capriciousness of their trimmings. One sees here the logical completion of the tendencies suggested above. For it is no longer a question of individual delicate balconies and sweeping cornices being flung out from the house; these secondary features have become so numerous and so accented that they dominate the effect. The whole looks as if it had been enveloped by a cobweb of bright ribbons which attract the eye and confuse the mind as to the form beneath.

Rare indeed in the mill cities are houses which show the degree of elaboration found in Gothic cottages elsewhere. One can point only to one in Lowell and another in Manchester. (Figure 59.) Barge boards are not infrequent, certainly they are the most common decorative feature, but generally what must be classed as Gothic houses are no more than cruciform in plan, and provided with deep roofs. In addition, one fine house in Belvidere is built of stone, has drip mouldings over the windows, and is surrounded by a continuous piazza. (Figure 52.) Not infrequently even the cruciform plan is dropped, and an ordinary rectangular house is crowned with a roof of four gables, one on each side. In some cases the simple three-bayed scheme is repeated with merely the addition of a fringe to the front eaves, perhaps a pointed window in the gable head, and oftentimes an unusual freedom in the treatment of the porches. (Figure 77.) Gothic forms were also quite charmingly adapted to double houses, either as identical separate units, or as a pair, where the additional size gave opportunity for a multiplicity of elements impossible at a smaller scale. (Figure 51.)

There are few Gothic houses in Lowell and similar towns that have any claim to distinction. As with the Greek house, the cause is partly the late acceptance of mature revivalism in these places. The Gothic Revival, like the Greek, came early into the repertory of the second phase of orthodox nineteenth-century architecture. For a few years it was universally popular, but it was soon found to be unsatisfactory except for two special building types, churches and castellated country mansions. After 1845 its use was increasingly limited to these two fields.[18]

But an even more important reason for the scarcity of Gothic houses is the symbolic significance of these buildings. The men of the middle of the nineteenth century did not in the least believe in art for its own sake. They were greatly concerned about the fundamental meaning of forms and styles. Andrew Jackson Downing, at that time the arbiter of taste in domestic architecture, remarked that the Gothic house displayed a "poetic, aspiring, imaginative idea embodied in the upward lines of pointed architecture. The man of common-sense views only, if he is true to himself, will have nothing to do . . . with picturesque and irregular outlines."[19] He was only expressing the common attitude. The Gothic house was abandoned to the intellectual left wing. It is noteworthy that the most prominent one in Lowell should have been built by a minister and called "the Manse." (Figure 52.) The simpler Gothic houses were erected by members of the lower middle class, who aped the dwellings of the more adventurous professional men, after a suitable lapse of time.

The Gothic house never became popular with the wealthy

citizens of Lowell. When these men sought to build something splendid, yet not oppressively formal, they turned to the Italian style in its various forms. This was the least hidebound of the various new manners. Indeed, it hardly consisted in anything more than a vocabulary of Renaissance forms which could be applied in almost any fashion desired.

The most splendid mansion of the Italian style was built in Belvidere during the late forties by the local architect James H. Rand.[20] (Figure 53.) He sold it to the Merrimack Company as a residence for the agent. It was a ponderous structure, reflecting in its cubic form some influence from the neighboring Nesmith and Lawrence houses. Unlike these, however, it was extraordinarily complicated in plan with ells and wings and porches and bows projecting in all directions. From one angle rose the square tower capped with a low pyramid roof that was an all but invariable feature of this style.

An idea of this mode of design at its best can be obtained from a house in Nashua. (Figure 64.) Here the nucleus is a rectangular gable-roofed block to which the other units are attached. In conception it is not essentially different from a Gothic house, except that the various parts are not as closely knit into a single whole. Rather it is a very carefully composed agglomeration of units, and these units are simpler, clearer, and heavier than is the case with the Gothic house. Thus, there are wide-spreading eaves, but these, instead of carrying icicles in wood, are supported by an array of opulently curved consoles. There is an open porch, but instead of suggesting a bower, with lattices resting on fanciful colonnettes, it is made up of a series of round arches springing from paneled columns. The whole feeling is rich and substantial, although varied and not stuffy.

The Italian manner was by far the most influential of all the styles. Thanks to its patronage by the wealthy during the forties, it spread through all classes of the population during the fifties, although in a modified form. But there were reasons for its popularity more fundamental than snobbism. The Italian was the latest to arrive of all the major revival modes that made up the second phase of orthodox nineteenth-century architecture. It was the *dernier cri* in 1845, in contrast to the *passé* Greek and the passing Gothic. Moreover, it made even fewer demands on the house than did the medieval manner. There was no need to adjust the design for a high roof or deep eaves. In its complete lack of a canon according to which the whole building must be organized, the Italian style anticipates the third phase of revivalism.

More important than all these is the fact that the Italian style adapted itself more easily than its rivals to the basic changes which were taking place in the feeling for architectural form. It was inevitable that there should be a reaction away from the excessive complexity and diffuseness of composition which characterized the finest houses of the forties. This change towards a more compact organization of solider masses could take place only within the limits of the Italian style. That was the only one of the revivals whose decorative elements could be omitted without a complete loss of character. As one contemporary observed, "the highest recommendation of the Italian style . . . is . . . that although it does not reject the application of porticoes and columnar supports, a higher degree of expression and dignity is often obtained without them."[21] But the Italian style when sobered down in this fashion really constituted something new. It was recognized as such by the men of the time, who dubbed the simplified form the "bracketed style."

As its name implies, the leitmotif of the new style was the console or bracket. It is the development of the use of the bracket and of the form of the bracket which best epitomizes the aesthetic trend. In Lowell, it is possible to divide the evolution into three stages.[22] There is no sharp dividing line between these stages, but the culminating monuments of each are quite distinct.

In the forties, brackets were intended to provide some relief on the bald under-surfaces of the wide-spreading eaves. The members were small, horizontal in direction, closely and evenly spaced. (Figure 64.) The second stage which began in the very last years of the decade reached its climax in the early fifties. The brackets then attained an extravagant size. Generally they were arranged in pairs, spaced wide apart, and they seemed to hang from the eaves far down the wall. (Figures 66 and 68.) The third stage began in the mid fifties and continued on, after the Civil War, at least in the houses of the lower middle class. At that time the corbel was introduced in the same shape as the bracket, and the consoles were reduced in size and increased in frequency in order to obtain some reasonable relationship between the two similar forms. Simultaneously the extreme projection of the eaves was modified, and the brackets tended to approximate isosceles triangles, extending downwards no further than they did outwards. Pairing of units was given up, and interest shifted from the creation of occasional bold accents, to the achievement of an effect of unemphatic and continuous richness. (Figure 67.) Finally, the consoles became smaller and smaller, and eventually disappeared altogether in favor of the corbel which in one form or another survived down to the Colonial Revival and the present day.

The development of the form of the brackets themselves closely paralleled this evolution in the manner of their use. In the first two phases they were made up of two portions, a large upper portion which was S-shaped and which united the eaves to the wall, and a smaller lower portion which varied in shape and which served to anchor the larger unit at its lower end. (Figures 64, 70, and 72.) In some houses of the forties a series of plain, projecting beams appeared to support the eaves. The earliest brackets were little more than an ornamental version of this same motif. (Figure 64.) Soon, however, an acorn-shaped pendant was added at the outer end and the height of the unit was increased. (Figure 62.) The next step was to pierce the sides of the panel, so that the bracket became a horizontal beam and a vertical post connected by a serpentine strut. (Figure 70.) In the huge brackets of around 1850 this last was the dominant element, linking as it did the pendant on the top outer corner with the anchoring unit at the bottom inner corner. (Figures 66, 71, and 72.) But the great difference between the brackets of the first and those of the second phase was the fact that in the latter the separate parts were treated plastically, with ornament both on the sides and on the intrados. In the most elaborate examples the parts were given naturalistic forms. The anchor portion became a tightly curled leaf, the strut sprang from an elaborate rosette, while the pendant was notched or acquired petals like a flower. (Figures 71 and 72.)

In the third phase the shape of the console was completely changed. (Figure 67.) The old tripartite division into anchor, strut and pendant was discarded, and the bracket tended to approximate a solid triangle with an irregular hypotenuse. In the larger units there was frequently a big projecting circular element. In the smaller ones a single circular hollow divided the form into identical upper and lower halves. Although the richness of decoration was retained, naturalistic forms were increasingly replaced by geometric ones. (Figure 73.)

A second striking feature of the bracketed style was its preference for square houses. This corresponded to a general trend in American domestic architecture. Throughout the middle nineteenth century cubic hip-roofed houses became increasingly important; correspondingly gable-roofed types decreased. There were many reasons for this. The gable-roofed house was closely associated with Greek forms, and tended to go out of favor with them. The square houses brought out more clearly the beauties of flaring eaves which grew ever more popular, and provided an admirable foil for projecting porches, bows, and cupolas. But most of all it was the snobbish symbolism of the square house that made it such a success.

In the eighteenth century, with the growth of the seaports and the rise of a commercial class, there had come to be a distinction between the pseudo-English architecture of the merchants and the simpler buildings of rural New England. The seaboard style in domestic architecture culminated in the development after the Revolution of the great four-square merchants' houses of Newburyport, Salem, and Beacon Hill. Once and for all these established the pattern which the mansion of a conventional New England gentleman was expected to follow. It is because of this accepted pattern that Boott's hip-roofed residence was to his contemporaries a hallmark of the owner's wealthy respectability.

As the square house increased in popularity, so the gable-roofed house declined. Although these last continued to be numerically important at least until the eighties, they became less and less respectable with every decade. Good enough for Squire Boott's parsonage in the twenties, by the Civil War it was the pettiest form of petty bourgeois dwelling, and ten years later only a jerry builder would consider it.

As Downing pointed out the square house was the type which appealed to "the man of common sense views only." "He will naturally prefer a symmetrical, regular house, with few angles, but with order, and method, and distinctness stamped upon its unbroken lines of cornice and regular rows of windows."[23] There must have been many clients of this sort in Lowell, for both the Greek and the Italian styles were adapted to suit the square house. For example, in the forties a Mr. Fletcher built himself a mansion that is nothing but a corruption of the style of the Nesmith and Butler houses. (Figure 60.) The earlier scheme has been enlivened by cutting panels into the pilasters, and the projecting cornice is accented by paired consoles. As is so often the case at this time, the strong color contrasts between wall and trim give an effect of restlessness and destroy the fine balance between decoration and form that had been achieved in Belvidere.

A simpler house on Mount Vernon Street reflects more happily much the same point of view. (Figure 61.) Here the corner pilasters are mere strips at the edges, leaving unbroken the expanses of the clapboarded surface. The house is crowned by a cupola, whose shape is echoed in the projecting porch. There is a definite consciousness of the design as a composition of three cubes. But it is primarily the defining rims of these blocks which are stressed, first by the pilasters, but above all by the boldly jutting cornices. These two represent middle-class taste. More refined and more reserved is an upper-class house on Andover Street in Belvidere. (Figure 62.) This reflects just the reverse tendency in the architecture of the forties. Here it is not the outlines that are stressed but the isolated features within them. There is the usual sharply projecting cornice, but what really catches the attention is the emphatic character of the six window groups and the door. Conceived as individual units, they are centripetally designed and richly if soberly detailed.[24]

There is a very similar but more elaborate house facing the South Common in Lowell. (Figure 63.) It is also somewhat later, as is evident from the increased complexity of the plan and the greater variety of Italian detail which is displayed. In fact one senses here the beginnings of a fundamental change in taste. Whereas in the Belvidere mansion one is impressed by the fragility of the central block and the lightness and openness of the decorative elements, here they have coagulated and become integrated to the main block which has grown more solid. The porch has been enlarged and is carried by four Corinthian columns close together, instead of the Tuscan columns wide apart. The flaring cornice no longer seems to be flung outwards. Rather it forms a rich belt around the top of the building, binding the whole together. But the most striking change of all is that now the wall surfaces are drafted to suggest masonry. There is thus a revival of the feeling for texture and a conscious lessening of the contrast between wall and trim.

Characteristic as these square houses are, they are not the most conspicuous houses of the forties. It is only with the dominance of the bracketed style in the fifties that the cubic house really comes into its own. Only then does it overshadow all other types and forms of dwelling. The first bracketed mansion in the grand manner was built in 1852. (Figures 66, 71.) In that year William

Livingstone built himself what is certainly one of the handsomest residences in Lowell.[25] This great cube commands one whole quarter of the town. On one side a long wing is thrown out, on the others a variety of porches and balconies project. Above there are the spreading eaves, and finally a cupola. The massing has a magnificent simplicity. Despite the richness and quantity of the detail, the building retains much of the explosive feeling of the forties, thanks to the boldness of the decorative forms and the enormous distances between them.

A few hundred yards away stands what can only be a somewhat later imitation of the Livingstone house.[26] (Figure 67.) The elements remain much the same, cupola, porches, consoles, quoins. The effect of the building as a whole has changed. The great fantastic forms of the earlier mansion have been tamed down. While there a simple conception was executed at enormous scale and with amazing daring, here there is an extraordinary complexity, a cramming of the maximum variety of forms into the minimum of volume. The hipped-roof is interrupted by a gable, giving the whole a definite axis. The chimney has broken loose from the cupola, and, most significant of all, the open porches and balconies are here replaced by a series of solid bow windows. Whereas one was bursting outwards in all directions in an astonishing variety of forms, the other is compressed, a congestion of massive units.

The medium by which a knowledge of all these various styles was introduced into Lowell must have been the architectural handbooks. American "Builders' Guides" had been appearing in increasing numbers since the end of the eighteenth century. Whereas the first ones included little but structural and ornamental details, in the later volumes whole building projects played an important part.[27]

It is rarely possible to pick out an actual house and point to the handbook from which the design was derived. Rather, the handbook projects served chiefly as means of indicating the manner in which the increasing multitudes of details might be worked into a large composition. The practice apparently was not to copy the whole scheme literally, but to get hints from it and in the actual building dispose the details as suited one's personal taste.[28] (Figures 65, 66.)

As might be expected with such a casual introduction to the historical styles, very soon most unorthodox hybrid buildings began to appear. This was particularly the case once romantic architecture was taken up by the lower middle class. The unusual smaller houses were apt to be more extreme than the larger houses, partly because of the greater ignorance of their owners, partly because of the inherent conservatism of that type of self-made man who alone in Lowell was able to build a large house. Thus it is among the smaller houses that one finds valiant attempts to combine Classic and Gothic styles. In one instance in Lowell the normal three-bayed type is graced with a correct Ionic entrance, pointed windows, and cusped barge boards. (Figure 78.) In another example the typical portico house has been provided with Gothic dormers and a back porch of pointed arches. At Manchester, New Hampshire, there is a cruciform house in a simplified Italian style with porches in the corners. This conception is carried even further at Rochester, New Hampshire, where the addition of a staged tower and pendulous consoles makes one think of an eighteenth-century garden temple in the Chinese style.

The conservative members of the lower middle class stuck to the three-bayed house, which remained unchanged, save in details. In the fifties, the magic console brought the form completely up to date. It was applied in this manner or that, according to the dictates of the moment. (Figures 69, 70, 72, 73, 75.) In these houses, too, the old simplicity of the block is exchanged for a more elaborate composition of the masses. This was achieved largely by the ubiquitous sprouting of bow windows. (Figure 69.) In them likewise lightness, vivid contrasts, and the expansive feeling in the earlier decade are replaced by richness, solidity, and compression in the later. Thus did the lower middle class follow the lead of the upper.

More important, although much less interesting than either of these categories, were those petty bourgeois and proletarian houses which attempted to get completely away from the gable-roof tradition. It is they that foreshadow the important development of the post Civil War period, when the overcrowding became so acute that there was a great wave of cheap construction. In the fifties a new type of multiple dwelling appeared. It consisted of a great rectangular block crowned with an almost flat roof. This form was occasionally repeated at a smaller scale for individual houses.

This same spirit of experimentation shows itself in the smaller wooden blocks of industrial housing. At Nashua, New Hampshire, for example, there is a whole series of wooden units belonging to the Nashua Company. Each is two stories high and crowned with a low-pitched gable roof. (Figure 80.) The distinctive and charming feature is the way in which the housing terminates at either end in a sort of pavillion, emphasized by four gables. This gives a pleasant rhythm to the design of the street.

Indeed, the greatest contribution of the small buildings was in their collective effect. As a group composition there was little difference between the upper-class residential district of a Federalist seaport and Belvidere.[29] But there was an enormous contrast between the ordinary bourgeois street of Lowell in the twenties and in the fifties. This is evident at once if one compares such planned groups of uniform units as the boarding houses of Worthen Street with the three-bay houses of Dane Street. (Figures 74, 75.) In one case the repetition of the horizontal eaves line and the unbroken plane of the front walls draws the eye inevitably down the street. In the other, the saw-tooth effect made by the successive gables and the strong plasticity of the façades tempts one to investigate each unit in turn.

It is curious that this difference of style becomes even more pronounced if one turns from these regular schemes to a common street, built at haphazard. The corridor aesthetic of the early period is emphasized by the common practice of combining the houses in long strings. In such a composition as Lower Appleton Street, the effect of motion down a vista is actually strengthened by the contrasting accent of the church façade. (Figure 76.) Further up the same street, in a section completed immediately after the great land sale, the irregular spacing and the differing styles of the houses make it almost impossible to consider them except as a series of individual buildings. (Figure 77.)

VIII

FULLY ROMANTIC ARCHITEC-
TURE, 1845-1865: PUBLIC
BUILDINGS AND MILLS

T HE FIRST concern of the citizens of Lowell had been to provide themselves with houses. These hastily built dwellings
proved inadequate once the city started to expand and grow prosperous. It was the resulting shortage which caused that great
activity in domestic building and that intense interest in domestic
architecture during the forties and fifties. But the commercial
and religious buildings had been among the most substantial and
elaborate structures put up during the first two decades of the
city's growth. There was as yet slight cause to rebuild those already erected and little demand for additional structures. Accordingly the churches and stores of this period are few and of no
great interest.

For the stores a simple formula was evolved. (Figure 81.)
The buildings were increased considerably in height, either by
multiplying the number of stories or by enlarging the individual
floors, or both. The windows were given an arched form and surrounded by a raised moulding, while the whole would be crowned
by a cornice carried on consoles. It is an index of the extent to
which the city was already built up as well as an indication of
the artistic point of view of the times that the designs are rarely

conceived except as façades. The cornice barely turns the corner, the ornamental features of the front are not repeated on the flanks —when there are any visible flanks. Corner stores, of course, display two adjacent façades. A slightly different form of decoration involves the use of arched corbel tables below the cornice and occasionally of pilaster strips.

It is noteworthy that in all these buildings the trim and the wall are of the same material—an indication of their comparatively late date. It is further remarkable that the stores continue to a great extent their early simplicity of character. These decorations were essential at that time; to build without them would have been old-fashioned. But the stores remain at heart traditional functional structures, and there is very little feeling that they serve as a display, as an individual advertisement for the concerns inhabiting them.

The churches of this period are more substantial buildings than their predecessors; they are also more conventional. The experimental days were over, and the new buildings represent merely one or another out of the multitude of accepted types. The last structure with any considerable individuality is the High Street Church, which was started by the Episcopalians in the early forties and sold to the Congregationalists, still incomplete, in the middle of the decade.[1] It represents the next stage after Dr. Duesbury's building, showing an even greater wealth of misapplied Gothic detail. Originally it was a very porcupine of a building, prickly with tall pinnacles. The aisle façades were enlivened by a series of battlemented gables; the windows are filled with perpendicular tracery, the buttresses provided with set backs. But, despite the attempt to indicate on the exterior the existence of a nave and aisles within, the basic scheme remains unchanged. It is a typical work of a period when, thanks to the increasing number of publications, builders became drunk with a superficial knowledge of Gothic detail without any conception of medieval building forms. Parallel cases are the Lee Street Church of 1850 and the Freewill Baptist Church of 1853.[2] Both are barnlike structures, devoid of

towers. Both face the street with their short ends. Both are mod-
ishly decorated, the former in a simplified round-arched Gothic,
which at that time passed for Romanesque, the latter by a series
of pilaster strips and an amazing double corbel table in brick.

A further evolution is represented by St. Patrick's, built in
1854, and St. John's, finished in 1861.[3] (Figure 79.) Here the
Gothic revival is shown ripened to an archaeologically impeccable
maturity. The former, with its complete symmetry, its elaborate
and rather mechanical tracery, foreshadows the hardening of forms
and unimaginative coldness that characterizes so much of the respectable Gothic architecture of the later nineteenth century.
However, particularly in the smooth sheet of wall at the east
end, there is a hint of the astonishing effects of scale which P. C.
Keeley was to achieve in the ensuing period. The latter, with its
symmetrical tower, and deep, broken roof, derives from the formula which Richard Upjohn devised for suburban churches.[4] It is
hardly to be distinguished from such a building as his St. Paul's,
Brookline, or indeed from any of the Episcopalian churches that
were being built at about this time in neighboring mill cities, like
Nashua and Lawrence.

What the foregoing groups of buildings lack in interest is more
than made up by the public buildings. It is here that one finds
exploited to the utmost that desire for display lacking in the
commercial buildings and that adventurous attitude towards design which had ceased to characterize the churches. The first public building in Lowell which illustrates the full romantic trend
was the new railway station, built in the late forties. This was a
sober, Italianate building with a T-shaped façade. Two stories
high, made of brick, it was crowned by a corbelled cornice which
curved majestically around the corners. The stem of the T was a
projecting pavilion supported below on arches, adorned above
with a series of round-headed windows and carrying an extraordinary pseudo-baroque clock, perhaps the base of a never completed tower.[5]

But, while this building preceded by several years all other public edifices in the new style, it was not, aesthetically speaking, as revolutionary as the original station had been. This is proved by the case of a neighboring town, Manchester, New Hampshire.[6] Here the city fathers had put up a town hall in 1841 of the conventional barn-cum-pilasters type. Unfortunately this burned down shortly, and in 1845 they built them another. In a characteristic burst of local pride they called upon Edward Shaw, a Boston architect, for designs, and erected what at that time was considered to be the handsomest building in the state. (Figures 82, 83.) "It is of a very peculiar style of architecture, nothing of the classical or pure about it, but still a fine looking structure," as one contemporary remarks.[7] "The design of the architect was that the building should have been entirely of stone, the columns hammered and the wall of ashlar work; but the committee deviated from his plan, and the building is of stone, . . . while the walls are of brick." It consists in the usual fashion of a low ground floor for shops and smaller rooms and of a tall upper floor for the hall proper. At one end rises a tower, crowned with an octagonal lantern, adorned with the inevitable pinnacles. The whole is spiced with delightful Gothic detail, octagonal buttresses, bands of quatrefoils, battlements, tracery, all those favorite forms culled from Pugin's *Specimens*. But while their application is anything but Gothic, it is nowise haphazard but is carefully considered and effectively executed. One realizes that for years American architects had been starved of variety in detail, and that it was this which the Gothic revival provided them. But here, as in the best early romantic buildings, the new discovery does not run away with the designer. At bottom there remains a splendid sense of proportions and of the relationship of masses, while the detail merely gives a needed touch of fantasy to the severe regularity of the scheme.[8]

At Lowell the corresponding building is the Court House, built in 1850.[9] (Figures 84, 85.) Here the style is Romanesque, and the design even more charming. The building is more complex in form, since, in the best Rhenish manner, there are two sets of projecting transepts, one of them crowned with a cupola. The skyline is further varied by a row of dormers. The material is brick, profusely relieved by wood trim. One could hardly ask for a more convincing proof of the interest of the forties in outline and decorative forms than this building provides. The surface of the brick is of a glassy smoothness; the detail crisply cut, boldly projecting. The cornice makes a vivid crinkly pattern around the upper edge, and the horizontal line is repeated by a deep carved band in the center of the building. The windows are large, with thin muntins, so that they appear as black holes, their outlines emphasized by the surrounding mouldings. The design is conceived wholly in terms of a careful arrangement of these lines and neatly limited patches upon the blank surface behind. As in all the characteristic buildings of the forties, the effect is tense, high strung. This is achieved not only by the pizzicato accenting of the surfaces, but by the sharp definition of the building blocks themselves and by their proportions. Almost every section is slender and tall, whether it be a transept, a porch, or a dormer. Almost every angle is acute.[10]

Contemporary public school buildings were too much under the dominance of a canon to reflect the more extreme aspects of romantic style, but this was not true of private schools. Beside St. Patrick's, and presumably contemporary with it, is a parochial school. Closely hemmed in on either side, it is an extremely simple building, offering a plain, windowed wall to the east, and the same to the west, with the addition of a projecting turret in the center. Yet, in the smoothness of the surfaces, in the crisp forms, in the delicate yet precise cornice, there is a kinship to the courthouse, even to the Nesmith house.

Again, as with private buildings, there comes a gradual change, and the excitement of novelty generated by the first impact of romanticism gives way to lushness and a certain ponderous well being. This development is indicated in Lowell by the prison, built in 1856, from the designs of James H. Rand.[11] This is a tripartite granite structure, the center a pile of Romanesquoid masses, the wings conventional Italianate blocks. Once again the new solidity and bulging heaviness of the form, the rediscovered richness of texture, the absence of contrasts between wall and trim are striking. Once again, clumsy as is the design, its clumsiness is not the result of a superfluity of ideas whose adjustment to one another has not worked out, as is sometimes the case in the forties. Here it is a question of insensitivity. The design is a matter of rote. The architect knew all the answers.[12] (Figure 87.)

Generally speaking, the mill architecture of the early nineteenth century is of two sorts. In England and New England, where industry quietly evolved out of handicrafts, industrial architecture developed slowly from the simple utilitarian structures of the locality. But in other parts of Europe and in the southern United States, where manufacturing was exotic, an institution imported and fostered by men of wealth, industrial architecture was assimilated to the prevailing monumental style, in terms of which its patrons thought. Their factories were designed just as other buildings were designed, primarily for aesthetic effect. Thus von Klenze, called upon in 1826 to plan the royal Bavarian bronze foundry, produced a small-scale version of one of the palaces lining the Ludwigstrasse. Chisholm's Mill in Charleston, South Carolina, three years later, with its arched windows, duck walks, and quoins, offered a last pale reflection of the High Georgian.[13]

This state of affairs continued in the mid nineteenth century, except that as manufacturing developed its requirements became more complicated, while the formulas of monumental design grew increasingly archaeological and became ever less adapted to the painless solution of new problems. The necessary compromises made for greater absurdities. The Salt Works at Königsborn are forced to suggest a medieval church, the chimneys of the power station in Rome simulate the columns of Trajan and Aurelius, while in Charleston of the mid forties, Bennett's Mill is made to recall the splendors of an eighteenth-century Palladian country house.[14]

The fact that industry in the British Isles and in the northern United States was in the hands of the unaesthetic bourgeoisie enabled the strong functional tradition of industrial architecture to continue. However, once manufacturing had come to play an important part in the national economy, once the individual concerns became prominent institutions, then, industry was forced to accommodate itself to the prevailing architectural code as a means of expressing its newly recognized significance and responsibilities. Boott had realized this, and met the problem by planning his establishment monumentally, but in the terms of the flexible eighteenth-century tradition. By the 1840's this way out was no longer satisfactory because Georgian was completely outmoded. Moreover, in the established centers, just where the need for display was most acute, the large-scale rebuilding such a program would have entailed was out of the question. No, manufacturing buildings must be adjusted to fit inside an architectural framework determined by the principles of the high romantic styles, and the styles themselves must be so simplified that a mere touch of detail here and there would lend an air of respectability to a whole great old barn of a building.[15]

At Lowell and her fellow towns common sense and the simplicity of the native tradition exercised a restraining influence, but occasionally the millowners drew a deep breath and plunged into an archaeological solution, complete with all the fixings.[16] The largest example is probably the Print Works at Manchester, New Hampshire, executed in 1853 in the Italian style.[17] (Figure 88.) Here the stair tower terminates in a belfry, the window heads are arched, and the wall ends in a deep, corbelled frieze. Generally such efforts were reserved for smaller buildings, such as the Romanesque control house of 1848, on the Merrimack Canal in Lowell, or the Kilburn Printing Company, built in the 1850's in front of the Merrimack Company, which affects a picturesque rusticity.

In the building, and particularly the rebuilding of mills themselves, the effort was to obtain a respectable effect by the use of
striking features that would command the attention and permit
the bulk of the structure to be left much as it always had been.
In 1844 there was an addition built connecting the two Stark
Mills in Manchester, New Hampshire.[18] At the same time the old
double-pitched roofs were replaced throughout by flat coverings.
The group was given a new monumentality by carrying the
stair turrets above the roofs to produce a series of towers. Since the
original mills were not exactly in line, the whole composition
formed a handsome echelon of masses, very impressive in the
narrow mill yard. In Manchester this device became the stock
procedure when rebuilding a mill. It was applied in 1844 and
1850 for the Stark Mills, in 1855 for the Manchester Company,
and in 1859 for the Amoskeag.[19]

At Lowell the same principle was followed, although differing
slightly in its application. In the early fifties when two of the
Massachusetts mills were linked together and crowned with flat-
tened roofs, the middle unit was emphasized by a pair of twin
turrets at either corner, so that the new portion stood out like a
church from a group of monastic buildings. (Figure 86.) This
system was adopted, although less spectacularly by the Lawrence
Company, and it was used again in the fifties and sixties by the
Massachusetts and by the Boott. The greatest variety was displayed
in the form of the turrets which were always slender and rarely
as dominating as those in Manchester.

With the Merrimack Company the problem was somewhat
different, for here two of the original mills burned down in 1855
and were rebuilt anew.[20] The remaining old mill in the center
row was then torn down and reconstructed to match. Here the
octagonal turrets were placed at the corners, and the rich cornice
was carried all about the whole structure. But the greatest addition to the Merrimack plan was the new dressing mill, built in
1863. (Figures 91, 92.) A tall square tower rose from one corner
of this structure, which was originally two, subsequently four,

and finally six stories high and which stood at the outer edge of the yard next to the counting house.[21] The dressing mill was thus by far the largest and most prominent building in the group. No expense was spared to make it architecturally worthy of its position as the façade of the largest and oldest factory in town, the most venerable manufacturing corporation in the country. The mill itself was a rectangular block, plain, except for the rich string courses marking the levels of its successive cornices. But upon the tower was lavished all the wealth of motifs evolved in two decades of romanticism. The solidity of its form and the uniformity of its material marked it as a characteristic monument of the second phase of the style. The elaborate detail seemed to grow out of the very fabric. But while its design had none of the awkwardness of experimentation that sometimes marks the work of the forties, it was still fresh. It had a freedom from archaeological conventions and a liveliness not usual at the period. Thus it epitomized the best features of the age. The striking new building focused into a single composition the park, the row of huge elms, and the great barracks of the "New Block" of boarding houses. It dominated everything by its sheer height and the beauty of its design. It remained the center of attention even in the face of the white elephant of a public school built adjacent to it at the turn of the century. The conception was grand, the execution original. The whole had an individuality that never characterized the older group of buildings, embedded as they were in tradition.

Yet these results were not achieved without sacrifices, sacrifices which the romantic age cheerfully made. Thus the Merrimack dressing mill summarized its period as much in the values it destroyed as in the values it created. The rebuilding of the plant in the sixties finally transformed the original orderly and urbane sequence of building blocks around an open court into a network of dark canyons winding between towering walls. (Figures 2, 92.) All sense of the mills as three-dimensional forms disappeared; one felt only the vast brick masses slowly choking the free space.

Romanticism, by its emphasis upon the quality of the few striking features, permitted an unrestrained philosophy of laissez faire to control the design of the bulk of a group of manufacturing buildings. Thereby it completely changed the aesthetic values of industrial architecture. For from the Civil War, until the Great War, at least, the interest of factories is the appalling impressiveness of rampant materialism, unchecked by any save financial and mechanical considerations, or else the accidental or self-conscious charm of inconsequential elements here and there.[22]

IX

CONCLUSION

THE CIVIL WAR marks the end of an epoch in the history of
Lowell. The cotton industry was sharply affected by the
general business depression which started in the late eighteen
fifties, and with the opening of hostilities the executives closed
down the mills.[1] Thus there was a break of more than eight years
in the normal economic life.

This break was particularly disturbing to Lowell because it
followed three and a half decades of almost uninterrupted prosperity. Her citizens were not people to accept such a misfortune
stoically. Even in the late forties many of the ablest young men had
set off for California because the increasing crystallization of
social and economic life had limited the possibilities at home.[2]
After 1857 hard times were reflected in an actual drop in population, an amazing reversal of the trend.[3] Finally, with the closing down of the mills, the Yankee farm girls were forced to
return to their homes.

The hiatus of the Civil War was more pronounced in architecture than in any other phase of civic life. The history of building is apt to be an alternation of boom and depression, and great
changes in the amount of business activity intensify the swing.[4]

Because the first twenty-five years of the community's independent existence were a period of much building, a slackening
in the pace of construction was to be expected during the fifties.

But what was more significant than the decline in building in this decade was the stagnation of architecture as an art. Compared to the astonishing developments of the preceding years, the most that one can discern is a gentle evolution. As a climax to this period of limited activity, there were eight years of nearly complete quiescence. From 1857 to 1865 little was accomplished save the rebuilding of the mills.

In every sphere the revival was as sudden and as rapid after the war as the decline had been before it. The revival soon became a boom, but the new prosperity did not in the least mean a return to old conditions. After 1865 the whole tone of life changed. Industry, society, and architecture alike manifested the transformation.

In cotton manufacturing there was a revolution in the management. The sixties saw the retirement of a second generation of executives. But even more important than the appearance of a new group of leaders was the adoption of new principles of administration. For the cotton mills the first twenty years of Lowell's history had been an era of profitable paternalism. The succeeding period, by contrast, was one of nepotistic mismanagement.[5] Control had passed into the hands of the selling agents, the bankers of the corporations, and their interests were not always identical with those of the stockholders.[6] The incompetence of the friends and relatives whom they installed as chief executives was matched by the bitterness of the subordinates.[7] Unable to rise, these "noncommissioned officers," became petty tyrants over the rank and file of the employees.

All might have escaped the punishment of their mistakes, except that for some years the widows, the orphans, and the thrifty young merchants of the city itself had been investing their savings in the stocks of the cotton corporations. When the dividends began to fall off, when the Middlesex Corporation was forced into bankruptcy, it was these new stockholders who brought the crisis to a head.[8] For the second generation of the bourgeoisie were just becoming men of substance when they saw not only their earnings but their little capital jeopardized. It is small wonder that prominent and aggressive citizens like Ben Butler, James Cook Ayer, and Charles Cowley denounced the administration of the textile industries. Thanks to them, a change of policy was inevitable.

The whole economic problem was complicated by the fact that the development of the railroads had brought down the price of coal. It was now possible to run steam mills cheaply enough so that they could compete with water mills.[9] Therefore the source of energy ceased to be the factor which determined the location of an industrial plant, and transportation facilities became the paramount consideration.[10] New factories were built not inland but along the seaboard. The favorite locations were in decaying commercial centers like Newburyport and New Bedford, for they offered a double advantage. On the one hand, the steam mills benefited from cheap, water-borne transportation; on the other, impoverished sailors and fishermen provided a large supply of helpless and exploitable labor.[11]

Lowell could not maintain its leadership in the face of such odds. During the last third of the century it was forced into the second rank of cotton-manufacturing cities. Indeed, only a pitiless labor policy enabled it to keep in the running at all. Actually, competition had been forcing the executives to economize ever since the depression of 1837. Working conditions had been growing less and less attractive, what with a gradual speed-up of production and a relative lowering of wages. After the Civil War, with the mills of Lowell obliged to rival newer and more favored plants, the original idealism had to be entirely jettisoned. The companies drove their employees yet harder and debased still further the standard of living. Most of the New England farmers had migrated to the more fertile West. The remaining native girls would have none of the mills under these new conditions. Their places were taken by immigrants, and Lowell became a city of the foreign born.[12]

So it is that, although the city experienced great prosperity during the last third of the century, its character was completely different from what it had been before. Lowell had been the leading exponent of a new path to economic salvation. It became one of a group of competing mill towns, successful because well established and skillfully if ruthlessly administered. It had been the darling of an important and adventurous clique of American capitalists. It now became the livelihood of a well-trained bureaucracy. Its history had been dramatic. Its citizens, aware of the world-wide interest focused on their actions, had behaved histrionically.[13] Its evolution became an uneventful progress in which the important problems were not those of Temperance, Slavery, and the Ten-Hour Day, but the improvement of the water system, the introduction of horse cars, and the formation of a local historical society.[14]

The character of building changed because inevitably architecture reflected the decline in the importance of the city and the transformation of its interests.[15] Building changed, furthermore, because for the first time it was forced to adjust itself to much that had been erected before. The city was no longer working out its pattern. Rather, it was filling in and modifying a framework already defined.

It seems logical, therefore, to carry this book no further. As was said at the start, it was written as a preliminary study leading towards a synthesis of nineteenth-century American architecture. The history of Lowell was only a means to that end. Between 1820 and 1865 the city was an unusually complete microcosm of the whole field. It was a community rich in normal nineteenth-century buildings, yet it illustrated the impact of new problems upon the native architectural tradition and it presented an interesting example of city planning and housing. After 1865 this was no longer the case, and the subject may properly be dropped.

To be sure, Lowell continued to offer a cross section of much of the building industry in the period after the Civil War, but her architecture was no longer the architecture of a pioneer settlement. Of course the city was confronted with a fresh series of challenges, as what city was not. But the difficulties were less pressing here than elsewhere. They were acknowledged, they were deplored, they were not promptly and independently surmounted. Nothing built in Lowell since the eighteen sixties has been as progressive as were the mills of the early nineteenth century. Nothing in recent times can match the originality and distinction of the first housing developments and the initial layout of the town. Qualitatively, the whole architectural history of Lowell since 1865 has been an anticlimax.

It seems hardly worth discussing the buildings of the postwar period in detail. What is needed next for the study of American architecture is the investigation of some entity that will be as illuminating for the last part of the nineteenth century as Lowell was for the years between 1820 and "the Great Rebellion." Here only three things remain to be considered, by way of conclusion. The recent melancholy history of Lowell and its sister towns must be sketched. The reasons for their decay as planned communities must be analyzed. Their outstanding architectural achievement, their housing, must be evaluated in terms of the present day.

Ever since the 1840's an increasing number of Irish girls had been employed in the cotton mills.[16] While they may have accelerated the decline in the standard of living, they were treated as the equals of the native workers, and their presence did not affect the social position of the working class to any great extent. After the war, matters were different. Then virtually the entire unskilled labor force was made up of immigrants, and this fact immediately brought about a fundamental change. The immigrants were completely dependent upon the cotton industry and they formed a permanent proletarian population. Wave after wave of foreigners rolled in, the Irish replacing the English, the French-Canadians replacing the Irish, and the Greeks replacing the French-Canadians. Some of them brought with them ideas of unionism and the class struggle. All together they created racial, religious, and linguistic problems which were more than the fatherly discipline of the corporations chose to cope with. Most of the executives lost patience. It was simpler to sell off the company houses than to try to perform the functions of a miniature League of Nations in the midst of interminable national feuds and international riots.[17]

The first third of the twentieth century brought to Lowell the final liquidation. Labor costs rather than transportation costs became the factor which controlled industrial efficiency. Southern mills, less hampered by social legislation, and supporting a lower standard of living, began to offer New England serious competition.[18] Naturally, it was the older factories of the North that felt this most keenly. Despite the brief prosperity of the World War years, several of them went out of business in the early twenties, and when the recent depression came, those that remained were operating at a small fraction of capacity.

Low-cost housing was now a luxury none could afford. Where they were able to, the companies sold off the remaining boarding houses for rooming establishments and let the apartments of the skilled employees degenerate into tenements, in the modern sense of the word.[19] Where they could not even avail themselves of these sordid possibilities, they tore down the housing to save taxes. Here and there the land might be used for a gas station or a parking space; otherwise it was just left gaping in vacant lots. Today it is nearly impossible to see in the rows of decrepit wooden dwellings or the files of blackened barracks the vestiges of model housing. No amount of imagination can conjure out of the jungle of weeds and debris and rusting spur tracks the vision of a trim and rationally planned city. As a physical reality, the Lowell that early travelers described, the Lowell that old prints still reveal, has all but disappeared. (Figure 1.)

The breakdown of the utopian community was prompted by the decline and collapse of its cotton industry. But just as it would be wrong to state that the formation of the city was exclusively determined by the needs of textile production, so it would be a mistake to maintain that the disintegration of the settlement was entirely the result of the migration of the cotton industry. In both cases manufacturing initiated the action. The direction which this action followed, and the speed with which it progressed were the outcome of forces far deeper than the fortunes and misfortunes of a single business.[20] To understand the form which Boott gave to his town, it is necessary to take into account Francis Cabot Lowell's social philosophy and ideals, the Anglo-Saxon tradition of housing, and the contemporary vernacular architecture. To comprehend the destruction of Lowell as a utopia, that destruction must be seen against the background of nineteenth-century architectural thinking in general. To explain the catastrophic extent of this destruction, Lowell must be considered as a typical purveyor town, and its precipitate collapse should be recognized as an example of the violent fate which generally overtakes this kind of community.

Throughout the western world, the last years of the eighteenth and the first years of the nineteenth century were a period of enthusiastic city planning. In England the practices developed during one hundred and fifty years of orderly urban expansion made possible the spectacular culmination represented by resorts like Brighton, by the work of Nash in London, by the New Town in Edinburgh. On the Continent the return of the courts to the cities initiated a long series of ambitious urban extensions. The earlier desire to lift the faces of buildings and districts here and there was succeeded by the wish to canalize the further development of whole communities in a determined framework.[21] Planning in the grand manner was even taken up in America, what with L'Enfant's designs for Washington and Paterson and Woodward's project for Detroit.[22]

The remainder of the nineteenth century was given over to the rapid destruction of the schemes laid out during its first decades. For the division of labor that resulted from the Industrial Revolution entailed the creation of a host of highly specialized new building types, each with its stringent functional requirements. There was no provision for these in the great *partis* designed on abstract aesthetic principles. Meanwhile, the whole conception of the desirability of large-scale planning was sapped by romanticism with its emphasis on the individual unit. And so when practical considerations demanded that the limitations of the old projects be disregarded, romantic considerations justified the disruption of the status quo and prevented the formation of an alternative framework. Laissez faire was the order of the day.[23]

The history of Lowell follows exactly this same pattern. The initial period of order and forethought is succeeded by an epoch of expansion and chaos. It must not be thought that this identity is the result of imitating Europe. On the contrary, both the laying out and the later evolution of the town are natural native developments which parallel similar occurrences abroad. The conception of setting up a new and ideal community certainly does not derive directly from foreign precedents. In a pioneering country like America the idea of founding a town in the wilderness grows quite naturally out of local conditions.[24] The method of planning this settlement is even more distinct from practice elsewhere. On the Continent a great scheme of gardens, public buildings, and majestic streets would be projected and slowly filled up. In Lowell there was only a functionally disposed nucleus. Within this nucleus the basic idea was a central highway parallel to the river, with the industrial plants on one side and the bourgeoisie opposite. The conception clearly derives from local tradition. Outside this planned kernel the remaining property was platted as rigorously as possible with a gridiron of streets. So far from contemplating a grand scheme and pursuing an orderly development, only areas likely to see immediate use were even laid out on maps, and great gaps remained for years which some accident or other kept from being developed.[25]

But the fact that the initial conception was less ambitious, and therefore less restricting than the extensive schemes of Europe made very little difference in the long run. To the men of the middle of the century one plan was much the same as another, and the history of Lowell is the typical tale of the breakdown of a city plan, partly through its inadequacy, partly because of uncontrolled selfishness.

The plan, indeed, had to give way even before it went into effect, thanks to the unexpected arrival of the Irish, for whom no provision had been or was made. It was strained by the real-estate policies of the Locks and Canals Company. For by holding the best land off the market during the first twenty years, they warped the development of the town. It was broken in a minor way when the Merrimack Company replaced Boott's wooden houses with a great brick block, and it collapsed entirely with the rebuilding of the mills during the Civil War. In short, its integrity was maintained, by and large, until the mid sixties. Then, like the social system it expressed, it disintegrated with increasing rapidity.

The process was natural at that stage in architectural history. Lowell could not remain aloof from the universal destructive forces of romanticism and materialism. But their disrupting influence was increased because they concurred with tendencies generated by another cycle of development, the evolution of Lowell as a purveyor town.[26]

It is characteristic of this urban type that development is a cycle, running over a shorter or a longer period of time. The driving force is the relationship of the citizenry to the dominant institution. This relationship is rarely stable, because there is always a lag between the evolution of the institution and the evolution of the town. Typically, the institution creates the town, and at first completely controls it. However, the very success of the institution soon builds up so large a town that the citizens begin to have a corporate consciousness and it is no longer possible to rule them directly. By the time the institution ceases to progress, the town may have reached such a size that for a time it "snowballs," regardless of the fortunes of its parent.[27] Then a balance of power is struck. This is upset by the decline of the institution which always precedes and is more precipitate than that of the town. The stage is set for the dramatic finale. The citizens, having progressed from the level of parasites to the status of purveyors, now become the scavengers of the institution that nurtured them. In a single dramatic incident they symbolize their superiority. The farmers of Cluny dynamite the apse of St. Hugh to erect therewith a stud stable for cart horses. The burghers of Manchester, New Hampshire, buy up the largest cotton mills in the world for a paltry $5,000,000.

Lowell cannot be said to have reached this climax as yet. But for many years it has displayed that division into more or less hostile groups which is characteristic of every mature purveyor town. The deep cleavage between the citizens and the Corporations has played a great part in permitting the decay of the social system as originally set up and, latterly, the destruction of the model housing. For in the first line it was the citizenry who made it possible for the living conditions of the proletariat to be depressed. What force could national public opinion exert when the local bourgeoisie did not even protest the deterioration? Feeling themselves a group completely apart from the employees of the mills, the residents of the town did not admit that it was their duty to insist on the maintenance of decent standards. On the contrary, they hastened to profit from the crowding together in slums of the Irish and the French Canadians.

The disappearance of the housing springs again from this same opposition. The town has always recognized that housing was a great asset. But it was the property of the Corporations, and the city felt no responsibility to preserve this advantage. When the manufacturing concerns went out of business, the city made no move to save the property. And so the housing has been torn down, or is rapidly decaying.

Changed economic conditions forced the Lowell system to be discarded in the years after the Civil War. All that remained of the architectural entity which the system created fell to pieces during the nineteen twenties. Nothing of Francis Cabot Lowell's utopia has stood the test of time.

Nor can it be claimed that his scheme exerted any appreciable influence upon later industrial settlements. By the time that other mass production industries arose, the problem of motive power had been solved by the use of coal, and the problem of labor supply by mass immigration. It is true that where it was not possible to locate industries near large population centers, one finds the company town. But later company towns differ markedly from the Lowell group. They were generally small. The inhabitants always formed a permanent proletariat, and the corporations owned and controlled every organization and institution in the town in a way that had not been possible earlier. Later company towns are enlargements of the earliest cotton manufacturing villages; they are in no way connected with Lowell and its fellows.

Thus the textile cities of central New England are sports in the general line of American industrial evolution. Transitory as ideal communities, unimportant as models, it is scarcely surprising that they have been almost completely forgotten. If they are remembered at all, it is as sociological curiosities. Their architecture is always ignored. Yet, natural though this neglect is, it is not deserved. For it is precisely their architecture and particularly their housing which has a vital significance for us today. It is important because, like similar unprecedented and issueless nineteenth-century creations in its essentials, it is amazingly modern. Like the Crystal Palace, like the neo-classic commercial buildings, it is a singularly pure embodiment of those qualities which are sought after in architecture today.

The housing projects executed during the renaissance and baroque periods can be divided into two classes, the princely and the paternal.[28] The most complete exemplification of the princely type is to be found in the baroque capitals. Uniform dwellings conceived as members of a series were essential components of these settlements. Their primary function was to provide an ornamental approach to the palace on one side, just as the formal gardens served as a foil for it on the other. The dwellings, like the gardens, were designed almost wholly in terms of their external effect.[29] But the very fact that the whole town was planned as an entity meant that the housing was logically related to every institution in the place.

The second type of housing project was the result of a tradition of charitable paternalism inherited from the Middle Ages. Ultimately, perhaps, it was the feudal system which made individual aristocrats feel that it would be laudable or advisable to provide their personal employees with suitable living quarters. During the sixteenth, seventeenth, and eighteenth centuries, sporadically, but all over Europe, rich men put up little groups of cottages for their dependents. The houses they built show two striking characteristics. In the first place they are generally conceived as the solution of an isolated problem, the housing problem.[30] In the second place they are always practical, geared to the functional requirements of living. Generally, in contrast to the pomp and pretentiousness of the courtly housing, these buildings are simple and traditional in style.[31]

The housing of the New England mill cities combined the best features of both these earlier types. Baroque fashion, the settlement is conceived as a whole. The housing is placed within this whole according to the part it will play in the life of the residents. It is carefully related to the mills on the one hand, and to the shops, public buildings, and churches on the other. But this relation is purely a functional one. The dwellings are not designed to form a handsome approach to the mills. On the contrary, like the houses of the manorial settlements, they are planned merely to provide decent shelter efficiently. Like them, too, they fall wholly within the vernacular architectural tradition.

Precisely because this housing embodied elements from both these types, it was preëminent in three respects. It was comprehensive in conception, it was efficient in operation, and it conformed to folk custom. It is these very qualities which are the ideal of every designer of housing today. Because the factory dwellings of Lowell realized them, perhaps they can suggest clues to the solution of our immediate problems.

But it must be recognized that the present importance of nineteenth-century buildings in general, and of these buildings in particular, is not to be found in their superficial characteristics. Lowell and her sisters are not models for modern practice. Given independent, unmarried labor, the company town with its tenements and boarding houses worked well enough. But under contemporary conditions of employment, a similar design could hardly be tolerated. Today such paternalism would be as much an anachronism as some of the physical characteristics of model homes a century ago. It would be as primitive and outmoded an arrangement as a dwelling with no central heating, a large bedroom with but a single window, and a backyard where privies alternated with pig-pens. These houses are significant, not because of the technique by which they solved the housing problem, but because of the fact that they did solve it. For this fact gives us an insight into those social forces which once refused to permit the existence of slums, and which must be called into play again if we are ever to rid ourselves of that evil.

The general situation a century and a quarter ago was not so basically different from the situation today as one might suppose. Then, as now, it was impossible for industrial workers to provide adequate shelter for themselves, despite exceptionally high wages. Then, as now, the enlightened public recognized the desirability of decent living quarters. There is only one paramount feature which distinguishes that period from our own. At that time it was recognized that proper housing was not a reward won by the able, but the right of all.

The way in which this principle was slowly forgotten is one of the tragedies of American social history. It was allowed to lapse, partly because immigration created a rift between the dominant native stock and the foreign-born workmen, partly because the forces striving for social betterment became exclusively focused upon the slavery question. Eventually the old point of view was replaced by a directly contrary attitude, the Victorian attitude par excellence.

This was imported from England. There, at least in the towns, the Industrial Revolution had brought about a widespread debasement of living conditions. It had also created a powerful urban middle class, a class which during the nineteenth century took over the initiative in architectural matters. Confronted by the reality of universal and appalling slums, it was natural that a wealthy manufacturer or a Tory philanthropist did not consider good housing either a necessity or an obligation. Instead, he thought of it as a charity, a sop to be thrown to the proletariat. This point of view appears in America as early as the middle of the century. Our business men no longer considered it desirable that all the laborers should dwell in abodes fit for "respectable mechanics in rural villages." Instead, a selected few were to be provided with pretentious warrens put up by pious foundations for the relief of the deserving poor.

Consciously or unconsciously, this smug attitude remains the belief of most good people today. The housing problem should be solved, of course; but *the American Way* is on the one hand to encourage rugged individuals to own their own homes, and on the other to look out for the unfortunate and the unfit by private bounty. Government low-cost housing projects smack of modernistic architecture, boondoggling, professorial reformers, and other unpleasant associations. Yet it is hardly any longer necessary to demonstrate that this Victorian ideology is unequal to the present-day task. When paternalism was possible, the American public forced industrial promoters to provide low-cost housing directly out of their own pockets. Now that paternalism is no longer possible, the American public must supply the housing indirectly, through taxes and government projects. But government intervention is raised above the level of political expediency only if decent shelter is recognized on the same terms as decent education, as a birthright, not as a privilege. This, indeed, is the only possible democratic point of view.

Our initial task is therefore a fundamental change in ideology. Such a change should not be hard, for the early textile cities prove that it is not a question of dropping our time-honored native attitude in favor of some foreign "ism." We have merely to reëstablish the one point of view which is peculiar to this country. Thus, the early textile cities are important because they are a historic declaration of our attitude toward low-cost housing. Far more explicitly than any document could, they state the American position. It is not individualism, not the merchant-bountiful and not the slum, but it is the belief that proper housing is a universal birthright which constitutes our native tradition.

APPENDICES

I

THE ECONOMIC BACKGROUND

Previous to 1640 the early settlers of New England had lived chiefly by exchanging supplies with the newcomers. When the stream of Puritan immigrants ceased, this source of income disappeared. Cattle, the chief stock in trade, dropped from £25 to £5 a head in a few months.[1] Lacking a staple with which to trade, even the settlers on the coast were forced to achieve that measure of economic self-sufficiency which difficulties of transportation made necessary for the frontiersmen right up to 1880.[2]

Although the colonies soon developed sufficiently so that they could have produced articles for export, manufacturing continued, because the normal economic growth was deflected by the Navigation Acts. Previous to 1651 the settlements had enjoyed economic freedom, but thereafter they were treated as possessions to be exploited.[3] As a result, "New England and later the Middle Colonies, not being allowed to exchange their normal products for England's manufactures, were forced to begin manufacturing for themselves."[4] The local legislatures responded to the necessity by passing laws such as this of 1651: "that all hands not necessarily employed on other occasions, as women, girls & boyes, shall, & hereby are enjoined to spin according to their skill & abilitie."[5] Free spinning schools were started in Boston and elsewhere.[6] The emphasis on textiles is very significant. The Navigation Acts destroyed the Dutch trade, which had hitherto supplied most of the cloth.[7]

Before the 1760's manufacturing had been a matter of economic necessity.[8] But the addition of a tax to the customary 100 percent mark-up in the price of English goods between London and New

York gave other grounds for avoiding importation wherever possible.[9] In New England societies such as the Daughters of Liberty
applied pressure against the purchase of English goods.[10] Homespun
became fashionable. The great increase in manufacturing that resulted served our ancestors in good stead, for the almost complete
self-sufficiency of many homes helped greatly in winning the Revolution.[11] The Continental army was supplied with homemade clothing.
It is difficult to exaggerate the amount of domestic manufacturing
during the war.

There followed, however, a brief but violent reaction. Beginning
even before the Treaty of Paris, this reached its high point in 1784.[12]
The country was flooded with foreign goods. But the hard times
which followed and legislative encouragement put many people back
into homespun very soon.[13] "When the people returned to their home
manufactures after their sad experience with foreign commodities,
they did it with a conviction that industrial dependence was as detri-
mental to their prosperity and happiness as political."[14] By 1790,
according to Phineas Bond, the British Consul in Philadelphia, "in
the four eastern states, viz. New Hampshire, Massachusetts Bay,
Rhode Island and Connecticut, the people manufacture much larger
quantities of woolen for their own use than they did before the war
. . . 40,000 yards of coarse New England linen have been sold in
Philadelphia within the last year. Among the country people in
Massachusetts Bay coarse linens of their own making are in such
general use as to lessen the importation of checks and even of coarse
Irish linens nearly two thirds."[15] The situation continued essentially
unchanged until the inauguration of the embargo in 1810. This
measure, by destroying the merchant's income from exports as well
as preventing importation, was doubly effective in fostering native
manufacturing.[16] Accordingly home production boomed until the
end of the war with England. Once more the country was flooded
with foreign goods. Then in 1816 the first tariff was passed, and a
duty of 82 percent soon drove the cheapest foreign goods from the
market. Thereafter American activities were placed on a wholly
new basis. See R. M. Tryon, *Household Manufactures in the
United States, 1640-1860,* and C. F. Ware, *The Early New England
Cotton Manufacturer;* also J. L. Bishop, *A History of American
Manufactures.*

II

THE SITE OF LOWELL

I

THE site on which the city of Lowell developed was a highly irregular piece of property. On two sides it was bounded by the Merrimack River, which here makes a turn of almost a right angle, from a direction almost due northeast to a direction almost due southeast. Perhaps a mile below the curve the Merrimack is met by the Concord River, which here runs slightly west of north but turns sharply a few hundred yards before its mouth, so that it actually makes a junction at right angles with the larger stream. A mile south of this the Concord is joined by a small brook, known as River Meadow Brook, which has a very winding course, but runs in a generally northeasterly direction. (Figure 1.)

These three streams describe four sides of a rough pentagon. The fifth side, did it exist, would be longer than the rest, as the course of the Brook and of the Merrimack above the turn are almost parallel. In general the land is low, and in places it was swampy, though there are hills near by, notably across the Concord River in an area later called Belvidere.

Something less than a mile above the turn are rapids on the Merrimack River, known as Pawtucket Upper and Lower Falls. The Pawtucket Canal led out of the Merrimack just above the Upper Falls, and running southeast, then east, and then northeast, joined the Concord River at the point where it changed direction, just above its mouth. Very roughly, the canal follows the curve of a quarter circle, struck from the great bend of the Merrimack as a center and with a radius of about a mile. There were originally four sets of locks on the Canal: the Guard Locks, about a quarter of a mile from the Merrimack; the Minx Locks, a few hundred yards below the point where the Canal was crossed by the upper highway (the Pawtucket-Boston road); the Swamp Locks, half-way between the two highway bridges; and the Lower Locks, just below the bridge which carried the lower highway (the Concord Road) over the Canal. (Figure 1.)

At the time of purchase there were several roads across this area. Above the falls, but below the mouth of the canal, there was a bridge over the Merrimack, known as Pawtucket Bridge. Over the Concord, between its junction with the canal and its mouth, there was another bridge. There was a ferry over the Merrimack just above the mouth of the Concord, called Bradley's Ferry, and finally there was a bridge across the Concord, well to the south, a few hundred yards above the mouth of the River Meadow Brook. One road ran almost due south from the Pawtucket Bridge, eventually crossing River Meadow Brook and finally meeting the main road from Chelmsford to Boston, outside the limits of the town. This we will call the Pawtucket-Boston road. The most important road was one which followed the course of the Merrimack River to a point just between the two falls and there split. One branch continued close to the bank and ended in a public landing just below the lower falls. The other turned in a southeasterly direction and crossed the Concord at the bridge near its mouth. This we will call the Merrimack Road. A third road ran in general northeast from the center of Chelmsford, skirting the north bank of the brook. Perhaps a third of a mile above the mouth of the brook, this road turned suddenly south, and a short distance beyond the point where it had crossed the brook, turned east again, and finally went over the Concord River on the upper bridge. This we will call the Brook Road. From near the first of its sharp turns a road swung almost due north parallel to the Concord until it intersected the Merrimack Road. This will be designated the Concord Road. Just below the point where it met the Merrimack Road, a short road ran at right angles to the bank of the Merrimack, leading to Bradley's Ferry.

There were several houses and mills on this tract of land. The two most important groups clustered around the sources of the two canals, called respectively Middlesex Village and Falls Village. In a small way both of these seem to have been thriving communities, although their prosperity was of recent date, as is attested by the houses, most of which were built in the second and third decades of the nineteenth century. A third group of houses was situated at the point where the Concord Road met the Merrimack Road, and there were still smaller clusters near the public landing and the upper bridge over the Concord.

It is difficult to be as specific about the mills. These establishments changed hands frequently, and in the records the same mills are referred to by different names. A map of 1794 (see *Illustrated History*, p. 156) shows a sawmill and a gristmill at the lower Pawtucket Falls, and a sawmill at the upper Pawtucket Falls. Between the mouth of the brook and the entrance of the canal there were two sawmills and an iron works, on the Concord. Just below the bridge over the brook there was a "clothier's mill" and just above it another sawmill and gristmill. This "clothier's mill" was of some importance, for here in 1801 Moses Hale established the first carding machine in the county. Written accounts differ from this description somewhat, as in ascribing the beginning of the saw and grist mills at the Falls to 1816, and of the iron works on the Concord to about 1821. There was also a flannel mill on the eastern bank of the Concord near its mouth.

Only two of the mills were of any significance in later times, and the authorities are in agreement as to the facts about these. In 1813 Captain Phineas Whiting and Major Josiah Fletcher started a cotton mill on the Concord River, just above the entrance of the canal. This was a small affair, 60 by 50 feet, and costing $2,500. In 1818 one Thomas Hurd purchased this cotton mill and turned it into a woolen mill. When Hurd failed in the hard times of the late twenties, his mill was bought up by Boston capitalists and became the nucleus of an important woolen factory in Lowell. Finally in 1818 Moses Hale and Oliver Whipple started a powder mill on the Concord River, just below the upper bridge. Farming and the mills supported the population of East Chelmsford, which was estimated at 200 in 1820.

In this area the Merrimack Corporation held various pieces of property, very irregular in shape. (Figure 1.) They owned (and their successors still do) a substantial strip of land on either side of the Pawtucket Canal. They owned all the land between the Merrimack and the canal, east of a line running about due south from the public landing, except for one long tongue of territory running south, close to the western boundary of the property, and a small rectangular piece on the west side of the Concord Road just south of its intersection with the Merrimack Road. They owned a roughly rectangular block bounded by the canal on the north, on the east by a part of the Concord Road, on the south by a part of the Brook Road, and on the west by a line running northwest, half way between the Concord Road and the Pawtucket-Boston Road. Finally they owned a long straight strip of land running southeast from a point just below the Pawtucket Bridge, and extending almost to the canal.

II

AFTER the Merrimack Road split, its main branch ran straight for quite a stretch, parallel to the lower course of the river. (Figure 1.) Then it made a great arc, at the end of which it turned slightly north, running straight until it intersected the Concord Road, in a direction due east, roughly parallel to the Pawtucket Canal. Then it turned slightly south, running parallel to the Merrimack once more until it crossed the Concord. In the city plan this was replaced by a road running directly from the bridge over the Concord to the lower end of the bow. Then the new street turned, running parallel to the river. This becomes Merrimack Street, one of the main arteries of Lowell. It was laid out in 1822. At least until 1826 it extended only as far as the edge of the company land, though its continuation and the arrangement of the streets around it was planned as early as 1825. This development consisted in running Merrimack Street through until it met the road to the town landing. The short straight stretch at the beginning of the old Merrimack Road was likewise run through in the opposite direction, crossing the Merrimack Canal, and then turning, as Merrimack Street turned, and running until it met the old Concord Road, just above the point where that crossed the Pawtucket Canal. Thus this road paralleled

Merrimack Street a convenient block's distance to the south. Another parallel road was made to the north, likewise starting from the road to the public landing. This, however, did not turn, instead it ran straight and intersected Merrimack Street just before that crossed the Merrimack Canal. These three "avenues," Moody Street, Merrimack Street and Lowell (Salem) Street, formed the basis for a gridiron of cross streets that covered this whole area.

The old Concord Road had run nearly straight south from the point where it left the Merrimack Road to a bridge over the Pawtucket Canal. Then it bent over towards the Concord River, and back again, before it crossed the River Meadow Brook. This road, largely outside of Company land, could not be altered. As Central Street, it retains much of its pristine form today. However, a new street was run from the bridge over the Pawtucket in a straight line south, continuing the line of the first section of the Concord Road, and joining Central Street once more just before they crossed the brook together. The streets east of Central Street ran from it in a direction at right angles to the Concord River; naturally, the streets to the west of Gorham Street, as the new highway was called, were parallel to the Pawtucket Canal, for their direction was established by the mills and housing on the south side of the Canal. The streets in the island of territory between these two thoroughfares followed a casually curving direction.

III

THE LIFE OF THE OPERATIVES IN LOWELL

Although, at any moment, living and laboring conditions throughout the mills of the city were uniform, over a period of years they
did change. They were maintained at the initial high level for about
fifteen years, and then gradually declined until the Civil War. This
decline was accompanied by a slow shift in the labor force, as the
Irish became an increasingly important factor in the mills. This
period ends with the ruthless and stupid closing down of the mills
during the Civil War. The next stage starts with their reopening,
manned almost entirely by immigrants. From then until the passage
of various restrictive laws at the end of the century, labor and living
conditions reached the nadir.

Like everything else Francis Cabot Lowell planned, his solution of
the problem of finding sufficient unskilled labor worked out to per-
fection. The vast majority of the girls were farmers' daughters from
the outlying parts of northern New England. Three times as many
came from New Hampshire and twice as many from Maine as came
from Massachusetts.[1] Bumpkins all, with queer-sounding names like
Samantha, Kezia, Leafy, and Florilla, they arrived dressed in "the
plainest of homespuns, cut in such an old-fashioned style that each
young girl looked as if she had borrowed her grandmother's gown."[2]
"All evidence agrees that need was not the chief motive which
brought girls to the mills."[3] "There were some who came to Lowell
solely on account of the social or literary advantages to be found
there. Some of the mill girls helped maintain widowed mothers or

drunken, incompetent, or invalid fathers. Many of them educated younger children of the family. . . . Indeed, the most prevailing incentive to our labor was . . . to make a gentleman of a brother or a son, to give him a college education," and President Walker of Harvard stated, "that in his judgment one quarter of the men in Harvard were being carried through by the special self-denial and sacrifice of women."[4] Others, no doubt, were motivated by more selfish aims, the desire for fine clothes or for a dowry, but whatever the driving spirit, for a time at least the supply of workers seemed inexhaustible. Despite the fact that very few of the girls stayed more than four or five years, the Lowell mills did not have to advertise to reach the labor market. They relied wholly on girls brought to the mills by friends already working there.[5]

Once in Lowell they invariably received work, starting as apprentices who earned about $1.80 a week, and working up to a wage that occasionally was as high as a dollar a day.[6] All paid $1.25 a week for board and lodging. In 1845 the average mill girl was said to be earning $3.15 weekly, or $1.90 more than her bare living expenses.[7] These were certainly better wages than women received in any other occupation. The standard pay for domestic servants was $.75 a week, and seamstresses received even less.[8] As mistress of a country school, a girl might earn a "paltry pittance a few months of the year, and be destitute of employment the remainder of it."[9] Work in other industries, such as manufacturing shoes or hats, was less profitable and more seasonal.

Lowell was therefore no sweat shop, and the proof of the fact is less in the wages paid than in the purchasing power of those wages. Even in those days it cost something to send a boy through Harvard. The savings of the mill girls deposited in Lowell banks alone amounted in round numbers to $100,000 in 1845.[10] Two sisters, working ten years, supported themselves and their widowed mother, built a house costing $600 (a pair of boarding houses cost only $500), bought a pew for $125, and had a cash balance remaining of $400.[11]

There is some dispute as to how long girls had to work to earn these wages. Certainly theirs was a six-day week, and, in general, their labor was light but constant. The hours varied with the season, but typically they lasted from sunrise to sunset, and the average for the year was probably twelve and a half hours.[12] This was not excessive, in view of the fact that the common workingday was twelve hours. To some extent the operatives preferred such a schedule. "The manufacturers in one town agreed to a reduction of hours at the operatives' request, but when the workers discovered that wages were to be reduced proportionately, they called for the longer hours again."[13]

There were of course important compensations. Thus there was plenty of time to sit and rest during the workingday, sometimes twenty or thirty minutes at a stretch, and everybody's attitude toward his work was casual.[14] On one occasion an important stockholder on a visit to the plant in Lowell was surprised to find that one of the mills was not running, and that all of the foremen had disappeared. He discovered them gathered in the attic, playing ninepins with appropriate parts of the machinery.[15] But even outside of exceptional events, there were more or less recognized vacations. If, occasionally, a girl wished to take a half day off, "two or three others would tend an extra loom or frame apiece, so that the absent one would not lose her pay."[16] This was possible because "two or three looms, or spinning frames were as much as one girl was required to tend, more than that being considered double work."[17] "Those of the mill girls who had homes generally worked from eight to ten months in the year; the rest of the time was spent with parents or friends. A few taught school during the summer months."[18] It must be remembered that "the cotton mill had been introduced into an industrially slack world. Men worked long hours, but they did not get the utmost possible out of themselves or others. It was necessary to acclimatize the rustic to machine production."[19]

The most convincing evidence that, whatever the hours, the work was not excessively fatiguing is the energetic fashion in which the girls spent their spare time. All activities tended to center around the churches.[20] Those, indeed, were the only social institutions in the city, and it was one of the mill regulations that everybody should go to church somewhere. Most of the occupations were educational, or at least uplifting in character. The chief attraction of Lowell was the possibilities it offered for improvement, and "very few were . . . without some distinct plan for bettering the condition of themselves and those they loved."[21]

Many of the girls were omnivorous readers, clubbing together and subscribing to various magazines.[22] One house with thirteen boarders received regularly fifteen newspapers and periodicals and borrowed five more. The titles speak for themselves: the Boston *Daily Times*, the *Herald of Freedom*, the *Literary Souvenir*, the *Edinburgh Review*, the *Young Catholic's Friend*, the *Star of Bethlehem*, the *Ladies' Pearl*, etc.[23] They also took books from the lending libraries, and although their tastes ran to historical writings and poetry, it is refreshing to know that "such books as . . . *Abellino the Bravo of Venice*, or *The Castle of Otranto*, were read with delight and secretly lent from one young girl to another." They must have nicely balanced other popular favorites, such as *Saint's Rest*, and *The Widow Directed*.[24]

Almost half of the operatives were connected with Sunday Schools, either as teachers or students.[25] Nor did this exhaust the desire for education. Many of the girls supported "themselves at Schools like Bradford Academy or Ipswich Seminary half the year by working in the mills the other half."[26] For those who did not there were the regular Lyceum lectures given by outstanding people like Emerson, and above all the Improvement Circles. These were groups of girls who gathered together, generally under the auspices of a minister, and read one another special pieces they had written for the occasion. Ultimately one such group published its pieces, and the result was the *Lowell Offering*, a periodical written and edited by the mill girls.[27] This so flabbergasted the European public that it was reviewed in the *London Times* and became the basis of a debate in the French Chamber of Deputies on the virtues of industrialism.

Less serious amusements fared badly. A theater was started in Lowell and failed. The "Museum" was not a great success, and "in 1836 a man was fined by the municipal authorities for exercising the trade of common fiddler; he was treated as if he had outraged the public morals, the magistrates fearing that the pleasures of the dance might tend to corruption of manners."[28]

The surrounding country was pretty, and picnics down the river were common, but, aside from religious and cultural fervor, what provided most diversion was a general consciousness of the picturesqueness of the scene.[29] It was exciting to live among girls from regions unknown, as Maine, New Hampshire, and Vermont were in those days. The population of the city itself was very mixed. Solemn Scots, fair-haired Germans, and peddlers from Poland rubbed elbows with Swiss organ grinders.[30] But above all it was the Irish who were a source of delight with their gayly colored clothes and thick brogue.[31] Then there was the endless stream of visitors from Andrew Jackson in whose honor the whole town had a holiday, to Mar Yohanan, a Nestorian Bishop who trudged through the mill yards in full regalia.[32] Once every summer "a fleet of canoes would glide noiselessly up the river, and a company of Penobscot Indians would land at a green point almost within sight from our windows. . . . Their strange endeavours to combine civilization with savagery were a great source of amusement to us; men and women clad alike in loose gowns, stove-pipe hats and moccasins. . . . Their wigwam camp was a show we would not willingly have missed."[33]

Of course Lowell was no Paradise. There were strikes, the first occurring in October, 1836, to protest the cutting down of wages and the abolition of the bonus of $.25 a head a week that had hitherto been paid to boarding-house keepers.[34] But in general there was less dissatisfaction with the work and wages involved in industrial employment than in the discipline which industrialism produced and the loss in the social status of the worker that accompanied his loss of independence. "The capitalists have taken to bossing all the mechanical trades, while the practical mechanic has become a journeyman, subject to be discharged at every pretended "miff" of his purse-proud employer," wrote the *New York State Mechanic* in 1842.[35]

In Lowell, the large corporations attempted to control every activity of the employees and every institution in the town. This control was so unquestioned that on one notorious occasion a company even undertook to dictate how its operatives should vote. Outside the Hamilton Mills appeared a notice reading: "Whoever, employed by this corporation, votes the Ben Butler, Ten-Hour ticket, on Monday next, will be discharged."[36] Such crass tactics were unusual, but the factory and boarding house rules were innumerable and covered every smallest corner of the operatives' lives. The printed rules, which were copious enough, were only a small part of the existing regulations.[37] These rules were implemented by a black list containing the names of everybody dishonorably discharged.[38] This list was sent around to all the mills in the city and in the neighboring cities and effectively prevented the culprits being rehired elsewhere. As a result all the operatives were placed completely at the mercy of the overseers. It was they who determined what constituted "habitual light conduct and conversation" or any other grounds for dismissal, and from their decision there was no appeal.[39] These foremen were substantial citizens, fathers of families, aldermen of the city, or deacons of the church. But even deacons were not above making passes at mill girls, and in fact, there was nothing in the Lowell system to prevent the overseers being what they later became, dishonest, petty tyrants.[40]

In the early times it was only the comparative scarcity of labor and the spirit of the employers, at once democratic and Puritanical, that made conditions bearable.[41] Caste lines were not sharply drawn, and there was a feeling of respectful equality between all working in the mill. The majority of the operatives "were as well born as their 'overlookers,' if not better, and they were also far better educated."[42] Lucy Larcom, working in the cloth room, was privileged to bring books to work. The agent, "a man of culture and a Christian gentleman of the Puritan school, dignified and reserved, used often to stop at my desk in his daily round to see what book I was reading."[43] "The most favored girls were sometimes invited to the houses of the dignitaries of the mills," and after hours it was quite usual for foreman and operative to teach side by side in the same Sunday School.[44] This genial spirit naturally affected the work. On the one hand the girl's own account of labor done by the piece was always accepted, and on the other "the feeling that the agents and overseers were interested in their welfare caused the girls, in turn, to feel an interest in the work for which their employers were responsible."[45]

The same spirit dominated the boarding house, around which centered whatever social life existed apart from the churches. The landladies were often people of refinement, mothers of mill girls, friends and advisers of their boarders.[46] Theirs was a hard lot. The rent they charged was fixed by the corporations, and the cost of food left them little profit.[47] They were obliged to compete against one another in the table they set, and the standards were very high.

Here is a description of conditions in a Waltham boarding house somewhat later.

The house bell was rung at six o'clock, and in half an hour we were all ready for breakfast, which, too, was ready for us. We had the best of beefsteak, with baked potatoes, boiled eggs, white and brown bread, biscuits, doughnuts, and snaps, butter and condiments, coffee and tea. Clean napkins were beside every plate. At a few minutes after twelve the great rush of hungry damsels is repeated. For dinner we had soup, scolloped oysters, roast beef and mutton, boiled potatoes, celery and pickles, pudding and pie, with tea, coffee and pitchers of milk. For supper we had cold meats, cheese, various kinds of bread and "fixings" and again coffee, tea or milk. . . . As for the appetites, so far as the stranger could take notice of such a thing, they were somewhat amazing to a man who is unaccustomed to sitting down at table with such an array of Yankee girls.[48]

It is easy to see how the architecture fitted the life. The long workingday and the three quarters of an hour or less allowed for meals necessitated a highly compact disposition of the buildings. The sober, democratic character of the community expressed itself in the simplicity, uniformity, and individuality of the residences. The structures were solidly built, and no expense was spared for upkeep, the houses being painted and thoroughly whitewashed every spring at the Corporation's expense.[49] The supply of water was abundant, and the yards and outbuildings more than adequate. The bedrooms displayed "an air of neatness and comfort exceeding what most of the occupants have been accustomed to in their parental homes."[50] The amount of living space was limited, there being little need for it, but after meals the girls used the dining room for recreation, and sometimes there was even a carpeted parlor where they might receive "gentlemen callers" on specified nights of the week.[51]

IV

THE DECLINE OF
PATERNALISM IN LOWELL

THERE is an excellent study of the decline of paternalism in Lowell, namely, George F. Kengott, *The Record of a City, a Social Survey of Lowell, Massachusetts* (New York, the Macmillan Company, 1912), pp. 28, 46-48. A few quotations reprinted here by permission of the Macmillan Company, publishers, will help illuminate this phase of the city's history.

"During the last few years the great industrial corporations of Lowell have disposed of much of their property (their boarding-houses, tenements, and great brick blocks outside of the mill yards) and have discarded the old paternal system of caring for their employees. The result is that the rents in houses formerly belonging to the corporations have been greatly increased, the price of board and lodging has been raised, and several families are now crowded into houses or apartments occupied a few years ago by one family.

"The English-speaking people who once occupied these corporation houses and tenements have moved in large numbers into outlying districts of the city and the suburban towns which have become accessible by the development of the electric car system."

"W. S. Southworth, agent of the Massachusetts Cotton Mills, made the following statement regarding the sale of the corporation tenements: 'During my twenty-six years at the Massachusetts Cotton Mills, the boarding-house and tenement system of that corporation has gradually declined and gone by natural course entirely out of existence.

" 'Consider first the boarding-house system for women. The houses were generally constructed with large rooms in which it was expected that from two to six persons would sleep. While the inmates were of the same racial type and especially while that type was the New England Yankee, there was no trouble; and because the city afforded no other resort, there was no clamor for an unobtainable privacy, nor was there often any expressed resentment at the rigid rules of the house, which required women to be in at a certain hour in the evening, to conduct themselves with propriety, and in the early days to attend church on Sundays, and to go to the hospital provided by the mills if they were sick.

" 'As time went on there was a gradual change. The city grew up around the mills, affording more and more opportunities for the renting of single rooms to those who wished them and would take their meals under another roof. Such opportunities, away from all restraint, attracted especially the younger women, who were generally more efficient workers in the mills. The gradual advance in the cost of living and the demands for a better table resulted in the claim of the boarding-house keeper that a single boarding-house yielded no profit and sometimes barely a living, and the corporation was called upon to put two or three houses under the charge of a single person. This resulted in a relaxation of rules. In addition to having a larger house, the boarding-house keeper also demanded the privilege of supplying meals to persons other than those lodging under her roof; and from this it gradually came about that the feeding of outsiders was the most remunerative part of the business, and there was a tendency to neglect the interests of the lodgers. When the mills began to draw upon the Irish and French-Canadians for workers, there was a demand for separation in the boarding houses, and the French particularly were necessarily in boarding houses by themselves. With the increased difficulty of finding lodgers, the rules became relaxed, and there was a strong temptation to "keep full" by taking in persons not employed by the corporation, or taking a few men boarders if they were offered. Both these courses were objectionable.

" 'As to the boarding-houses for men, it is to be said that in my day at least there was very little patronage of these, and I can remember but one or two among the 110 tenements of this corporation, and they were finally given up altogether. Men received higher pay than women, and could better afford to look out for themselves. Besides this, when it came to the mixing of races the houses became so troublesome that the police had to be resorted to frequently, and there was more or less scandal, leading to the abandonment of any attempt to maintain houses for men.

" 'Now as to tenements for private families; many of these were originally provided, and, in time, as it became more difficult to fill the boarding houses, for causes above outlined, and for others as well, more or less of the houses intended for boarders were converted into tenements for single families. It was thought desirable at the outset to keep near the mills the more important men employed by them, such as overseers, second-hands, and experienced mechanics, and these generally had the first choice of tenements; in fact, nearly all the tenements were filled by men of this class who had families.

" 'With the growth of the city it gradually came to be a sort of reproach with a man well able to live elsewhere that he retained a corporation tenement, and the men best able to do so began to refuse the offered tenements, and to find homes for themselves, pleading generally better air, or pleasanter surroundings, or a place for children to play, etc. rather than the true reason which was that they felt themselves too good to live in a corporation house. There was a feeling too, that living near the mills they were under a certain espionage which was irksome. So it came about that it was necessary to keep the houses, to let in people other than the most desirable.

" 'The rents placed upon the houses were in my day so much less than the rents on the street that the difference amounted to from $1.50 to $2.00 in favor of the tenant. Of those in the boarding houses the same could be said as to the board paid. The mill paid the boarding-house keeper a small amount per capita in order to keep the rate of board very low. In the old days the low cost of housing or of boarding appealed to the workers, and was in the mill offices alleged as a justification for a more moderate rate of wages; that is to say, the providing of a mill tenement or boarding house was reckoned a part of the wages.

" 'In the course of time this theory became distasteful to those who received those advantages, and it was finally entirely ignored. When the corporation could no longer see any advantage to itself in furnishing houses, when the best men refused to live near the mills, and the most desirable of the ordinary workers preferred to live elsewhere than in the tenements or boarding-houses offered them, the whole system was ready for abandonment. In the case of this corporation, so centrally located, the land values increased, the land became desirable for business buildings or was sought by those who were after investments which they could manage as they liked. When blocks of tenements were sold the rents were in some cases tripled, never less than doubled, and the character of the tenants changed completely.' "

William S. Southworth was perhaps the dominant personality among Lowell executives of his day. He was born in 1849. He came to Lowell in 1864, working there in various capacities until 1876. He then left Lowell, but returned in 1882 to become superintendent of the Massachusetts Cotton Mills. This is the beginning of the "twenty-six years at the Massachusetts Cotton Mills" to which he refers. He became agent of the mills in 1889. See the *Illustrated History of Lowell and Vicinity, Massachusetts,* done by Divers Hands (Lowell, Courier-Citizen Company, 1897), pp. 266, ff.

V

THE GROWTH OF THE CITY

BELOW, there is a chart of the increase in population in the city of Lowell from 1820 to 1865. The actual figures are: 1820—200 (from Coburn, rough estimate); 1826—2,500 (from *Courier-Citizen, Illustrated History*, p. 189); 1828—3,532 (from Keith); 1830—6,477; 1832—10,254; 1833—12,363 (from *Illustrated History*, p. 189); 1836—17,633 (from Keith); 1840—21,000 (from chart based on U. S. Census); 1846—29,127 (from Cowley); 1850—33,000 plus (from chart based on U. S. Census); 1855—37,554 (*Illustrated History*, p. 621); 1860—36,227 (from Coburn); 1865—30,990 (*Illustrated History*, p. 621). Figures for 1860 and 1865 vary somewhat, according to different sources.

In general one can see that the steady growth of the city depended almost entirely upon the growth of the manufacturing enterprises until 1828. Then the bourgeoisie appear, and the curve mounts rapidly. This curve keeps on rising evenly at a slightly decreasing rate until 1855. The depression of 1837 did not affect Lowell very much, causing but a slight slackening of the rate of increase, which was resumed almost immediately afterwards. After 1855, with the depression there is a marked falling off, which becomes intensified after 1860 with the Civil War and the closing down of the mills. The effect of this sudden change on the city must have been very profound. Certainly all the inhabitants were aware of it. The city picked up rapidly, however, and it is amazing that the rate of growth from 1870 to 1900 was even greater than from 1830 to 1860.

B. REAL-ESTATE ASSESSMENTS

Below is a graph of the increase in the assessed real-estate values of property in Lowell from 1830 to 1860. The total figures are: 1828—$207,900 (not shown); 1830—$768,000; 1836—$10.5 million; 1851—$19.8 million; 1860—$22.1 million. This total is broken down into three groups—the property owned by the large cotton manufacturing corporations, the property of all other manufacturing concerns, and the real estate of private individuals. There is no breakdown for the year 1828. In the year 1830 the three largest cotton corporations owned property worth $337,000, and the total owned by cotton corporations must have been approximately $400,000. The amount of property owned by other businesses was negligible. In 1836 the cotton corporations owned 5 million dollars worth, the other corporations 1.2 million dollars worth, and private individuals, 4.3 million dollars worth. In 1851 the cotton corporations owned 9.7 million dollars worth, the other corporations owned 1.2 million dollars worth, private individuals owned 8.9 million dollars worth. In 1860 the cotton corporations owned 9.7 million dollars worth, the other corporations owned 2.8 million dollars worth, private individuals owned 9.6 million dollars worth. The area at the bottom of the graph represents the property owned by the cotton corporations. The heavily hatched area represents the property owned by the other corporations. The lightly hatched area represents the property owned by private individuals. (Figures for 1826 and 1830 from the inventory of Polls and Taxable Property, figures for 1836, 1851 and 1860 from Keith.)

It is significant to notice that from the very beginning the property of the cotton corporations did not increase in value as rapidly as the other two forms of property. The part they played in the tax structure of the city became progressively less important. By contrast the role of private property became increasingly preponderant. It is interesting that despite the dropping off of population this continued to increase in value during the 1850's. Both these tendencies continued on in the post Civil War period.

The Inventory of Polls and Taxable Property reveals a certain number of curious facts for the early years. In 1826 there were 16 people in the town who had property in excess of $1,000. Of these the richest was Thomas Hurd, who owned a house and factory valued at $5,200. This was subsequently sold and became the nucleus of the Middlesex Company. The Merrimack factories were valued at $5,000 each, and the boarding houses at $500 a pair. The town included 682 polls.

In 1830 there were 20 people who owned property in excess of $1,000 in one district of the city alone. (There were six districts, although the first accounted for about 60 percent of the property.) Brick houses were valued at about $1,000. The parsonage was considered to be worth $1,500, the Moody House, $1,750.

In 1835 there were 13 property holders who were worth more than $10,000. Fortunes of this size comprised few large items, at this time. For the most part they were invested in one or two business buildings, brick blocks valued at from $5 to $7,000. Land values were noticeably higher. There were one or two really large properties, one of $47,000, another of $27,000, but for the most part they were from $10,000 to $15,000. A large hotel, such as the American House, was valued at $11,000.

LOWELL - INCREASE IN POPULATION

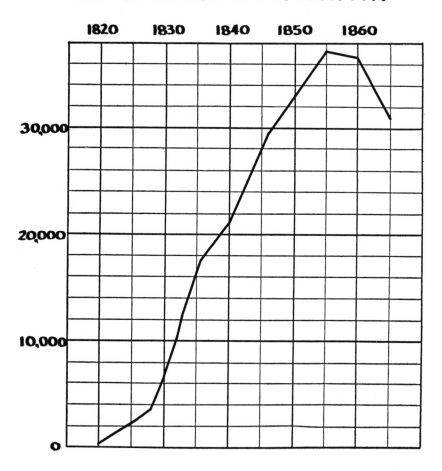

LOWELL - REAL ESTATE ASSESSMENTS

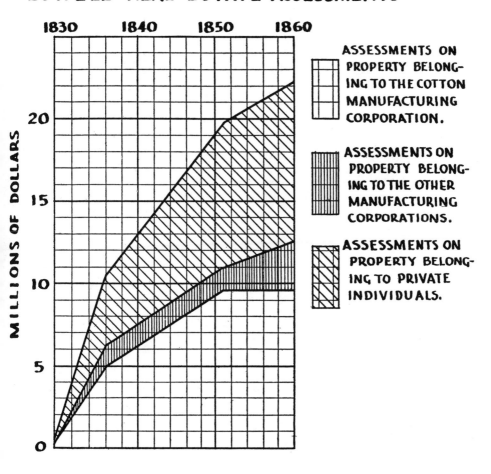

ASSESSMENTS ON PROPERTY BELONG-ING TO THE COTTON MANUFACTURING CORPORATION.

ASSESSMENTS ON PROPERTY BELONG-ING TO THE OTHER MANUFACTURING CORPORATIONS.

ASSESSMENTS ON PROPERTY BELONG-ING TO PRIVATE INDIVIDUALS.

VI

LISTS OF SOURCE MATERIAL

A. MAPS

The following is a list of the maps used in the writing of this book. Most of these maps are to be found in the possession of the Locks and Canals Company at Lowell. This company has a card catalogue of the maps in its possession. Most of their maps are stored in the attic and cannot be easily reached or identified according to their descriptions in the card catalogue.

1. "A Plan of Chelmsford, protracted by a scale of 200 rods to an inch. Surveyed Nov. 1794 by Frederic French. 23 miles to Cambridge Courthouse." Published in the Courier-Citizen's *Illustrated History of Lowell*, p. 157, with the note, "copied from the original map in the State House, Boston, Mass."

2. "A Plan of Sundry Farms &c at Pawtucket in the Town of Chelmsford, MDCCCXXI. J. G. Hales, Surveyor and Civil Engineer." In the Locks and Canals Company. This map has been published in *Proceedings . . . at the Semi-Centennial Celebration*, p. 32.

3. "A Plan of the Land and Buildings belonging to the Merrimack Manufacturing Company, with the neighboring Farms, Roads, etc. at Pawtucket in the Town of Chelmsford, MDCCCXXV. By George R. Baldwin." This exists in the Locks and Canals Company, and was used in determining the buildings existing in 1825, in the writing of this book.

4. "A Plan of Sundry Pieces of Land belonging to the Merrimack Manufacturing Company, Chelmsford, March, 1826, by Geo. R. Baldwin. Plan referred to by George R. Baldwin in his deposition in perpetuam, taken before me this day and annexed to said deposi-

tion. Cambridge, Dec. 4, 1868, William A. Richardson, Judge of Probate." Of this plan I have seen a photostat. I understand that in the middle of the century Baldwin, who had surveyed the land for the Merrimack Manufacturing Company in 1825, was asked by the Locks and Canals Company to make a deposition in perpetuam, against the possibility of law suits. To this deposition was attached apparently either a copy of his original map or a new map made from his notes. In any event, this map of which I have a photostat is very close if not identical with Number 3. I suppose that the original of this map exists in the Cambridge Court House.

5. "A Plan of the Buildings and Lands belonging to the Merrimack and Hamilton Manufacturing Companies and the Locks and Canals in the towns of Lowell and Dracut. J. C. Hales, 1827." Description taken from the catalogue of the Locks and Canals Company. I have never seen this map.

6. "A Plan of the town of Lowell and Belvidere Village, from measurements taken by Benjamin Mather, 1832." Description from the catalogue of the Locks and Canals Company. I have never seen the original. This map was published in *Proceedings . . . at the Semi-Centennial Celebration*, p. 96.

7. "A Plan of a Part of the City of Lowell, from a survey made in 1833-34 by U. A. Boyden, with additions by James B. Francis, 1837." In the Locks and Canals Company. Used to determine the dates of buildings before 1840 in the writing of this book.

8. "Map of the City of Lowell, surveyed in 1841 by I. A. Beard and J. Hoar, showing lands belonging to the Locks and Canals. 1841." This description is from the catalogue of the Locks and Canals Company. The map must be the original of the first published map of Lowell. I have never seen it, although there are several copies of the first published map of Lowell in the possession of the Locks and Canals Company. As published it does not show the lands belonging to the Locks and Canals. It also appears in Miles's, *Lowell as It Was and as It Is*. The published map, of which I was given a copy, was used in the writing of this book for dating buildings before 1841.

9. "Plan of Lowell Cemetery as designed and laid out by G. P.

Worcester, Civil Engineer. Drawn on Stone and printed by E. W. Bouve, Graphic Court, Boston, 1841." A copy of this exists in the Map Room of the New York Public Library. I know of no other.

10. "Plan of land in Lowell belonging to the Locks and Canals, by J. B. Francis, 1844." Description taken from the Locks and Canals Company catalogue. I have never seen a map exactly answering this description, but I suspect that it is the same as Number 11.

11. "Duplicate Plans of Land in Lowell." This is a book of plans showing land in Lowell owned by the Locks and Canals Company. It is dated 1844. This book is owned by the Locks and Canals Company. It shows the disposition of the various lots of lands with numerical references to the Book of Deeds. I used this map as a check against the real estate holdings shown on Map 3. It served to provide an indication of the land which had been bought between 1825 and 1844. I believe that this map must have been made with reference to the coming land sale.

12. "Catalogue of 113 lots of land in Lowell, including the Merrimack Hotel, 2 brick stables, 4 brick tenements and two wooden houses, belonging to the Proprietors of the Locks & Canals on Merrimack River. Which will be sold at Auction . . . on Tues. Ap. 15, 1845 (Weather fair or foul) at the Hall of the Mechanics Association, Lowell, Boston, Samuel N. Dickinson, Printer, 1844." This appears as a little booklet and exists in the Locks and Canals Company and in the Widener Library, Harvard University.

13. "New Map of Massachusetts compiled from the Latest and Best Authorities and corrected by permission from the survey ordered by the Legislature. Carefully revised and additions made in 1848. Boston, 3rd edition, published by Nathaniel Dearborn. Engraver & Printer, 104 Washington St." Inset map of Lowell. "Population in 1840, 20,816." Inset is unlike any other map of Lowell I have seen. I think it is derived from Benjamin Mather's map with additions. In New York Public Library.

14. "Plan of the City of Lowell Massachusetts, from actual surveys by Sidney & Neff, 80 Walnut Street, Philadelphia, published by S. Moody. Printed by F. Muhl, Phila." A copy of this map exists in the Locks and Canals Company. They permitted me to have it photostated. It was used to determine the buildings built between 1841

and 1850, in the writing of this book. This is the finest map of Lowell, for it shows not only pictures in the border of all the best houses and chief manufacturing establishments of the city, but beside each house indicated on the map is written the name of the owner.

15. "Map of the City of Lowell, Mass. by R. W. Barker, 1868." In the Locks and Canals Company. They kindly permitted me to have it photographed, and it was used to determine the public buildings and streets added between 1850 and 1868.

16. "Index Map of Lowell by Ripley, 1888." Description from the Catalogue of the Locks and Canals Company. I have never seen this map, as it covered material outside the scope of this book.

17. "A Survey of the City of Lowell, based on plans in the City Engineer's Office. Published for Miller & Lord, 93 Bay State Road, Boston, Mass. . . . Made and Copyrighted by the National Survey, Chester, Vermont, 1929."

B. VIEWS

1. General View of Lowell. Published at Sendfelder's Lithograph Co. Rooms, 123 Washington St., Boston, 1820. View is taken from next the Rogers House on Fort Hill, very good. Copy in the Lowell Historical Society.

2. General view of Lowell in 1826 from the South, oil painting by Benjamin Mather. Reproduced in Wilson Waters, *History of Chelmsford*.

3. General View of Lowell. Engraving, published in the *People's Magazine*, Vol. I, No. 26, March 8, 1834. View along the Merrimack Canal towards the Machine Shop, showing the pool in front of the Moody House. Excellent view of the Machine Shop. Copy in the Lowell Historical Society.

4. General View of Lowell. "From House of Elisha Fuller, Esq., Dracut, by E. A. Barrar, Pendleton Lithograph. Entered 1834." Copy in the Lowell Historical Society and in the New York Public Library, see Frontispiece. This view is reproduced in Hill's *Lowell Illustrated*.

5. General View of Lowell. "Sketched 1838, published 1839." Drawn by J. W. Barber. Taken from Dracut, extending from the Lawrence

Mill to the Museum. Poor. Copy in the Lowell Historical Society.

6. General View of Lowell. Signed by J. Hedge. From the top of the Lowell letter paper. Dated by William Goodwin (on the basis of Central Bridge) as after 1849, although not long. Poor engraving. Copy in the Lowell Historical Society.

7. General View of Lowell. Dated 1855. Colored print, shows the city from the Dracut side. Copy in the Locks and Canals Company. Reproduced in *A Chronicle of Textile Machinery*.

8. General View of Lowell. 1865. From the Tuxbury residence in Dracut. From a painting by J. B. Batchelder. Excellent. Copy in the Lowell Historical Society.

9. General View of Lowell. Water color, drawn from Dracut. No date. Dated by William Goodwin in the 50's. Less good than the Batchelder view. Copy in the Lowell Historical Society.

10. General View of Lowell. 1876. Birdseye view, colored. Excellent. Copies in the Locks & Canals Company and in the Lowell Historical Society.

11. General View of Lowell. 1883. Photograph, reproduced in Hill's *Lowell Illustrated*. Taken from opposite the mouth of the Concord, to contrast with the Pendleton Lithograph of 1834.

12. General View of Lowell. No date. Drawn by F. E. Lane, printed at T. Moore's, Boston. From the Dracut shore. Copy in the Lowell Historical Society.

13. General View of Lowell. No date. Taken from Dracut, and showing the city from the mouth of the Concord to the Lawrence Mill. Good steel engraving. Shows the Merrimack mills rebuilt, after the 1860's therefore. Copy in the Lowell Historical Society.

14. General View of Lowell. One of the "Merrimack Prints," oval, no date. Fine engraving. Copy in the Lowell Historical Society.

15. View of the Merrimack House, Lowell. Handbill advertising the house, dated May 6, 1835. Fine Pendleton Lithograph. In the Lowell Public Library.

16. View of the Second Universalist Church, Lowell. T. Moore's Lithograph. States that Dr. Duesbury was the architect, and that the building was dedicated in 1838. Copy in the Lowell Historical Society.

17. View of the Merrimack Block, G. Pelton, W. T. Goddard,

printer. Dated by William Goodwin in the 1840's. Copy in the Lowell Historical Society.

18. View of the Lowell Machine Shop in 1840. Drawing reproduced in *A Chronicle of Textile Machinery*.

19. View of the Market House, Lowell. Shows the market house before the addition of the belfry. This is dated around 1844 by William Goodwin. Copy in the Lowell Historical Society.

20. First Baptist Church, Lowell. Engraving, dated after 1846, by William Goodwin. Copy in the Lowell Historical Society.

21. View of the Boott Mills, Lowell. 1852. From *Gleason's Pictorial Drawing Room Companion*. Engraving, from the mill yard. Copy in the Lowell Historical Society.

22. View of the Court House, Lowell. Engraving, 1856. Published in Cowley's History, first edition. Copy in the Lowell Historical Society.

23. View of John St. from Merrimack St. Photograph, ca. 1868. Print in the Lowell Historical Society.

24. View of Merrimack St., Lowell, 1863. Photograph of Merrimack St. from John St. looking towards City Hall. Reproduced in *Lowell Illustrated*.

25. Corner of John and Lee Sts., Lowell. Taken before 1919, as it shows a marble, Italian-Gothic building which was torn down then. Copy in the Lowell Historical Society.

26. Old Northern Depot, Lowell. Photograph, no date. In the Lowell Historical Society.

27. Worthen St. Baptist Church, Lowell. Drawing, in the Lowell Historical Society, no date.

28. 1st Freewill Baptist Church, Lowell. Drawing in the Lowell Historical Society, no date.

NOTES

I: INTRODUCTION

1. They had found that the issues which exorcised Victorian architects were dead. What remained was a legacy of pressing architectural problems, problems which had grown almost unnoticed to critical proportions. Naturally, they rejected the standards of the immediate past that had produced the confusion which confronted them. Their analysis of this past was, of course, based on that rejection.

2. There were exceptional Victorians who admired buildings such as these. It is remarkable, considering the conservative approach of many academics today, that in the middle of the nineteenth century the man who discussed the Crystal Palace with the most intelligence and enthusiasm was not an architect, but a historian, and a respectable, even a conventional historian at that, James Fergusson. In his *History of the Modern Styles of Architecture*, 2d ed. (1873), on p. 556 he says: "A new style of architecture was inaugurated together with the first Exhibition of 1851, which has had already a considerable effect on a certain class of designs, and promises to have a still greater influence in the future. There is perhaps no incident in the history of Architecture so felicitous as Sir Joseph Paxton's suggestion of a magnificent conservatory to contain that great collection. At a time when men were puzzling themselves over domes to rival the Pantheon, or halls to surpass those of the Baths of Caracalla, it was wonderful that a man could be found to suggest a thing which had no other merit than being the best, and, indeed, the only thing then known which would answer the purpose; and a still more remarkable piece of good fortune that the commissioners had the courage to adopt it. . . . a man must have had much more criticism than poetry in his composition who could stand under

its arch and among its trees by the side of the crystal fountain, and dare to suggest that it was not the most fairy-like production of Architectural Art that had yet been produced. As re-erected at Sydenham, the building has far greater claims to rank among the important architectural objects of the world." He continues on p. 558. "Such a style would not, of course, be applicable everywhere, but there are so many buildings of this class now wanted for exhibitions, for railway stations, for places of assembly, and for floricultural purposes, that it is of great importance the subject should be studied carefully, as it is one of the few branches of the art on which a future of progress seems to be dawning. If such a development were to take place in even one of the most insignificant branches of the art, men would not long remain content to spend their money on even the correctest Classic columns or Gothic arches; once they perceived that these were not only absolutely useless, but actually hurtful, it might even come to be believed that the men of the nineteenth century practically knew as much of scientific construction, and were as refined in their artistic tastes, as our ignorant and hard-fisted forefathers in the thirteenth. When this is done the battle is gained, and Architecture again becomes a truthful art, and recovers the place from which she has been banished for centuries."

3. This point of view is so well known that it hardly seems worth documenting, particularly as any citation will make it seem as if I were picking upon an individual and making him an object of ridicule. However, unless I quoted something, it might seem as if I had misinterpreted the point of view in question. I therefore present two quotations because I believe they are typical and not extreme expressions of this attitude. The first is from W. C. Behrendt, *Modern Building, Its Nature, Problems, and Forms,* p. 71. The second is from J. M. Richards, *An Introduction to Modern Architecture,* p. 21. The first is quoted by permission of Harcourt, Brace and Company; the second, by permission of Penguin Books, Ltd.

"Tracing the line of creative building through the course of the nineteenth century, we will find it keeping aloof from the precincts of high architecture and taking its direction strictly among utilitarian buildings. In fact, the great achievements of the century in building, the works of historical significance, originated from the disciplined minds of the engineers rather than from the roving fancy of the architects. It is not the architecture of our modern city halls, libraries, and museums, designed for monumental display rather than for practical use, that first manifested the new spirit of building, but it is the new iron bridges and derricks, the furnaces and cooling towers, the silos and wide-spanned worksheds, in short the works of the engineers which wholly changed the face of the cultivated land. While architecture at this time was in general reactionary in its attitude and reminiscent in its effect, and even the best works of the leading academic masters revealed but vestigial ideas, the works of the engineers appeared as buildings of a really creative nature, announcing something new and pointing towards the future. In these impressive structures, a world of new forms was opened up, forms as new in their nature as they were strong and exciting in their effect."

"It was left to the engineers to use the new science creatively. With few exceptions any work of other than purely pictorial merit produced by architects after the industrial revolution had reached its height, owed its existence to the survival, for one reason or another, of eighteenth century conditions."

4. It is of course a question whether one can divide Victorian architecture into these two fields any longer. So many elements interpose themselves between the two, that one wonders whether this division is logical. It is possible to explain much of the excellent building of the early nineteenth century as the result of "the survival of eighteenth century conditions." But such an important achievement as the popular acceptance of the balloon frame during the nineteenth century is not the result of any such survival, nor is it an accomplishment of the engineers. It is a development of folk architecture, and folk architecture is one of those aspects of the nineteenth century which the dualistic view of the older generation cannot include. Even aside from folk architecture, however, there are fine buildings such as the commercial structures of the early nineteenth century (the Bristol Hotel in Providence, or the Quincy Market in Boston), and the series of New England covered bridges, which it is pretty hard to classify. Certainly they are not wholly folk architecture, nor yet are they engineering. At the same time they cannot be considered orthodox Victorian architecture, at least in the sense that the older generation understood that species. For the Bristol Hotel, see Henry Russell Hitchcock, Jr., *Rhode Island Archi-*

tecture, pl. 28. The best brief account of the revival of interest in nineteenth-century architecture which has taken place within the last few years, is in *ibid.,* p. 44.

5. There is no field in which it is possible to follow the progress of this process of centralization more easily than it is in architecture. For a century or so after the rebuilding of Versailles most important buildings were associated with courtly fiat settlements, that is they were rural or semi-rural. After 1750 there is a change, and during the nineteenth century the great edifices were almost exclusively metropolitan. Since 1900 there has been another change. The fact that progressive architecture today is by and large suburban, is one of the clearest indications that the city, as the Victorians understood it, is disintegrating.

6. The architecture of the Victorian city might be all these things, and still not be a fit object for a study of this kind, were it not for two other facts. The Victorian cities were complete, in a sense that modern communities are not, and they are quite distinct both from modern and from colonial settlements.

The Victorian city was complete, because its isolation and the comparative simplicity of its economic organization made it highly self-conscious. In its day it was an independent cultural unit to a far greater extent than any settlement can be at the present time, granted our dependence on the telephone, the automobile, the radio, and the movies. It is clearly distinct both from the commercial centers of the early republic and from the metropolises of the twentieth century, because it constitutes a definite transitional stage in the process of urban evolution in this country. This evolution can be divided into three phases. In the first the cities were commercial centers, located on the seaboard or on the great inland waterway routes. In the second the cities became linked together by the railroad and the telegraph. These inventions enabled the cities to draw upon the country as a whole, while an ever-expanding frontier encouraged them to specialize. But while steam knit the nation into a single economic organism, the individual city remained as much apart from the surrounding countryside as it had been in the Middle Ages. In the last phase, with the advent of the telephone, electricity, and particularly the automobile, the country is becoming gradually organized into a small group of more or less uniform economic regions, each surrounding and tributary to a large metropolis. The individual city has either developed into the center of such a region or has become a satellite of that center. The Victorian city was compact. This kernel has now exploded into a system of satellite suburbs around a central nucleus. As a complementary process the countryside is beginning to focus inwards to a single dominating point. Finally, the disappearance of the frontier and the development of backward regions has caused the division of labor to become local rather than national, and the life of the individual city has grown to be increasingly diversified. The second phase covers roughly the reign of Queen Victoria, although it came finally to an end only with the development of the automobile, after the first World War. See R. D. McKenzie, *The Metropolitan Community,* Chapters I, X.

7. The challenges which the Victorian architects had to face may be divided into three great categories: those, like reënforced concrete, light wood construction, or the elevator, which have to do with the introduction of new materials and new techniques into the art of building. Those, like the railroad station or the department store, which represent the emergence of wholly new institutions for which appropriate shelter had to be provided. Those, like housing and city planning, which have always existed, but which, in the nineteenth century, assumed quite new and acute forms. The Victorians, facing these challenges for the first time, did not by any means succeed in finding adequate answers for most of them. But they did attack them boldly. Gifted with extraordinary creative imaginations, they produced solutions of startling originality. Some of these formed the basis upon which a successful and standard form was ultimately worked out. Others, like prefabrication, were issueless, and have been all but forgotten. But even they are important. Where the definitive answer to the difficulty has still not yet been found, they may suggest to us new and pregnant approaches. See below, Chapter IX, Conclusion.

8. More than any other type, the industrial cities were the product of technological developments. Individual examples were always rendered out of date as technique evolved till now even the species itself may be gradually disappearing. It is therefore possible to divide the industrial settlements of the last century and a half into a series of chronological groups according to the successive technological factors which one after another were paramount in determining industrial efficiency and therefore controlled the location and development of these manufacturing communities. In the cotton industry, the first of these groups would

be made up of the towns founded between the Revolution and the eighteen forties, during the period when water provided the motive power and the source of this power was the primary consideration in locating an industrial town. This group also falls into two sub-groups, the small towns of southern New England, and the later mill cities of central New England. See Chapter II. Already in the 1840's there were those who maintained that the steam mill was more economical than the water mill. After the Civil War, this proved to be the case. The rise of the railroads and the consequent cheapness of coal thus establishes the second great group of textile cities, towns like Fall River and New Bedford. For a time the old inland cities like Lowell remained flourishing, but the really progressive centers were along the seaboard, where they were able to capitalize on the advantages of cheap maritime transportation. See Chapter IX. The third great group of textile cities would be those located in the South. The Southern mills began to compete with those in New England after 1880. At first, their advantage was their proximity to the source of raw material, but as they grew larger and demanded more than could be supplied locally, this advantage tended to disappear. A more secure competitive benefit was provided by the cheapness of labor in the South. This became increasingly marked with the progress of social legislation in the North. The boom years of the war gave the New England mill towns a brief respite, but since the early 1920's they have been towns of the dead. See E. G. Keith, *The Financial History of Two Textile Cities,* and M. T. Parker, *Lowell, A Study of Industrial Development.*

9. In Rhode Island there were cotton-spinning mills started as early as 1793, and communities grew up around them. Individually these communities were small, but in some cases a large number of them were clustered close together and eventually came to form a big settlement. For example, Pawtucket became a center of mill operations, and was incorporated a town in 1862, a city in 1885. These overgrown village clusters were something quite different from the cotton-manufacturing centers of mid New England, which were planned as cities right from the start. For a discussion of the Rhode Island settlements, see Chapter II, particularly note 46. For the intentions of the founders of Lowell, see Chapter III, and particularly note 40.

10. Lowell was a great self-advertiser. The supply of dedicatory addresses, inaugural sermons, and miscellaneous published boastings

of the Board of Trade is even more copious than usual. Of greater importance, however, is the skill with which the town has always managed to focus outside attention upon itself. Lowell, the infant prodigy, performed to the oh-ing and ah-ing of French economists, English divines, and monarchs from the South Sea Islands. Lowell, the bright young man, with a propensity for prostituting farmers' daughters, became the vortex of a whirlpool of discussion. Lowell, the promiscuous, sire of a cardinal, and a racial problem, was an obvious "case" for sociological study. Lowell, the senile, crippled by corruption, made a splendid study in urban retrenchment, unique at that scale.

II: THE BACKGROUND OF LOWELL

1. See Appendix III.
2. See J. Leander Bishop, *A History of American Manufactures,* Chapter XIV.
3. See W. R. Bagnall, *Samuel Slater and the Early Development of the Cotton Manufacture in the United States,* p. 44.
4. The first mill which was certainly designed expressly for spinning was the one built by Slater for Almy & Brown in 1793. See *ibid.,* p. 47. The mill still exists and is used as a museum. It is discussed below, Chapter IV, note 14.
5. See C. F. Ware, *The Early New England Cotton Manufacture,* p. 29.
6. *Ibid.,* p. 64.
7. According to the Census of 1810 there were 54 mills in Massachusetts, 26 in Rhode Island, 14 in Connecticut, 12 in New York, 1 in Vermont, and a total of 109. To this must be added 64 in Pennsylvania. The United States total was 238. "From 1809-15 more than 50 mills were under construction in New England, grouped in a compact area extending from Providence northwest along the valley of the Blackstone and southwest along the valley of the Pawtucket and over the Rhode Island borders into the neighboring townships of Massachusetts and Connecticut." "The mills around Providence increased from 41 to 169 between 1809 and 1815, and the spindles from 20,000 to 135,000!" From H. C. Meserve, *Lowell, an Industrial Dream Come True,* p. 38. Quoted by permission of the National Association of Cotton Manufactures. In C. F. Ware, *op. cit.,* there is on p. 37 a table taken from an article by Clive Day on "The Early Development of the American Cotton Manufacture," published in the *Quarterly*

Journal of Economics, XXXIX (1925), 452. This table shows the cotton mills erected in New England from 1805 to 1832. The figures given there differ from those in Meserve. Also they are not consistent within themselves, or rather two different sets of summarizing figures are presented. I have no way of knowing which set of the three is preferable. It is not important, however, as the general results are very similar.

8. See C. F. Ware, *op. cit.*, p. 27.

9. *Ibid.*, p. 135.

10. *Ibid.*, p. 30.

11. *Ibid.*, p. 135.

12. *Ibid.*, p. 125.

13. "Steam did not come to supply the energy for cotton manufacturing at all generally until railways made transportation of coal convenient and cheap after the Civil War. Slater tried to use steam power in 1828, a factory in Salem was equipped with steam in 1839, and several companies after 1842 were steam operated, but the fact that these companies were always specifically designated as 'steam mills' indicates that this was a distinguishing feature, not a method in common use." *Ibid.*, p. 82. Quoted by permission of the publisher, Houghton Mifflin Company.

14. "Slater's Labor Force in 1816 was typical of a 'family mill.' It was made up of, 1 family with 8 members working; 1 family with 7 members working; 2 families with 5 members working; 4 families with 4 members working; 5 families with 3 members working; 8 single men; 4 single women." *Ibid.*, p. 199. Quoted by permission of Houghton Mifflin Company. Derived from the *Slater Papers*.

15. The only discussion of these mill villages which has been published appears in Henry-Russell Hitchcock, Jr., *Rhode Island Architecture*, Chapter IV. See especially Plates 33 and 34. Mr. Samuel Green of Ipswich, Mass., is preparing a much needed study of early Rhode Island industrial architecture and housing which should be definitive.

16. See Nathan Appleton, *Introduction of the Power Loom and Origin of Lowell*, p. 9.

17. In "re-inventing" the power loom, Francis Cabot Lowell, an amateur mathematician, collaborated with Paul Moody, a brilliant mechanic. For the authoritative account, see *ibid.*, pp. 8-11. Appleton states: "Mr. Lowell's loom was different in several

particulars from the English loom . . ." He also discusses the other devices that Lowell and Moody invented.

18. *Ibid.*, p. 14.

19. See C. F. Ware, *op. cit.*, p. 64.

20. Actually there was also a fourth problem, the question of sales resistance. This is so much less important than the others that I have relegated consideration of it to the notes. There was some difficulty in persuading people to buy the cloth. Their dislike was based to a considerable extent on the unfamiliarity of the product, for it was not until the invention of the cotton gin in 1793 that this fiber could be used, and it was some years before it became common. Fortunately, the public became accustomed to it fairly soon, and the curious prejudice against native goods likewise disappeared rapidly. "At the time when the Waltham Company first began to produce cloth there was but one place in Boston at which domestic goods were sold. This was at the shop in Cornhill kept by Mr. Isaac Bowers, or rather by Mrs. Bowers. She said everybody praised the goods, and no objection was made to the price, but still they made no sales. . . . I soon found a purchaser in Mr. Forsaith, an auctioneer, who sold them at auction at once at something over thirty cents." Appleton, *op. cit.*, p. 11.

21. See C. F. Ware, *op. cit.*, p. 7.

22. Wages for the children ranged from 33¢ to 67¢ a week. The superintendent might earn as much as $2.00 a day. Store pay was necessary on account of the small amount of currency in the communities and the limited working capital of the companies. It was of course very costly for the employees. See *ibid.*, pp. 29, 243 ff.

23. *Ibid.*, p. 249.

24. *Ibid.*, p. 213.

25. *Ibid.*, p. 203.

26. See Appleton, *op. cit.*, p. 15.

27. This system of labor has been tried elsewhere in the modern world, where, as in New England, it was necessary to introduce industrial production into an agricultural way of living. The most notable instance is Japan. A curious analogy, as my wife has pointed out, is provided by the way in which Italian peasant girls work in convents making lace for a few years, and then return to their homes.

28. This is, I think, the generally accepted interpretation of the facts. However, there is another interpretation. Norman Ware states: "The contrast of the two systems (the Rhode Island child labor

system, and the Waltham boarding house system) is interesting because the scarcity of factory labor was probably as great in Rhode Island as in Massachusetts, which suggests that the Waltham system was the result of the Puritan traditions of the Boston Capitalists." See Norman R. Ware, *The Industrial Worker, 1840-1860*, p. 75. Quoted by permission of Houghton Mifflin Company.

I must emphatically disagree with this conclusion. It is fun to debunk the sometimes pompous Boston capitalists, but I think that at this point Mr. Ware has overreached himself. There is no suggestion that the mill girls regarded the moral regulation as superfluous, in any of the contemporary accounts of their life in the mills. There is, on the other hand, a great deal of emphasis on the moral effects of industrialism on the part of various leaders of public opinion at that time. These big cities might easily have developed into scandals, and certainly there were plenty of prominent men ready to pounce upon the least suggestion of indecency in connection with manufacturing. Furthermore, I think that Mr. Ware implies too great a difference in point of view between the "Boston capitalists," and the millworkers. Actually these Boston capitalists were not men of established wealth. The old wealthy New England families had for the most part fled the country at the time of the Revolution, because of their Tory sympathies. Those that remained were engaged in shipping, a distinctly more aristocratic pursuit than manufacturing, at that time. The Boston capitalists were for the most part new men and sprang from almost exactly the same background as their employees. For example, both Nathan and William Appleton, who were important promoters of textile corporations in Lowell and elsewhere, had started very humbly in the little town of New Ipswich, New Hampshire.

29. Their success was complete. The mills never had any difficulty finding workers. Few of the laborers stayed more than five years and many of them annually paid a visit to their families that lasted in some cases as long as three months. Thus there was no such disruption of the social system as that which occurred when the European peasantry left the farms for the mills. See Appendix III.

30. The working hours varied from time to time, and no doubt from place to place. It is also hard to find any great agreement on them. Miles's estimate in *Lowell as It Was and as It Is* seems definitely

too low. Probably 12½ for the year round is a good average figure. For a general discussion of the life of the mill girls in Lowell, see Appendix III. See also C. F. Ware, *op. cit.*, pp. 249 and following.

31. I cannot resist quoting at some length from Michael Chevalier's *Society, Manners and Politics in the United States: Being a Series of Letters on North America*, pp. 138-139, 143. "In France, it would be difficult to conceive of a state of things, in which young girls, generally pretty, should be separated from their families, and thrown together, at a distance of 50 or 100 miles from home, in a town in which their parents could have no person to advise and watch over them. It is a fact, however, with the exception of a very small number of cases, which only prove the rule, that this state of things has yet had no bad effects in Lowell. The manners of the English race are totally different from those of us French; all their habits and all their notions wholly unlike ours. The Protestant education, much more than our Catholic discipline, draws round each individual a line over which it is difficult to step. The consequence is more coldness in the domestic relations, a more or less complete absence of a full and free expression of the stronger feelings of the soul, but, in turn, every one is obliged and accustomed to show more respect for the feelings of others. What amongst us would pass for a youthful imprudence or a pretty trick, is severely frowned upon by the English and Americans, and particularly by the Americans of New England, who are, as has been said, double-distilled English. Nobody in this country, then, is surprised to see the daughters of rural proprietors, after having received a tolerable education, quit their native villages and their parents, take up their residence 50 or 100 miles off, in a town where they have no acquaintance, and pass two or three years in this state of isolation and independence; they are under the safeguard of the public faith. All this presupposes an extreme reserve of manners, a vigilant, inexorable and rigid public opinion, and it must be acknowledged, that under this rigorous system, there is a sombre hue, an air of listlessness thrown over society; but, when one reflects on the dangers to which the opposite system exposes the daughters of the poor, who have no guardian to warn and protect them, when one counts its victims, however slight may be his sympathies with the people, it is difficult to deny, that the Anglo-American prudery, all things considered, is fully worth our ease and freedom of manners, what-

ever may be their attractions. [Note] Mrs. H. C. Carey, in his *Essay on Wages* (p. 89), quotes the following letter from the director of one of the factories in Lowell. 'There have been in our establishment only three cases of illicit connexions, and in all three instances the parties were married immediately, several months before the birth of the child, so that in fact we have had no case of actual bastardy.' "

"Lowell, with its steeple-crowned factories, resembles a Spanish town with its convents; but with this difference, that in Lowell, you meet no rags nor Madonnas, and that the nuns of Lowell, instead of working *sacred hearts*, spin and weave cotton. Lowell is not amusing, but it is neat, decent, peaceable, and sage."

32. See Appleton, *op. cit.*, p. 7.

33. See C. F. Ware, *op. cit.*, p. 139.

34. Of course merchants of Providence also ventured their money in a small way. Almy & Brown are the outstanding instance of this, but apparently the amount of money they put up was not great, rich though the Browns were, and enterprising though their experiments with manufacturing proved them to be. See *ibid.*, pp. 30, 125.

35. Perhaps the most striking example that is connected with Lowell is the case of William Appleton. Starting from humble origins, he managed to accumulate $4,000 in capital as a storekeeper. He came to Boston and invested the money in shipping. After six years he retired with $60,000. See R. Bagnall, *Contributions to American Economic History, Sketches of the Manufacturing Establishments in New York City, and of Textile Establishments in the Eastern States*. There is a biography of William Appleton in connection with the Hamilton Company in Lowell.

36. "By 1834 seven-eighths of the merchants of Boston were identified with New England cotton mills as stockholders, directors or agents." Malcolm Keir, *Industries of America—Manufacturing*, p. 299.

37. See C. F. Ware, *op. cit.*, p. 60, quoted by permission of Houghton Mifflin Company.

38. *Ibid.*, pp. 61-62, quoted by permission of Houghton Mifflin Company.

39. *Ibid.*, p. 62.

40. Certain other modifications which Lowell and his associates introduced are worth mentioning. They concentrated on producing coarse and cheap goods, for it was these which were most in

demand. In 1816 they had managed to get a tariff placed on their only competitors, the mills in India. The cloth, once it was produced, was not parceled out among a scattered group of jobbers. All of it was turned over to a single agent, who alone was responsible for sales and received for his pains a commission of one percent. James Montgomery in *A Practical Detail of the Cotton Manufacture of the United States of America*, p. 162, states: "The factories at Lowell produce a greater quantity of yarn and cloth from each spindle and loom (in a given time) than is produced in any other factories without exception, in the world." This was because in America power was cheap and labor, even unskilled labor expensive, so that there was a great advantage in running the machinery fast.

41. See C. F. Ware, *op. cit.*, p. 145.

42. In the other seaboard trading cities the natural place to invest money was in the means of communication tying the port to the West, which was booming at just this time. The city that was perhaps most likely to compete with Boston in financing manufacturing was Philadelphia, but Philadelphia had a tradition of craftsmanship which stood in the way of mass production.

43. In New England the inland river sites were linked to excellent ports by a network of turnpikes and canals. Very shortly railroads were introduced also. Lowell was fortunate in being located near the head of the Middlesex Canal which connected the Merrimack with Boston Harbor. In general, however, freight was carried over the road until the advent of railways. Even Lowell sent little freight by the canal. It was, however, the standard means of transportation for passengers who could not afford to hire a carriage of their own. The trip from Boston took a whole day. See H. J. H. Robinson, *Loom and Spindle; or, Life among the Early Mill Girls*, p. 28.

44. See C. F. Ware, *op. cit.*, pp. 14 ff.

45. Alfred Vagts has already discussed the parallel between the organization of armies and of manufacturing. See his *A History of Militarism*, p. 34, and his study "The German Army of the Second Reich as a Cultural Institution," in C. F. Ware, ed., *The Cultural Approach to History*, pp. 184 ff.

46. Until Mr. Samuel Green's study of Rhode Island industrial architecture appears (see above, note 15), all remarks on the character of the first mill villages are very tentative. It is quite possible that I am making too strong a distinction between the "hamlets" of

Rhode Island and the "cities" of central New England. But after some little reading and a couple of visits to the Rhode Island sites and discussions of the matter with Professor Russell Hitchcock and Mr. Green himself, I feel the distinction very clearly. It seems to me that the Rhode Island settlements were not communities, properly speaking. They were small groups of houses clustered about the mills. At a later time churches appeared, but before 1820 there were practically no communal buildings, with the exception of the stores. These last were owned by the manufacturing companies, and were really a necessary extension of the mills. One cannot, therefore, speak of villages, that is, balanced and organic groupings of people. What one has are dormitories, set down in the middle of the countryside, and, however distinguished the planning, it is dormitory planning. It is never focused upon the church or other community activities. There is apparently one place in Rhode Island that is an exception to these statements, namely, Slatersville. That gives the appearance of a village, to a greater extent than any of the others. Yet it is significant that this community, although one of the earliest, if not absolutely the earliest, was never imitated afterwards. And I have the impression that even in Slatersville the communal quality was a matter of appearance rather than a living reality.

47. Again, there may be people who feel that I emphasize too strongly the different relationship of the Rhode Island hamlets and the New England cities to their respective capitalists. But whatever the theoretical state of affairs, it seems to me that in practice the Rhode Island settlements were administered completely paternally. That is, one man decided what should be built and where, what should be done and where, and he made himself responsible for carrying out the program. In central New England, on the other hand, while there is no denying the preponderant influence of the corporations and of leading executives like Boott, yet the whole population expressed a collective will very early; witness the program of school building on which the town of Lowell embarked in 1833 despite the opposition of Boott and all of the corporations. There was, in fact, a balance of power struck. The very fact that employees of the mills took part in outside activities (particularly those associated with the churches), loosened up the hierarchical organization of society. Mill girls in their descriptions of life in Lowell often refer to the democratic effect of teaching Sunday School together with men who during the week were

junior executives. Such experiences tended to break down the normal caste snobbism. Although, generally speaking, the executives identified themselves with the interests of the stockholders, there were cases in which the executives took the part of the employees and forced unpopular policies upon the owners of the business. One can hardly imagine this happening in Rhode Island.

48. I don't know whether there is a recognized name for these towns. I have never come across it, and so I found it necessary to invent the term *purveyor town*. This is not altogether satisfactory, but it is the best name I can think of.

III: THE FOUNDING OF LOWELL

1. One positive fact and one negative fact can be cited in support of this statement. Positively, there are the remarks which Appleton makes on Francis Cabot Lowell. "His care was especially devoted to arrangements for the moral character of the operatives employed. . . . He is entitled to the credit of having introduced the new system in the cotton manufacture, under which it has grown up so rapidly. For, although Messrs. Jackson and Moody were men of unsurpassed talent and energy in their way, it was Mr. Lowell who was the informing soul, which gave direction and form to the whole proceeding." See Nathan Appleton, *Introduction of the Power Loom and Origin of Lowell*, p. 15. If one remembers that the housing of Lowell was designed not for the comfort of the employees so much as for their moral preservation (see Appleton's remarks quoted above, p. 13), this statement will be seen to clinch the matter. For the negative fact, see below, note 25. It is pointed out there that the story of the founding of Lowell is told in great detail by several people in a position to know. Due credit is given to the contributions of everybody concerned. If somebody other than Lowell had been responsible for the conception of the social organization, it is hard to believe that they would not have been mentioned in this connection.

One curious thing emerges from Appleton's statements quoted above, namely, the subordinate position given to Boott, at least by implication. Although a leading stockholder in the Merrimack Company, Appleton apparently considers him as the first employee of the company, rather than as the equal of the founders. This description of his position is bolstered up by a passage from Boott's own diary, in which he refers to Nathan Appleton with some deference (see below, Chapter IV, note 2). It must be re-

membered that most of the history of Lowell has been written by
citizens of Lowell. Boott was the leading representative of the
cotton corporations on the spot, and he unquestionably acted
with great independence. Naturally, therefore, the local historians
tended to exaggerate his importance within the whole setup. An
estimate of the real situation is complicated by the fact that the
relationship of the agent to the directors was not fixed at this
period. It varied from company to company. The best proof of
this is the misunderstanding that took place between Samuel
Batchelder and the directors of the Hamilton Manufacturing
Company in Lowell. See Samuel Batchelder, *Introduction and
Early Progress of the Cotton Manufacture in the United States.*

2. Appleton, *op. cit.,* p. 14, states: "It is remarkable how few changes
have been made from the arrangements established by him, in
the first mill built at Waltham. It is also remarkable, how accurate
were his calculations, as to the expense at which goods could be
made. He used to say, that the only circumstance which made
him distrust his own calculations, was, that he could bring them
to no other result but one which was too favorable to be credible."

3. See C. F. Ware, *op. cit.,* p. 66.

4. *Ibid.,* p. 70.

5. Appleton, *op. cit.,* p. 13, describes conditions in 1816. "In June,
1816, Mr. Lowell invited me to accompany him in making a visit
to Rhode Island, with a view of seeing the actual state of the
manufacture. I was very happy to accept his proposition. At this
time the success of the power loom, at Waltham, was no longer
a matter of speculation or opinion: it was a settled fact. We pro-
ceeded to Pawtucket. We called on Mr. Wilkinson, the maker of
machinery. He took us into his establishment—a large one; all
was silent, not a wheel in motion, not a man to be seen. He informed us that there was not a spindle running in Pawtucket,
except a few in Slater's old mill, making yarns. All was dead and
still. . . . We saw several manufacturers; they were all sad and
despairing."

Further evidence on this score is given in C. F. Ware, *op. cit.,*
p. 66: "The success of the Waltham company is particularly
striking in view of general business conditions in the country
during its early years and the fate which mills of the older type
were suffering. The combination of the post-war slump, the dump-
ing of British goods on the American market after the peace, and

the collapse of the western currency sent numbers of the old producers to the wall. 'Half the spindles' in the vicinity of Providence and Fall River were said to be idle in 1816. The number of manufacturing companies which received charters in the state of Massachusetts fell from thirty-four in 1814, to twenty-three in 1815, to eight in 1816, none in 1817, two in 1818, one in 1819, and three in 1820. Some mills failed, others struggled feebly along, closing down temporarily or partially." Quoted by permission of Houghton Mifflin.

6. Appleton, *op. cit.,* p. 15.

7. Migration westward was stimulated by the embargo. It did not, however, seriously begin to deplete the population of New England until some time later. Generally speaking, the high point in New England agriculture and the maximum farm population was in the 1830's.

8. See C. F. Ware, *op. cit.,* p. 80.

9. See Appleton, *op. cit.,* p. 17.

10. As the titles "agent" and "treasurer" will recur constantly, it seems wise to define their functions here. In the early New England corporations, the president performed the duties of the modern chairman of the board. He called and presided at meetings of the directors and of the stockholders. He did very little else. The president of the company in the modern sense—that is, the chief executive officer—was the treasurer. The treasurer had his office in Boston generally, at least after the companies were well started. He was in charge of all the financial activities of the company, although this job was less onerous than one might suppose, because the selling was in the hands of the selling agents, who were also the bankers of the corporations. The agent was "vice-president in charge of production," that is he lived at the mill and was responsible for everything concerned with output, including, of course, the housing and the relation of the corporation to the town.

11. Appleton, *op. cit.,* p. 18.

12. The simplicity of their requirements was very striking. Proximity to capital, to market, to raw materials, to labor, was not considered, as is proved by Boott's efforts to purchase land and power rights at Gardiner, Maine. Water power, and plenty of it, was all they sought. This demand for power at once limited the field of activity, since there were no suitable rivers in New England south of Boston. This fact confined the location of the towns of the

Lowell group to the larger river valleys of central Massachusetts, southern New Hampshire, and Maine. By contrast "A survey conducted by the National Electric Light Association and the Metropolitan Life Insurance Company during 1927 and in 1929 in 2,084 cities in the United States and Canada, revealed the following reasons given for plant location, arranged according to the frequency with which each was cited. 1). Markets: 2). Labor: 3). Transportation: 4). Materials: 5). Available Factory Buildings: 6). Personal Reasons: 7). Power and Fuel: 8). Cheap Rent: 9). Near related Industries: 10). Living Conditions: 11). Financial aid: 12). Taxes: 13). Mergers and Consolidations: 14). Cheap Land: 15). Near Parent Company: 16). Banking Facilities." From the *Architectural Forum*, March, 1937. Quoted by permission of the publisher.

13. Mr. Moody was Paul Moody, the mechanic who helped Lowell re-invent the mechanical loom and other devices, see above Chapter II, note 17. Moody became the chief mechanic of the Boston Manufacturing Company and later the agent of the Lowell Machine Shop.

14. Appleton, *op. cit.,* pp. 17 ff.

15. "The river has a mean discharge of 8,020 second-feet, producing in a descent of 30 feet a theoretical motive force equivalent to about 27,000 horsepower." M. T. Parker, *Lowell, a Study of Industrial Development,* p. 60.

16. See Bagnall, *Contributions to American Economic History,* section on the Proprietors of Locks and Canals on Merrimack River.

17. See Appleton, *op. cit.,* p. 23.

18. See S. A. Drake, *History of Middlesex County, Massachusetts,* II, 62.

19. In later years it became part of the folklore that the hated Kirk Boott had bought up the property at unjustly low prices. "He came to Chelmsford, and saw the great Merrimack River and its possibilities, and set himself shrewdly to work to buy land on its banks, including the water-power. He represented to the simple farmers that he was going to raise fruit and wool, and they, knowing nothing of 'mill privileges,' believed him, and sold the greatest water-power in New England for almost nothing. When they discovered his real design in buying the land, and the chance for making money they had lost, they were angry enough." H. J. H. Robinson, *Loom and Spindle; or, Life among the Early Mill Girls,* p. 9. Quoted by permission of the publisher, Thomas Y. Crowell &

Company. The actual facts are completely otherwise. "The whole purchase was made of the Pawtucket Canal and of most of the farms here before Mr. Kirk Boott had set foot upon the spot." From *Proceedings in the City of Lowell at the Semi-Centennial Celebration of the Incorporation of the Town of Lowell*, Address of John A. Lowell, p. 56.

That the Merrimack Manufacturing Company paid too low prices for the land is also disputed. Appleton and Jackson employed a certain Thomas M. Clark to do the buying. In 1821 he was the agent of the Locks and Canals Company, but at the time that the Pawtucket Canal had been built, he was the clerk of the company, and in that capacity he had learned to know the yokels of Chelmsford and their ways. He bought four farms, and paid good money for swamp land. Indeed, as his son stated later, "There was one farmer who believed that he (Clark) was insane, and therefore he was unwilling to take the trouble to make the deeds, transferring his farm, until 'Squire Wright' signed a bond of indemnity, to the amount of two hundred dollars, guaranteeing him this sum in case it should turn out that he had taken the trouble for nothing. He was firmly satisfied that my father would never pay such prices if he was not insane." *Ibid.*, Rev. Mr. Clark's address, p. 58.

Later, of course, prices soared in the neighborhood. The case of the Cheever farm is a good illustration. "This farm contained 110 acres, nine undivided tenths of which were bought for one thousand eight hundred dollars. The owner of the other one tenth had agreed to convey it for two hundred dollars, but dying suddenly insolvent, it was sold by order of the courts, the Locks and Canals Company giving for seven and a half tenths thereof upwards of three thousand dollars. The remaining two and a half tenths were bought afterwards for nearly five thousand dollars." The price of the last portion per acre was just 100 times the price of the first portion purchased. From H. A. Miles, *Lowell, as It Was, and as It Is*, p. 26. One need shed no tears over the money the Merrimack Manufacturing Company had to spend acquiring this small piece of land. For most of the lands they bought at $200 an acre "were afterwards sold at from twelve cents to a dollar per foot, a year later." J. Bayles, *Lowell, Past, Present and Prospective*, p. 8.

20. The Company was capitalized at $600,000. The principal stockholders were Nathan Appleton and Patrick Tracy Jackson, 180

shares each. Kirk Boott and John W. Boott, 90 shares each. Paul Moody, 60 shares. Subsequently others were admitted to small holdings. See Appleton, *op. cit.*, p. 22.

21. In his capacity as agent, Boott was paid a salary of $3,000 a year. The Merrimack Manufacturing Company bought from the Boston Manufacturing Company joint rights in Lowell's basic patents. It also bought up the contract which Paul Moody had with the Boston Manufacturing Company, and thereafter he was permanently associated with Lowell.

22. There is no written record telling who was responsible for the layout of Lowell. Manchester, New Hampshire, was laid out by Ezekiel A. Straw, at that time a cub engineer, replacing the regular engineer who was sick. The job was not considered a matter of the first importance apparently, and it seems likely that it was turned over to the most competent engineer available.

The only person connected with Lowell who had an engineer's training was Kirk Boott, who had studied at Sandhurst. There is reason to believe that he was a draughtsman (see below, Chapter IV, note 64) and, finally, he was such a domineering character that it is hard to believe that he would have permitted anyone else to lay out what he, at least, always thought of and treated as *his* town.

23. The Boston Manufacturing Company built a few houses for their employees and one very large block. Most of these were ranged along a road which ran parallel to the river and bounded the plant on its inner side. The long block was behind them. The development was closer to the kind of dormitory settlements that were made in Rhode Island and was not really comparable to Lowell and later cities. By 1825 there was a community attached to the Boston Manufacturing Company in Waltham, albeit a small one. Here is the description of Bernard, duke of Saxe-Weimar: "About four hundred and fifty workmen are employed, who live in different buildings belonging to the factory and form a particular colony. They have two schools, a church, and a clergyman." From S. A. Drake, *History of Middlesex County, Massachusetts*, I, 185.

24. From J. L. Bishop, *A History of American Manufactures*, I, 411. This remark is ascribed to Tench Coxe, who was Hamilton's undersecretary. The society was incorporated in 1791 and acted on Coxe's suggestion by founding Paterson, New Jersey. L'Enfant provided them with a plan, which, however, proved too ambitious,

and the project languished. The town was revived again on a new basis many years later. See Chapter IX, note 22.

25. It is worth considering at this point whether or not Lowell was related to any of the earlier English utopias. These have not, so far as I know, been studied as a group, and my statements here are based on an examination of all the books in the Avery Library, Columbia University, which have material on English utopias. As positive statements they cannot be taken except with a grain of salt. The remarks with regard to the influence which these utopias did not have on Lowell are, however, more trustworthy. Ever since the late eighteenth century various people had concerned themselves with improving living conditions of the proletariat. Architects, like Wood, set about designing model cottages for farm and factory laborers (see Chapter IV, note 37) and Gandy even went so far as to outline a whole ideal community. But the most famous and comprehensive scheme was that published only a few years before Lowell was started. In 1818 Robert Owen brought out his *New View of Society*. This was a project for constructing coöperative towns, based on both industry and agriculture, and presented complete, with a bird's-eye view rendering. One might suppose that the advanced humanitarian opinions of this eminent Scottish cloth manufacturer, no less than the success of his ventures at New Lanark, would have commended him at once to the attention of Lowell's associates. Recently it has been suggested that such was the case. A writer in *Lowell, a City of Spindles* (p. 121) implies that the social arrangements of Lowell were inspired by Robert Owen's experiments in Scotland. But all the evidence indicates that the founders of the cotton industry in America were uninfluenced by, if not indeed completely ignorant of, Owen's or any other social utopia. The story of the creation of Lowell is recorded by well-informed contemporaries in great detail. Although we know that in 1811 Mr. Lowell visited British factories and studied the machinery whenever he could, and although we know he was at that time considering the social aspects of the industrial problem, there is no mention anywhere of Owen or of New Lanark. This is not really surprising, for, as Mr. Lewis Mumford has pointed out, Robert Owen was a woolen manufacturer, and Francis Cabot Lowell was chiefly preoccupied by the Lancashire cotton manufacture. Moreover, in 1811, Owen was not yet completely master in his own house. As far as can be judged from his autobiography,

his plans at this time lay in improving the lot of the workmen by good wages and a new method of education, rather than by founding special communities for industrial activities. Owen's and the other English utopias had little direct part in the formation of Mr. Lowell's ideas, and it was these which guided the creation of Lowell.

26. If a precedent must be found for such a simple conception, it is that type of New England village where the main street runs parallel to the river. Examples of this type may be found in the Connecticut Valley.

27. The land for these facilities was often given to the town by the landowning corporation. The fact that as early as 1838 land was reserved in Manchester, N. H., to form a public park is significant. The idea of the public park was something new, the first example being in Birkinhead, according to Lewis Mumford. It shows the degree to which the New England capitalists were abreast of their times.

28. Of course in the case of a really large development it was necessary to have more water power available. Then two canals were dug, parallel to one another and separated by about a hundred yards. This, of course, made two islands for mills. The classic instance of this scheme is Manchester, New Hampshire.

29. The most perfect large-scale instance is Manchester, New Hampshire.

30. See Appendix II, A.

31. See Appleton, *op. cit.*, p. 24.

32. See Appendix II, B.

33. It was as inconceivable a hundred years ago that a mill should be built without housing as it would be today that a boarding school should be built without dormitories. Visualized in these terms, and with this degree of immediacy, it is obvious why the housing was placed where it was.

34. See Appendix II, A. The two through ways were the road from Chelmsford along the Merrimack River (which we call the Merrimack Road) that formed the basis for Merrimack Street, and the road running from the ferry across the Merrimack by the mouth of the Concord, due south parallel to the smaller stream. This we have called the Concord Road. It was the basis for Central Street, Gorham Street, etc.

35. See Appendix II, B.

36. It may be hard to see the F, and harder yet to visualize it when

in the city itself. In the frontispiece, however, it is quite apparent. The stem of the F runs SE along the Merrimack; the head of the F runs SW along the Pawtucket Canal and ends in a great seraphlike blob running due west. The cross bar of the F runs SW from the Merrimack along the Merrimack Canal.

37. In evaluating the plan of Lowell, it is interesting to compare it with Manchester, N. H., which was laid out a few years later, and which likewise was on a great scale. Manchester was more simply planned on a scheme of parallel strips. Owing to the public spirit of William Amory, it was provided with a whole series of parks, adjoining or near to the main street. But the absence of any logical cross axis has meant that Hanover Street has been arbitrarily selected to serve as a focus to the town, and that the shops and warehouses have overrun the area behind the main street. The area around the parks has been spoiled, as a result. The residential district has been pushed further out than was originally intended, because no provision was made for expansion.

The scheme of Lowell was more supple, if less neat, than the contiguous zones of Manchester, and it has resulted in a minimum of blighted areas. The real estate policies of the landholding corporation forced the petty bourgeoisie to congregate in the area east of Gorham Street, and this, the Chapel Hill district, has retained its character to the present day. In later times, with increasing wealth there came a need for elegant residences, and these were situated across the Concord River in the hilly territory known as Belvidere. This area, slightly removed and definitely marked off, has also retained its character. Between the Merrimack and the spinal column of the town, Merrimack Street, there was little space and this was so filled with stores, public buildings, and mills that it, too, has held up until recently. The slum quarters have thus been forced out of the center into districts where land is less expensive. Moreover, it is in just these areas that the city was able to buy parks, when, with the sale of the company land in the mid-forties, it undertook to do so. Accordingly, at least in one case, the open space is surrounded by the houses of those who need it most.

38. For the real estate which the Merrimack Company owned see Figure 1 and Appendix II, A. The land was transferred by the Merrimack Company to the Locks and Canals Company at the time the latter was resurrected.

39. According to a completely reliable source, but one which prefers not to be mentioned by name, the Locks and Canals Company had loaned money to various of the manufacturing corporations. It did not have the ready cash with which to finance the digging of a new canal, in order to obtain more power. The stockholders of the Corporations were to some extent the same as the stockholders of the Locks and Canals Company. Rather than call these loans, and endanger the manufacturing corporations, it was decided to raise the money by selling off the real estate, and to reorganize the Locks and Canals Company so that it became a wholly owned subsidiary of all the manufacturing corporations collectively.

40. Two chance remarks survive which give a clue to what the founders of Lowell hoped was to be the future of their settlement. Appleton, *op. cit.*, p. 19, writes: "Our first visit to the spot [the site of Lowell] was in the month of November, 1821, and a slight snow covered the ground. The party consisted of Patrick T. Jackson, Kirk Boott, Warren Dutton, Paul Moody, John W. Boott and myself. We perambulated the grounds, and scanned the possibilities of the place, and the remark was made that some of us might live to see the place contain twenty thousand inhabitants." " 'It was in this year,' [1824] says Mr. Batchelder, 'I well remember the prediction of Mr. Patrick Jackson. He remarked that their purchase of real estate at the Falls comprised about as many acres as were contained in the original territory of Boston before it was extended by encroachments on the tide waters; and,' he continued, 'if our plans succeed as we have reason to expect, we shall have as large a population on our territory in twenty years as we had in Boston twenty years ago.' " *Semicentennial Proceedings*, Reminiscences by Dr. John O. Green, p. 66. This last guess proved extraordinarily accurate. In 1804 the population of Boston was 26,000. In 1844 the population of Lowell must have been 27,000, as by the State Census of 1845 it was 28,841. None the less it would seem that both of these statements were merely off-hand wishful estimates. Lowell gives no evidence of having been designed to accommodate 25,000 people, or indeed any particular number of people.

41. The outstanding instance of this in Lowell was "The triangular tract at the head of Central street . . . sold by the Locks and Canals Company to Patrick Tracy Jackson of Boston, who paid for it what was then regarded as the extravagant price of thir-

teen cents a foot." See F. W. Coburn, *History of Lowell and its People*, I, 181. Quoted by permission of the Lewis Historical Publishing Company. The investment paid handsomely, as well it might, for in early times it was certainly the finest piece of property for commercial purposes in the city.

42. It is Chevalier who gives the most lyric description of the city as it appeared in the middle thirties. "The town of Lowell dates its origin eleven years ago, and it now contains 15,000 inhabitants, inclusive of the suburb of Belvedere. Twelve years ago it was a barren waste, in which the silence was interrupted only by the murmur of the little river of Concord, and the noisy dashing of the clear waters of the Merrimac, against the granite blocks that suddenly obstruct their course. At present it is a pile of huge factories, each five, six, or seven stories high, and capped with a little white belfry, which strongly contrasts with the red masonry of the building, and is distinctly projected on the dark hills in the horizon. By the side of these larger structures rise numerous little wooden houses, painted white, with green blinds, very neat, very snug, very nicely carpeted, and with a few small trees around them, or brick houses in the English style, that is to say, simple, but tasteful without and comfortable within; on one side, fancy-goods shops and milliners' rooms without number, for the women are the majority in Lowell, and vast hotels in the American style, very much like barracks (the only barracks in Lowell); on another, canals, water-wheels, water-falls, bridges, banks, schools, and libraries, for in Lowell reading is the only recreation, and there are no less than seven journals printed here. All around are churches and meeting-houses of every sect, Episcopalian, Baptist, Congregationalist, Methodist, Universalist, Unitarian, &c. and there is also a Roman Catholic chapel. Here are all the edifices of a flourishing town in the Old World, except the prisons, hospitals, and theatres." Michael Chevalier, *Society, Manners and Politics in the United States: being a series of Letters on North America,* translated from the third Paris edition, pp. 128-29.

IV: THE FIRST BUILDING CAMPAIGN

1. See Appleton, *Introduction of the Power Loom and Origin of Lowell,* p. 23.

2. Boott continues: "Moody declared that this was 'the best wheel in the world,' N. Appleton became quite enthusiastic. In the afternoon he spent an hour looking at the wheel, after which

he returned home by Andover." It is a great pity that the Boott diary has disappeared, for if this one quotation is any sample, it would give personal impressions of the major characters of the founding of Lowell, which cannot be found elsewhere. The diary is known only through Bagnall, *Contributions to American Economic History*, p. 2157.

3. The scene was a striking one, for the wheel was a wooden affair, 30 ft. in diameter. This was because "Mr. Moody said he had a fancy for large wheels" (Appleton, *op. cit.*, p. 24), and his partners amiably permitted him to indulge himself. Small wonder he considered it peerless. The casual attitude illustrated by this fact is typical for the founding of Lowell. All the important decisions seem to have been arrived at informally, coöperatively, and in a carefree spirit of adventure. Nathan Appleton says that he put up money for Waltham just to see the experiment fairly tried. Lowell's premises were logical, but Appleton well knew that every other attempt at mechanical weaving in America had proven a failure. Bagnall opines that most of the other original stockholders in the Boston Manufacturing Company felt the same way. But the Merrimack Manufacturing Company was a different matter. All parties had complete faith in that venture, after the signal success at Waltham. And so the stockholders could afford to be free and easy, humoring Moody on the mill wheel, Boott on the matter of the church, and so forth.

4. The original intention was to have the machinery for the Merrimack Manufacturing Company's mills made in the machineshop at Waltham. As soon as the founders realized that other concerns might establish themselves in Lowell, they recognized that the facilities for making machinery at Waltham were inadequate, and they decided to start a new machineshop.

5. See above, p. 24.

6. See Appleton, *op. cit.*, p. 23.

7. Apparently it was only a question of digging. However, it is sometimes said that a new method of introducing the water into the mills was tried at the Merrimack Company. This was developed in imitation of some powder mills already established by Oliver Whipple on the Concord River not far away. I don't know any way of checking up on this statement. A supply of day laborers seems to have been one of the few things that Francis Cabot Lowell had not prepared for. At first Boott relied on local talent. However, in April, 1822, thirty Irish immigrants appeared.

They had tramped twenty-five miles from Charlestown, in search of employment. Boott sallied forth and met them in a saloon. He refreshed them suitably at the company's expense, and hired them forthwith. In a few years the original pioneers were augmented by hundreds of their fellows, and the men from County Dublin and County Cork soon came to form the principal supply of unskilled labor in the city. Incidentally their presence created a housing problem, discussed above, see p. 39. See F. W. Coburn, *History of Lowell and Its People,* p. 170.

8. There were five Merrimack mills built one right after another during the early years. Apparently they were identical in form, so that it is impossible to tell which was built first. The first one was completed on September 1, 1823; by 1826, when Lowell was set off from Chelmsford as a separate town, two more were running, and the final pair were almost finished. One of them burned in 1829, and was immediately replaced. See Drake, *History of Middlesex County, Massachusetts,* II, 62, 64, 66.

9. The seventeenth and eighteenth century American water mills have never been seriously studied as far as I know. There are a good many of them, and one sees them not infrequently. They are rarely, if ever, dated or datable. I can base my statements only upon old mills which I have seen in one place or another. The identity with contemporary domestic architecture may be backed up by the case of the barnlike structure in which Gilbert Stuart was born. "For a hundred years after Gilbert Stuart's time, a grist mill was operated in this building." Federal Writers Project, *Rhode Island, a Guide to the Smallest State,* p. 335. All the mills built in East Chelmsford before the advent of the Merrimack Manufacturing Company must have been of this domestic variety. It is possible that one of these early mills survives today in a structure whose original function cannot be determined. This is located on the River Meadow Brook, just at the point where it is joined by the Wamesit Canal; that is just above the bridge which today carries Lawrence Street over the stream. It may have once been part of the sawmill or the clothier's mill which appear at about this spot on the map of 1794. It may well be a later structure. Bagnall says that Moses Hale's mill (see Appendix II, A) was still standing in the eighties "on the corner of Gorham and Congress Streets, near the bridge." It had been moved there from its original location. It certainly does not seem to be standing there now. It is just pos-

sible that this structure is Hale's mill, assuming either that Bagnall made a mistake, or that the old structure was moved once again, since his time. In any event, it is a typical primitive mill, both in its appearance, and in the difficulty which one encounters in dating it.

10. According to the Salem *Mercury* it was "a plain three story building of brick, measuring about sixty by twenty-five feet, with a pitched roof and a deep basement, on one end of which moved a heavy pair of horses to furnish rotary power." Quoted in H. C. Meserve, *Lowell, an Industrial Dream Come True,* p. 30. When Washington visited the establishment on his tour of the eastern states in 1780 it had 40 employees. The concern failed very soon. For the reasons, see C. F. Ware, *The Early New England Cotton Manufacture,* p. 20.

11. There is of course no reason to believe that this building was built for a mill. It may well have been taken over by the mill and adapted. Even if it had been built for the mill, I would not for a moment imply that it represented the first use of masonry construction in a mill. It is merely the first indisputably dated example which I have run across. No doubt, when stone or brick was a common building material, mills were built of masonry, just as houses or barns were. For example, there is a mill partly of stone at Washington's Crossing, Pa., that is called pre-Revolutionary. See James Cawley, *Historic New Jersey in Pictures,* fig. 164. The significant thing about the Beverly mill is the fact that brick, while not unusual, was definitely not the ordinary building material in Massachusetts at that time. It shows that a mill was considered as something special, not merely a utilitarian building like a barn, or else that it was considered worthy to be housed in such a superior class of building, which was then already in existence.

12. This was rented by the firm of Almy & Brown and later purchased by them. It was swept away by a freshet, see W. R. Bagnall, *Samuel Slater and the Early Development of the Cotton Manufacture in the United States,* pp. 43, 46.

13. *Ibid.,* p. 47.

14. The building is still in existence. At present its aspect is quite different from its appearance when Slater was manager, since it has been enlarged several times. However, subsequent additions continued the curious disposition of the roof, as well as the original width and height (twenty-six feet, two stories and an

attic), so that the part of the present building next to the river gives one a good idea of the initial structure. The first change was made a few years after the mill was built. It was extended eastward towards the river and increased in length by fifty feet. Under the administration of Almy, Brown & Slater the building was enlarged toward the west. This brought its total length up to one hundred and forty feet (*ibid.*, p. 47).

I know of no trustworthy illustration of the mill in its original condition. Edward Field, *State of Rhode Island and Providence Plantations at the End of the Century,* shows a picture of it in its original form, which Mr. Samuel Green tells me is derived from a painting that is a nineteenth-century reconstruction of the original mill, albeit an accurate reconstruction. The most easily accessible pictures of the mill in its present form are to be found in Henry Russell Hitchcock, Jr., *Rhode Island Architecture,* pl. 29, and Federal Writers Project, *Rhode Island, a Guide to the Smallest State,* facing p. 66. It may be presumed that the building was open from end to end inside because there was only one adult overseer looking after the labor force. See C. F. Ware, *op. cit.,* p. 23.

In the present state of our knowledge it is quite impossible to say whether the design of this mill was an adaptation of English models, like the machinery, or whether it was determined wholly by the American tradition. The study of mill architecture was just beginning in England during the months preceding the war. The only published material on English mill architecture that I have come across is a few paragraphs in the mid-nineteenth-century work, W. T. Fairbairn, *Treatise on Mills and Millwork,* Chapter V. From this it would appear that the earliest English mills were very similar to those in America. This was also the conclusion that the modern students arrived at, although their investigations were very far from complete. The question is really a trifling one. Whether it derived from England or not, Slater's mill was certainly very close to the American vernacular tradition, as Hitchcock points out, *op. cit.,* p. 39. The only feature which might be an importation is the monitor roof. I know of no examples on American 18th-century buildings. On the other hand, I know of no English examples either. Certainly, in the form to which it had evolved by 1840 it was unknown or forgotten in England. See James Montgomery, *op. cit.*

15. Edward Field, *op. cit.,* p. 347, makes the statement, "The mill

of Almy, Brown and Slater was for many years, and probably up to the beginning of the War of 1812, the largest and best equipped cotton mill in the country." This is putting it too strongly. Mr. Samuel Green has literary evidence of a six-story mill erected in the middle of the first decade of the nineteenth century, and certainly the Lippitt mill, built in 1810-11, was larger if not better equipped.

16. See C. F. Ware, *op. cit.,* p. 37.

17. See Hitchcock, *op. cit.,* p. 39.

18. *Ibid.,* pl. 31.

19. *Ibid.,* pl. 30.

20. See Bagnall, *Contributions to American Economic History,* p. 1998.

21. When the mill was placed at right angles to the direction of the current, only one belt was needed, although this was some four hundred feet long. It was likely to break, and this stopped the whole mill for half a day. The plan of having the mill parallel to the direction of the current was "generally adopted about Lowell and considered the most unobjectionable of any that has yet been tried." This involved two water wheels, which ran a driving drum from which two belts ran up to the main drum on the first floor. From this another belt ran up and ran another driving drum on the third floor. Instead of many pulleys and wheels, there were only a few, as each driving drum was set in the middle of an axle and ran all the machines on the floor.

American mills were run on belts rather than on gears, as was usual in England, because it was impossible to get gears as well made over here as they were in England. Belts were more efficient than the clumsy native gears. See James Montgomery, *op. cit.,* pp. 19 ff.

22. See Bagnall, *Contributions to American Economic History,* p. 2025.

23. *Ibid.,* p. 2123.

24. Appleton, *op. cit.,* p. 28, makes the statement: "The second mill built at Waltham contained 3,584 spindles, spinning No. 14 yarn, with all the apparatus necessary to convert cotton into cloth. This was taken as the standard for what was called a mill power, or the right to draw twenty-five cubic feet per second on a fall of thirty feet, equal according to Mr. Francis Lowell to about sixty horse power." This unit was standard throughout northern New England. It is very hard to find trustworthy illus-

trations of the mills in Waltham. In the Waltham public library there is a series of small oil paintings of the various mills and boarding houses of the Boston Manufacturing Company in their original condition. Some of these paintings were based on old prints, it is said. These paintings are not uncommonly reproduced, as in *Illustrated History of Lowell and Vicinity, Massachusetts*, p. 218, or *A Chronicle of Textile Machinery, 1824-1924*. I have never seen any copies of the old prints, so I cannot vouch for the accuracy of the paintings. However, the public library in Waltham does have an old photograph of the third mill erected by the Boston Manufacturing Company.

In Lowell itself there were more than thirty mills of this new standard type by 1840. See Miles, *Lowell as It Was, and as It Is*, p. 59 and also Frontispiece. Only one of these survives today. This is the long structure of the Merrimack Print Works. But it has been remodeled, and it is so encased in later building that it is almost invisible, and does not give nearly as vivid an impression of the appearance of the original factories as can be obtained from old drawings. The best source of these is the series of lithographs forming the border of the Sidney & Neff map, no. 12, Appendix VI, A.

To judge from these, the handsomest version of the type in Lowell itself was the Machine Shop, built in 1824. Here, as in Slater's mill, the stair tower projected more than usual; perhaps because, as in the latter, the stairway was rectangular rather than circular. Otherwise it is a typical specimen. The machine shop changed hands in 1845, and was rebuilt at that time. The illustration of it was published a few years after this rebuilding. I have no way of knowing how thorough the rebuilding may have been. I doubt if it affected the exterior to any great extent, although I believe that the pilasters and entablature of the stair tower, and perhaps even the whole of the stair tower, date from this period.

It might be well to mention here some other old mills. The best treatment of them is in Hitchcock, *op. cit.*, pp. 41 ff., although it covers only the Rhode Island material. There is an old stone mill belonging to the Pleasant Valley Manufacturing Company at Washington Hollow, New York. A plaque on the outside reads "Burnt 27th January 1815, rebuilt by Delaverne and Thwing in the same year." There is no evidence that it has been reconstructed to any great extent since. There is, or was, until recently an old mill at Rochester, New Hampshire. This is not dated by any records in the possession of the present owners, but the delicate detail of the brick entablature and the wooden cupola can hardly be later than the eighteen twenties, and may well be earlier. There is also a fine old mill at Laconia, New Hampshire, which although somewhat later in date than the examples mentioned above presents the Lowell type at a somewhat smaller scale. Indeed, it is the best indication of what the units of the Merrimack Company looked like now surviving. The interior survives unchanged, with its original wooden posts. At Amesbury, Massachusetts, there is a fine mill dating from the thirties probably, which has recently been shorn of its monitor roof and ruined.

25. Each unit was 150 feet x 40 feet, four stories and an attic high, and contained from 5,000 to 7,000 spindles. Thus they were a little longer than Slater's mill in its final state, twice as wide and twice as high.

26. It is impossible to say when this idea originated. Certainly the ultimate scheme had been determined upon as early as 1825, for in that year they all appear on a map. See Appendix VI, A., No. 3.

27. See above, Chapter II, note 31, where Chevalier compares Lowell with its cupolaed mills to a Spanish town with its convents.

28. See Montgomery, *op. cit.*, p. 22. The beams were about 14 inches x 12 inches. Every other beam would be supported, and there would probably be two rows of posts. Thus the bays were not quite square. Montgomery goes on to discuss the difference in construction between English and American mills: "Instead of large beams laid across the house for supporting the floors, the Factories in Great Britain have joists about three inches by ten; these are laid on their edges about twenty inches apart, with one inch flooring above, lathed and plastered beneath, or sheathed with thin boards. The joists are also supported in the center by a beam about eleven inches by six, running from end to end of the building; the pillars are of cast iron, and placed right under this beam: the beam does not rest on the pillar, but on a cast iron case, which passes up on each side of the beam, and meets together above; so that, whilst the under part of this case rests on the top of the pillar, the upper part supports the pillar above; thus leaving the beam entirely free of the pillars in the rooms above; by which means the uppermost floors are supported on

columns of cast iron from the foundation; there is therefore no danger of such floors sinking in the centre. But in this country [America] where the cross beams rest on the top of the pillars, while the pillars above rest again upon the beams, the floors in the upper stories sink down in the centre, in consequence of the shrinking of the timbers, and the pressure of the ends of the pillars into the beams. The writer has seen some of these which have sunk down four and five inches in the course of four years." *Ibid.*, p. 20.

In view of the hue and cry that is being raised over the invention of balloon frame construction in the Middle West at about this time, it is interesting to notice that the English were familiar with its two essential principles, namely, continuous vertical supports from foundations to roof and the use of closely spaced light members instead of widely spaced heavy members. See S. Giedion, *Space, Time, and Architecture*, pp. 269 ff.

29. A number of mills with the original wooden posts remaining are still to be found in Rhode Island, notably the "Old Slater Mill" in Pawtucket, and the Lippitt Mill. There are also posts in Laconia.

30. This was particularly the case in Lowell, because the town was completely under the autocratic thumb of Kirk Boott. By temperament he was a Tory, and Rugby, Sandhurst, and staff work under Wellington in the Peninsular War brought out and sharpened all the fine points of his native disposition. I do not for a moment mean to imply that there was no contact across these social boundaries; there was a great deal. But it seems as if this friendly mixing of the classes was possible because basically the distinctions were so impregnable that no amount of contact could break them down. See H. J. Robinson, *Loom and Spindle,* p. 71.

31. For other sidelights on Boott's character, see *ibid.*, p. 10.

32. *Ibid.*, pp. 13 ff.

33. See Josiah Curtis, "Public Hygiene of Massachusetts," p. 513.

34. Miles, *op. cit.*, p. 67. He goes on to say, "These [boarding houses] are constantly kept clean, the buildings, well painted, and the premises thoroughly whitewashed every Spring at the Corporation's expense." It should be remembered that it was only good economy for the companies to build and maintain their properties well.

35. Actually the houses were very good as housing. On that point

the authorities are pretty well agreed. The one criticism that was made was in regard to the ventilation. The bedrooms lodged two, four, six, or even eight, two in a bed. They often, indeed usually, had but one window. Conditions in the mills themselves were even worse. In winter, thanks to the fact that they were lit by oil lamps and that the windows were kept sealed, the temperature rose to 90°. Josiah Curtis, in his report to the American Medical Association on hygiene in Lowell sums up the whole case against the life of the operatives in a single sentence. "There is not a State's prison, or house of correction in New England where the hours of labor are so long, the hours of meals so short, or the ventilation so much neglected, as in all the cotton mills with which I am acquainted." Curtis, *op. cit.*, p. 531, note.

Coming from a physician, this is a statement of great significance. Yet there are certain reservations which should be made. In the first place it was written in 1849, definitely after the Golden Age, when hours of labor generally were being shortened and only the cotton mills were out of step. At that time the mills, like the boarding houses, were being strung together in long rows, with a consequent loss of light and air. It seems probable, also, that accompanying this loss of ventilation was a growing appreciation of the importance of fresh air. Significantly, it is the casual visitors at the middle of the century, not the girls who actually worked in the mills in the early period, that object to the stuffiness. It is logical to conclude that the original mills and boarding houses were adequate for the demands of the twenties. It was the rise in general standards of health and the sacrifice of comfort to economy and efficiency in the later mills and boarding houses that produced the situation which so aroused Curtis. It is striking that at least one early visitor was favorably impressed by the ventilation in the Lowell mills. "The whole discipline, ventilation and other arrangement appeared to be excellent, of which the best proof was the cheerful and healthy look of the girls," wrote Captain Basil Hall, R. N., in 1827. See Drake, *op. cit.*, I, 186.

36. An exception was the case of John Bull's row, which was built by the Merrimack Manufacturing Company in 1830, one and a half stories high. Later another story was added. See text, p. 47.

37. See John Wood, *A Series of Plans for Cottages or Habitations of the Labourer, Either in Husbandry or the Mechanic Arts*, p. 3.

38. *Ibid.*, p. 3.

39. *Ibid.*

40. Wood says: "In order to make myself master of the subject it was necessary for me to feel as the cottager himself, for I have always held it as a maxim and however quaint the thought may appear, yet it is altogether true, that no architect can form a convenient plan, unless he ideally places himself in the situation of the person for whom he designs." John Wood, *A Series of Plans for Cottages or Habitations of the Labourer,* p. 3. Wood goes on to give excellent practical suggestions, such as that the cottages be "close adjoining so as to appear as one building, that the inhabitants may be of assistance to each other either in case of sickness or any other accident." *Ibid.,* p. 6.

41. These were the houses of the Chelmsford Glass Works, a company established in 1802. See, *The Lowell Book,* p. 6. There was at least one string of three units, a story and a half in height, each dwelling having a central chimney and two windows on either side of the door. It is highly likely that the housing was built shortly after the factory was started, for it was located in a very sparsely inhabited district. If that is the case, this would be the earliest American industrial housing development, as the first Rhode Island examples, such as Slatersville, are slightly later. This fact has some significance. Obviously, industrial low-cost housing did not start in Chelmsford, in the plant of a tiny glass factory. It must have originated elsewhere in America; in fact it was probably not uncommon, to judge by the rapidity with which the idea was taken up in the cotton industry. It remains to find the earlier examples. The resemblance to Wood's design is almost certainly not the result of direct copying. It arises from the fact that Wood, unlike Gandy and other English designers, planned his cottages in the vernacular style which was common to England and America.

42. According to the *Inventory of Polls and Taxable Property* for the year 1826, in the Lowell City Hall, the Merrimack Company owned 30 dwelling houses and 6 two-story houses. "In the tenements of the Merrimack Company there were 967 persons; 299 males and 668 females." Drake, *op. cit.,* II, 64. "Tenements" is here used to include boarding houses, of course.

43. In general, statements of this sort can be confirmed by the maps. In this case Appendix VI, A, No. 3 is the relevant source, although this is dated 1825. The next two streets were presumably laid out shortly thereafter, to accommodate the new housing built

by the Merrimack Company before 1830. As is noted elsewhere, the maps must be used with some caution, as frequently there is no distinction made between actually existing streets and projected streets. Of course, in this instance there can be no question as to the existence of Dutton and Worthen Streets and the alley between.

44. This ground plan was recently in the possession of the Merrimack Manufacturing Company. The plan shown in Figure 5 is redrawn from the original, as it was not practical to reproduce the original.

45. It is not possible to determine the exact number. As far as one can judge from the survivors, the thirty dwellings of the Merrimack Company were all pretty nearly the same size. The six two-story houses (none of which have survived) must have been smaller. If one assumes that these latter accommodated something more than ten persons each, one must assume that the larger houses accommodated something less than thirty persons each. As will be seen from the description below, it is not easy to fit many more than twenty people into this house. As the two-story houses were valued at the same amount as each dwelling house (that is each pair of boarding houses), namely $500, it is possible that they accommodated many more than ten persons, which would bring the average down somewhat. The whole problem is complicated by the fact that it is impossible to make the figures given in the Inventory of Polls and Taxable Property agree with the buildings shown on the maps. The building consisted of a main block two and a half stories high, and 31 feet x 42 feet. Behind this was a single story shed extending some 40 feet to the rear. The interior was divided into two halves by a party wall, and the entrances were side by side in the middle. The center portion of the ground floor was occupied by a long, narrow, dark hall, out of which the stairs rose in a single straight flight. The front of the house had two square rooms opening into one another by a large door. The ell likewise had two large rooms.

Miles (*op. cit.*, p. 67), writing in 1840, states "the front room is usually the common eating room of the house, and the kitchen is in the rear. The keeper of the house has her parlor in some part of the establishment, and in some houses there is a sitting room for the use of the boarders." Here, it would seem that the two rooms in the ell were kitchen and dining room, the two rooms in the front the parlor and bedroom of the landlady. One of these might have been a sitting room for the operatives, in which case one would assume that the large door was a later change. The existing arrangement would have left the landlady little privacy. I believe, however, that this was one of the houses where the operatives had to use the dining room for a sitting room. As there are only four large and two small bedrooms upstairs, it seems unlikely that one of them would be sacrificed to the proprietress. At the very back were two smaller rooms, one of them serving as woodshed and for storage, the other being the washroom and containing the only running water in the house. This single supply was considered ample by all commentators. On the second floor there was a tiny hall in the center of the house surrounding the stair well, and four rooms—two small ones, front and back, and two large ones in the corners. On the third floor, thanks to the slope of the roof, there was only space for two rooms. The two front rooms below and the two large bedrooms on the second floor were heated by wood-burning fireplaces. The four large bedrooms held at least two double beds each, and the two small rooms at least one, making a total of ten beds, for twenty persons.

46. Mr. Lewis Mumford states that this is the traditional village platting, with a double unit instead of a single one. He feels there is a fire hazard in a wooden row which this plan eliminates.

47. That is, generally. There are exceptions, and very handsome ones too. This is notably the case at Somersworth, N. H. (Figure 12), which has perhaps the finest housing in New England.

48. See Chapter IV, note 35, p. 184.

49. Mr. Lewis Mumford has rightly pointed out that this statement holds true, strictly speaking, only for romantic suburbs and eighteenth-century towns and villages. Most of Baltimore, Philadelphia, New York, and Boston was built up during the nineteenth century in strict rows of repeating units. However, although real estate conditions in these large cities did not permit the full expression of the nineteenth-century point of view in street design, the general principle of stylistic evolution holds true even here. One need only compare the smooth surfaces of Tontine Crescent with the raucous plasticity of the projecting bay windows of the South End in Boston.

50. Mention American architecture before the nineteenth century, and one plunges immediately into a terminological problem. For

myself I eschew the word "colonial" except as it has strict political meaning, or is used in quotation marks. I prefer to use "Georgian," which avoids terms like "post-colonial." I consider that the Georgian falls into three phases, the early Georgian, a style of simple geometrically formed buildings, such as the Bruton Parish Church at Williamsburg; the High Georgian, which derives pretty directly from English precedent and is found indigenously in Virginia and elsewhere in the large cities—e. g., Westover; St. Paul's, New York; and the work of Peter Harrison—the late Georgian, which is found chiefly in New England, and which I use instead of the term "post-colonial." The pre-Georgian architecture of America I call "early American"; the post-Georgian architecture (Jefferson, etc.) I call "Federalist," or "early Republican." Needless to say in this sense the term "Georgian," has no more connection with the royal Georges than the term "Gothic" has with the Goths.

51. There is a view of the garden and pond in the Lowell Historical Society. Cf. Appendix VI, B, No. 3.

52. From Niles' Register of Baltimore for August 27, 1831. That book copied it from the Portsmouth, N. H., *Journal*. It is quoted in full in G. O'Dwyer, *The Irish Catholic Genesis of Lowell*, p. 8.

53. For conditions in 1849, see Curtis, *op. cit.*, p. 520. There he states: "At this date in a central district, bounded by Shattuck, Market, Central and Merrimack Streets [an area of roughly 3 and one-half acres in extent] we find the City Hall, and the offices of the mayor, city clerk, treasurer, and engineer and twelve physicians; the post office, city library, two churches, three banks, one grammar and three primary schools—embracing an aggregate of eight hundred and thirteen pupils, during the last year—ninety stores—many of our first class—two smithies, several machine shops, a foundry, coal and wood yard, three livery stables, and two hundred and fifty four tenements, inhabited by one thousand four hundred and forty five individuals. This district [that is the tenements] by the survey of the city engineer embraces only one fifteen thousandth of a square mile." "One week ago I entered a house in a central location and found it occupied by one store and twenty-five different families, I found one of the families to consist of a man, his wife and eight children—four of whom were over fifteen years of age—and four boarders." "About the same time it became necessary to visit another room, in the night, which contained only five hundred and thirty seven

cubic feet [roughly 9 feet x 10 feet x 6 feet], and no means for ventilation. For many hours, night after night, it contained no less than six individuals, three of whom were adults." (In the above quotation from Curtis, the items in brackets I have added. His parenthetical remarks I have placed between dashes.) Even more serious than the low level of the bad housing is the quantity of bad housing. In 1865 one third of the population of Lowell, 10,000 people, were of foreign birth. The conditions Curtis describes are typical of the way that most of them had to live.

54. The statements as to Boott's wealth are conflicting. The citizens of Lowell thought of him as exceedingly rich, like the Boston capitalists he represented. The Boston capitalists tended to deflate this estimate of his wealth, partly because they thought of him as an employee, partly as a reaction to the exaggerated estimates of the people of Lowell. I know of only three facts that can be cited which are relevant to this question. Boott's salary was only $3,000, which everybody admitted was low. The Merrimack Company was prepared to pay more, if they had to. In fact when it was a question of importing an Englishman to run the Print Works, they cheerfully paid more. Had Boott been in want, he could certainly have demanded and received a higher salary. Boott's house was assessed at $2,500, that is five times the value of a pair of boarding houses. Finally, Boott and his brother each subscribed $90,000 capital to the Merrimack Manufacturing Company, see above, Chapter III, note 20. They probably did not have to produce that much in cash, but the Merrimack Manufacturing Company paid dividends of 12 percent a year, on the average (see Chevalier, *op. cit.*, French edition, p. 199) so that Boott must have enjoyed a handsome income.

55. At a later period, when this land was needed for mills, Boott moved his house up to the place where Merrimack Street joined the old road to the town landing, now known as Pawtucket Street. After his death in 1837 the house was purchased by the corporations to serve as a hospital for their operatives. It is a hospital to this day, although no longer owned by the manufacturing companies.

56. Mr. Talbot Hamlin has pointed out the interesting resemblance of this building to the Jumel House, in New York. It is not at all impossible that Boott knew the Jumel House.

57. An engraving of this house was published in *The Builder's As-*

sistant, by John Haviland, Philadelphia, John Bioren, 1818-21, Vol. III, Pls. 109, 110. Haviland was an English architect working in Philadelphia. Presumably he designed the Moody House in Haverhill, which would account for its advanced character.

58. Compare this use of pilasters with those which dangle on the front of Bulfinch's University Hall, Harvard University, Cambridge.

59. See Drake, *op. cit.,* II, 105.

60. *Ibid.,* II, 104.

61. See Agnes Addison, "Early American Gothic."

62. See C. A. Place, "From Meeting House to Church in New England."

63. See the author's *American Gothic Churches, 1823-1893.*

64. I have assumed the existence of Boott as an architect based on three statements. "He made plans of the company's land, of every parcel which was disposed of in his time, and ground-plans and elevations of all the buildings which were erected." W. R. Bagnall, *Contributions to American Economic History,* p. 2192: "He was engineer, architect, draughtsman, conveyancer, clerk, moderator of the town meeting." John O. Green, in *Proceedings in the City of Lowell at the semi-centennial celebration,* p. 65. "Early in the Spring (1825), preparations were going on for building the church. Mr. Boott drew several plans and discussed them with his friends." "The original plan of St. Anne's Church building, as drawn by Mr. Boott contemplated the addition of thirty feet to its length [since made], to bring it into a proportional form." Theodore Edson, *Historical Discourse on the Occasion of the Fiftieth Anniversary of the 1st Introduction of Stated Public Worship,* pp. 11, 24. It seems to me unlikely that he did all this drawing just as a relaxation for a tired business man. I assume that these statements mean that he was the architect of all the buildings discussed above. It is extremely unlikely that there was another architect, some outsider, for not only could such an important individual hardly have escaped mention in all the multitude of accounts of early days in Lowell, but it was very unusual for architects to have any part in the creation of these towns. They were not even called in to design special buildings much before the forties. At about that time one J. H. Rand appears as the architect of several structures in Lowell. He seems to have been a local person, perhaps a builder who arrogated to himself this more pretentious title. The fact

that Haviland, an important Philadelphia architect, designed the house in Haverhill is therefore highly exceptional.

It must be remembered that architects were at this time a rarity in America. Perhaps the most vivid indication of professional conditions in the east during the twenties is James Gallier's account of his stay in New York in his autobiography. Therefore, if these buildings in Lowell are not the work of Boott, then they are the work of some one of the local contractors (whose names are known). Correction would be merely a matter of substituting one name for another.

V: A DECADE OF GROWTH

1. See Appendix VI, A, Nos. 3, 4.
2. See H. A. Miles, *Lowell as It Was and as It Is*, p. 59; also Nathan Appleton, *Introduction of the Power Loom and Origin of Lowell*, p. 29.
3. See *The Merchant's Magazine and Commercial Review*, XVI (New York, 142 Fulton St., 1847), p. 422.
4. Figures from Miles, *op. cit.*, p. 59. At the beginning of 1826 the settlement contained twenty-five hundred inhabitants. A bill was sent to the legislature asking for the creation of a new town. Appleton, *op. cit.*, pp. 32 ff., states: "It was a matter of some difficulty to fix upon a name for it. I met Mr. Boott one day, when he said to me that the committee of the Legislature were ready to report the bill. It only remained to fill the blank with the name. He said he considered the question narrowed down to Lowell or Derby. I said to him, 'then Lowell by all means,' and Lowell it was." In 1836 the town of Lowell had a population of 17,633, and it was incorporated a city.
5. The first buildings would have been even more temporary, except for the fact that after 1826, the Locks and Canals Company decided that "all buildings more than ten feet high, hereafter to be erected upon any of the lands then belonging to them, must be of stone or brick, with a slated roof." S. A. Drake, *History of Middlesex County, Massachusetts*, II, 64.
6. See C. F. Ware, *The Early New England Cotton Manufacture*, p. 66.
7. The first thing they had to do was to revise the existing corporate setup. As organized in the first half of the twenties, the Merrimack Company owned all the land and water power and also went in for manufacturing. Thus it would be both the

landlord and the competitor of any other concerns that might wish to establish themselves in Lowell. This was not a situation calculated to encourage rapid development. At the time of the purchase of the real estate, the Company called "the Proprietors of the Locks and Canals on Merrimack River" had been put into a state of coma. It was now resurrected. The Merrimack Company sold all the property in Lowell to the Locks and Canals Company. The Locks and Canals Company then leased to the Merrimack Company all the water power it needed and sold to the Merrimack Company the site that the manufacturing concern was actually occupying. It then offered to sell any other companies that might come along such land as they needed, and to lease them the necessary water power. Thus, all the manufacturing companies were placed on a common level of dependence upon the Locks and Canals Company, Drake, *op. cit.*, II, 63.

8. *Ibid.*, II, 64.

9. For the dates of the founding of the separate corporations, see the chapter on the Locks and Canals Company and the chapters on the separate manufacturing corporations in W. R. Bagnall, *Contributions to American Economic History*. The companies were located as follows: In 1825 the Locks and Canals Company built the Hamilton Company a new canal, starting just above the Swamp Locks, running parallel to the Pawtucket Canal a short distance to the south, and eventually debouching into the main canal once more. The Locks and Canals Company then sold them the lower half of the island they had created and additional territory for housing to the south of the new canal. The building of the Tremont, Suffolk, and Lawrence Companies necessitated the construction of still another canal. This was dug in 1831 and ran due north from the Swamp Locks, and then northeast, parallel to the Merrimack Canal, until it reached the river. On either side of this canal the Tremont and Suffolk Companies built a pair of mills apiece, while at the point where the canal joined the main stream, the Lawrence Corporation put up four mills. A final canal was dug in the late thirties for the Boott and Massachusetts Companies. This ran northeast out of the Pawtucket Canal, just above the Lower Locks, then turned northwest, and ran until it met the Merrimack Company, where it joined the river. Each company put up four mills between the river and the canal.

10. See Miles, *op. cit.*, pp. 76 ff.

11. *Ibid.,* p. 77.

12. Once more a matter of terminology. I use the term "double-pitched" roof to signify a gable roof.

13. In 1847-48 the Merrimack Manufacturing Company built on the riverbank a mammoth new mill equipped with 25,000 spindles, five times as many as its predecessors. (The number of spindles comes from Bagnall.) This was gigantic in size, even for that time. "Previous to the year 1806, the number of spindles contained in a factory seldom exceeded 1,000. In 1838, there were 26 factories in Lowell, containing 150,404 spindles, being a fraction over 5,371 spindles in each factory. At the present time (1851), there are two mills in Lowell containing 17,440 spindles." From R. H. Baird, *The American Cotton Spinner,* p. 31. (It is possible either that Baird failed to mention the new Merrimack mill, or else that Bagnall's figures are wrong.) The mill still exists. More astonishing even than its size is the enormous number of windows, which is striking even today. They make up almost two thirds of the wall area, instead of one third, which has been usual among better mills before. That this impressed contemporaries may be gathered from their attempts to render the effect in drawings. Unfortunately an upper story has been added, the cupola has been removed, and the lines of the roof changed, so that the intended effect can hardly be gauged from what now remains.

14. Drake, *op. cit.,* II, 64, says that by 1826 the Hamilton Company "had erected two blocks of houses with eight tenements in each, and were preparing to erect two more, one hundred and ninety-three feet in length and thirty-six feet in width." I saw a ruinous fragment of one in the summer of 1937. I do not doubt that it has been removed since that time. Drake's statements check with the maps.

15. The resemblance is really very striking. Massachusetts Hall was built in 1720 from the designs of John Leverett, the president of the University. Its similarity with buildings such as the "New Block" of the Merrimack Manufacturing Company (see text, p. 67), built a century and a quarter later, show the existence and persistence of a genuine tradition of folk architecture.

16. This arrangement is seen on a grand scale at Manchester, N. H. (Figure 21.) Here it is at its most attractive, for the ground rises sharply up from the bank of the river, and the boarding houses are stepped along the steep climbing streets. Moreover, with the

lavish use of space, characteristic of the planning of Manchester, there are large back yards between the houses, instead of the mere alleys found in Lowell. (Fig. 43.) Of course the boarding houses in these units were considerably larger than those originally built for the Merrimack Manufacturing Company. Fifty or sixty girls in each was the rule. See J. H. Burgy, *The New England Cotton Textile Industry*, p. 154. He quotes the figure from Harriet Hanson Robinson, who was a mill girl.

17. This is proved by the absence of many buildings in Lowell which did not belong to the Corporations. The population of the town was variously estimated. Edson, the rector of St. Anne's, said that it was about 600 when he first arrived in 1824. It is pretty generally agreed that it was about 2,500 in 1826. See Drake, *op. cit.*, p. 64. Of these almost one thousand were employees of the Merrimack Manufacturing Company, 263 more were employees of the Machineshop. In addition there were the employees of the Hamilton Corporation, perhaps 400 people—to judge by the number of tenements the company had built—and several hundred more who worked for the Locks and Canals Company. The number of citizens cannot have been large, therefore. Once they started to come, however, they came rapidly and in quantity. Lowell's growth was something completely new in America at this time, and amazed Europeans only less than the whole social system. For example, Captain Basil Hall, R. N., expressed very well the general point of view in 1827, when he wrote, "a few years ago, the spot which we now saw covered with huge cotton mills, canals, roads and bridges was a mere wilderness, and, if not quite solitary, was inhabited only by painted savages." Quoted *ibid.*, I, 185.

18. See Appendix V.

19. The best index of the increase in the number of private houses is the rise in the amount of property on which the bourgeoisie paid taxes. This could be computed from a study of the Lowell Inventory of Polls and Taxable Property, at great labor. Keith gives a small table, which is reproduced as a graph in Appendix V, and to which I have added certain information that I have gathered from the city documents.

20. Indeed, in some aspects there is actual retrogression, the number of hotels, for example, declined, thanks to changes in transportation habits after the introduction of the railroads.

21. The number of churches here cited is derived from the detailed

denominational history given by F. P. Hill, *Lowell Illustrated.*
It does not check exactly with flat statements such as are found
in Miles, *op. cit.,* and elsewhere as to the number of churches
active in Lowell at one particular moment. The history of the
individual churches is of an extraordinary complication. They
were forever merging, subdividing, appearing, disappearing, and
above all buying, selling, and moving church buildings. A very
few of these survive in any condition whatsoever, and of only a
few of those destroyed are there illustrations. Thus generaliza-
tions about the architecture must be based upon a very limited
knowledge of a small proportion of the monuments.

Here is a sample of denominational history. The first Methodist Church was on Chapel Hill and was dedicated in 1827. The
second Methodist Church, known as the Barnes Church, stood
at the corner of Market and Suffolk Streets and was dedicated
in 1832. The third Methodist Church, known as the Wesley
Chapel was opposite the Barnes Church, being purchased and
dedicated in 1837. "From the erection of the 'Barnes Church' in
1832, to the division of the Church in 1838, there was one church
organization with two congregations." One congregation worshiped in the Barnes Church about a year, when, the church
being sold, they returned for a few months to Chapel Hill, then
hired the town hall, then hired and returned to the Barnes
Church, whence they moved to their new buildings, the Wesley
Chapel in 1837. "The other congregation worshiped at Chapel
Hill until the Barnes Church was hired; then both congregations
united and held their services in the Barnes Church, but becoming straitened for room, a few months later, the chapel was
re-opened and occupied. In June 1838, the Church was divided
into the Chapel Hill Methodist Episcopal Church and the Wesley
Chapel Methodist Episcopal Church. . . . From the Chapel Hill
Church the St. Paul's has been developed, and from the Wesley
Chapel Church, the Worthen St. Church," dedicated in 1842.
(From Hill, *op. cit.,* p. 44.) Multiply this situation by three or
four so as to include the Congregationalists, the Baptists, the
Catholics, etc., also add the minor sects like the Unitarians and
the Universalists, and remember that any picture of any of the
church buildings may be referred to by any one of two or three
names, sometimes even five or six, if the building changes hands,
and you will get a picture of the sort of situation one is up
against.

22. The material on the real-estate development and on the houses is derived from a study of maps. There are a large number of maps of Lowell preserved in the Locks and Canals Company, a list of them will be found in Appendix VI, A. In general I have used two maps as a basis, the map published by I. A. Beard and J. Hoar in 1841, and the map published by S. Moody. I have compared these with earlier manuscript maps, and have marked on them relevant information. Both of these published maps show houses and other buildings, and so it is possible to arrive at an approximate date by their presence or absence on these maps. This method can not be followed too rigidly, as there must be many inaccuracies in drawing. Moreover, it was common practice in Lowell to move old buildings. Actually all that the presence on a map tells, unless it can be confirmed by stylistic character, is the date at which a given site was occupied. A like caution must be used with the roads. The maps were based partly on the roads in actual use, partly on roads which were planned (and in some cases never executed). It is impossible to tell just what the presence of a road in the map means. Even the city records do not provide any adequate check, for until the great land sale in 1845 most of the roads, though used by everybody, were private roads, belonging to the Locks and Canals Company. I have been as discreet as possible in using this data, and have tried to state if I was dating a building wholly on the basis of its presence or absence on the map.

23. See Appendix II, A.

24. This seems to be at variance with the statement in R. M. Hurd, *Principles of City Land Values*, p. 74. "In all growth, central or axial, great or small, the vital feature is continuity, the universal tendency being to add on buildings one by one, of the same general character as those which preceded them." Hurd's statement holds true, I believe, only for the development that takes place in the center of well established communities. The initial process of filling up a vacant area, either in the start of a community, or at the fringes of an old community, seems to follow the pattern by which modern cities expand through subdivision. "Subdividing activity is especially irregular and erratic. Instead of appropriating the land at the edge of the built-up urban area and extending the platted portion gradually outward, the more usual procedure appears to be that of reaching out past considerable tracts of unsubdivided property, establishing plats in isolated and far-

flung locations, and then gradually filling in the interstices." R. D. McKenzie, *The Metropolitan Community,* pp. 202-3. Quoted by permission of McGraw-Hill Book Company.

25. This practice continues in Lowell at least down to the fifties.

26. An example of the single square house in Lowell, before the coming of the corporations, is the Burkee House, which however was not a private dwelling but a tavern. An example of the five-window house was the Livermore House, "erected about 1750 by one Timothy Brown, the heavy lumber for its construction being obtained of Captain Ford at his saw mill near Pawtucket Falls." (From the *Lowell Book,* Chapter I.) For illustrations, see the *Illustrated History of Lowell and Vicinity,* pp. 192 and 194.

27. Here, later, the empty angle was filled in, making the house a square. An additional wooden ell was thrown out to the rear, and the gable of the original ell was turned into a clumsy gambrel.

28. In all probability this porch is a later addition, although cf. Figure 32.

29. See *Old Residents' Historical Association Contributions,* I, xxi. The hotels were as follows, the Stone House, the American House, the Mansion House, the City Hotel and another (name forgotten) on the site of the Belvidere Hospital, the Washington House, the Appleton House, and the Railroad Hotel, two on Middlesex Street (Howard House and Lowell House [?]), and the Merrimack House.

30. Another smaller hotel which is surviving today is the Lowell House, otherwise known as the Eagle Hotel, on Middlesex Street. The building is similar to a large multiple dwelling. Another structure which should be included in this category is the large house which appears on the map of 1852 labeled "Water Cure Establishment." It is a charming and unique L-shaped structure with two stories of open porches at the angle and a cupola crowning the hipped roof. It was built probably in the late thirties by the same Elder Thurston who erected the First Freewill Baptist Church.

31. See Chapter III, note 43.

32. The building of this church was one of the most dramatic episodes in the whole history of Lowell. The construction brought to a head all the latent anti-Catholic sentiment of the Yankee community, and on the night of May 18, 1831, the native elements tried to wreck the acre and the new building. There is an

excellent account of the ensuing riot in G. O'Dwyer's, *The Irish Catholic Genesis of Lowell,* p. 16.

33. The first Baptist Church is still in existence, although much altered by a restoration in the 1890's.

34. See C. A. Place, *Charles Bulfinch, Architect and Citizen,* p. 36.

35. See *The Lowell Offering and Magazine,* written and edited by factory operatives, I, 173.

VI: THE IMPACT OF ROMANTICISM

1. See S. Giedion, *Space, Time and Architecture,* p. 24.

2. This belief originated in the nineteenth century itself. It was in fact this dogma which launched the nineteenth century on the quest of a new style, a nineteenth-century style. In applying it to the Victorians, we are taking them at their own disparaging estimate of themselves, just as the Victorians believed that Renaissance architecture was nothing but imitation, because Renaissance architects laid so much stress in their writings on copying the Antique. James Fergusson in his *History of the Modern Styles of Architecture,* 2d ed., p. 3, makes the statement: "there is not perhaps a single building of any architectural pretension erected in Europe since the Reformation, in the beginning of the sixteenth century, which is not more or less a copy, either in form or detail, from some building either of a different clime or different age from those in which it was erected. There is no building, in fact, the design of which is not borrowed from some country or people with whom our only associations are those derived from education alone, wholly irrespective of either blood or feeling." The implication that the buildings of these imitative styles of architectural art, are inferior to the buildings of the true styles, is obvious, even in this brief quotation. No critic today would damn the Renaissance and Baroque periods out of hand as Fergusson does. But we think nothing of retaining his condemnation of the nineteenth century, which is based on just the same arguments.

3. See above, pp. 41 ff.

4. See above, p. 71.

5. This third mode of design is the High Victorian style, referred to below in Chapter IX, note 15. It is the outcome of the effort to create a truly modern style mentioned in the preceding note. This style has not as yet received sufficient attention. There were, of course, later phases of nineteenth-century architecture. The

High Victorian or third phase may be considered to have lasted until the eighties, perhaps even the nineties, depending on whether one considers Richardson and his followers an outgrowth of this style or as something new. In any case, after the nineties there is a definite split. On the one hand there is the modern movement stemming out of Richardson. On the other there is the contemporary reactionary movement. This likewise stemmed from Richardson, although in a different way. To mention but two links, McKim and White both worked in Richardson's office, while Ralph Adams Cram admits that Richardson was one of the major formative influences in his career. These later phases have no importance for this study, so we will not discuss them further.

6. The history of the public buildings is also somewhat complicated. The functions of the various buildings changed, and the names depend on the functions. Thus the Market House became the Police Station. Furthermore the history of the schools (an administrative unit under the direction of one teacher) is quite different from that of the school buildings, each of which might contain two or more schools. The only reliable guide that I have found is the *Annual Reports of the Receipts and Expenditures of the City of Lowell*, which, in addition to the annual expenditures, lists the city-owned property with the assessed value of the buildings. Unfortunately, this document only begins in 1838, and care must be taken as the Reports are published for the year following the expenditure.

7. See S. A. Drake, *History of Middlesex County, Massachusetts*, II, 66.

8. See *Illustrated History of Lowell and Vicinity, Massachusetts*, p. 171.

9. See *Contributions to the Old Residents Historical Association, Lowell, Mass.*, VI, 263.

10. Subsequently a cupola was added in the middle of the roof ridge of the Market House. All but the base of the cupola has been removed.

11. See Charles Cowley, *Illustrated History of Lowell*, p. 99.

12. Barristers' Hall was used as a church, first by the Universalists, then by the Methodists. It is frequently called the Central Methodist Episcopal Church. For an illustration, see Cowley, *op. cit.*, p. 99.

13. $500 was the value of one of the wooden houses, such as No. 22 Dutton St. which contained a pair of boarding houses.

14. The corporations at this period paid most of the taxes; naturally they were not any too anxious for the community to embark on a big program of public spending. A great and dramatic fight took place in town meeting, with Kirk Boott leading one faction, and the Reverend Theodore Edson the other. When Edson carried the majority of votes, Boott was so incensed that he never went into St. Anne's again.

15. There are some apparent exceptions. Thus the fact that the Howard St. Primary School is end-on to the street is a proof of its comparatively late date. The Edson School, which stood until recently on the South Common, originally faced on South Street. Highland Street, running close by its south end, was a later addition, built long after the school.

16. A plan and an elevation of the Lowell high school of 1840 are to be found on pp. 112 and 113 of H. Barnard's *School Architecture*. The school had one great school room and two smaller rooms on each floor, also two entrance halls with coat racks. If there were any sanitary facilities, they must have been in the basement. This plan was apparently fairly typical of schools built up to that time. Generally the two floors were administered as separate schools, each with its own principal. In 1856, however, this scheme of organization was given up, the various school houses were remodelled, and the schools were graded by years, much as at present. The new plan was inaugurated in the otherwise conservative Centralville Grammar School. See *Lowell, a City of Spindles*, p. 29.

17. The extent of school building is reflected in the city budget. The amount of money spent on maintaining the schools increased from $15,000 in 1837 to $55,000 in 1855.

18. See above, p. 65.

19. This was pointed out perhaps for the first time by Henry-Russell Hitchcock, Jr., in the first chapter of *The Architecture of H. H. Richardson and His Times*, pp. 4, 5. "At the time of Richardson's birth in the late thirties the Greek Revival had become without any question the national style in architecture and building. For the last time in this country architects and carpenters, engineers and farmers of the East, the South and the West, all built in a single homogeneous way . . . The Greek vernacular, once established, lived on as the basic style of the nation almost down

to the Civil War. There was little internal development within the style except the substitution of square pilasters for proper columns, or the use of skeleton supports of wood or metal, made light and transparent in order that porches and piazzas should not complicate the plain solid cube of the house. It was against a very real regimentation of architecture that the generation active just before Richardson reacted, out of boredom perhaps as much as anything else, beginning to destroy the Greek Revival just as soon as it was firmly established." Quoted by permission of the Museum of Modern Art. This Chapter presents what is certainly the best general account of American architecture of the middle third of the nineteenth century.

20. That is to say those members of the first group on which any information can be found. See Chapter V, note 21.

21. The opposition between the sects was very real in Lowell. The older denominations combined to curse upstart groups like the Unitarians and the Universalists. The Episcopalians were also newcomers to upcountry Massachusetts, but ranting against them would hardly have been safe, in view of Boott's convictions. See Drake, *op. cit.,* II, 77.

22. See *The Lowell Offering and Magazine,* written and edited by factory operatives, I, 152.

23. *Ibid.,* p. 304.

24. According to some accounts the building was first erected in 1828, but it is impossible to know whether at this time it had a portico or not.

25. See Cowley, *op. cit.,* p. 96.

26. See *The Lowell Offering,* II, 48.

27. See Cowley, *op. cit.,* p. 88.

28. See *The Lowell Offering,* I, 263.

29. "The Freewill Baptist Church was built largely of money belonging to over one hundred factory girls, who were induced by Elder Thurston's promises of large interest to draw their money from the savings-banks, and place it in his hands. These credulous operatives did not even receive the interest of their money, but believing in him as an elder of the church, they were persuaded even a second time, to let him have their savings." H. J. H. Robinson, *Loom and Spindle,* pp. 21, 22. Quoted by permission of the publisher. Less than ten years after the building was finished, it was attached for debt, and the minister narrowly escaped being arrested on a charge of swindling. Ben Butler and

Fisher Hildreth, two aggressive young bourgeois, took it over after a lawsuit and converted it into a theater. To this a museum was added. The two were not profitable and in 1856 it was rearranged as a lecture hall and offices. Finally, in 1865, as the lecture hall did not pay, it was entirely devoted to offices. The building was struck by lightning and caught fire on three different occasions.

30. Double houses are comparatively rarely found in Lowell after the later thirties. Strangely enough the large multiple dwellings persist much longer, indeed they have really never disappeared.

31. Single houses of the three-bay type, i.e., half double houses with the doorway on one side of the façade, are found in other parts of the country at a much earlier date than they appear in Lowell. They are the normal late Georgian type of house in the Connecticut Valley, for example.

32. "About such and such a date" in this book generally means within five years one way or the other. In the nineteenth century in America it is almost always possible to fall within those limits, just on stylistic grounds. Here, specifically, the New Block is not found on the map of Lowell surveyed in 1841 and is shown in an engraving published in 1849. The New Block is also different from, and less advanced in style than, some additional housing which the Merrimack Manufacturing Company erected before 1850, and probably in the last years of the 40's. (Figure 68.) The date 1845 seems about right, therefore.

33. There were a few later blocks, one of them illustrated in Figure 68. It was this group which was referred to in the preceding note. The date of their erection may be determined by the fact that they appear on the map of 1850 and not on the map of 1841. They are also obviously later in style than the New Block. They differ from the latter only in details of their exterior form; however, in their size and general conception they are much the same. To be sure, on the evidence of contemporary plans which existed until recently in the possession of the Merrimack Manufacturing Company, it is possible to say that these blocks were composed entirely of tenements, whereas the New Block was made up of boarding houses.

34. See W. R. Bagnall, *Contributions to American Economic History*.

35. Notably the Appleton, the Tremont, and the Suffolk, in addition to the Hamilton. Illustrations of all these will be found on the

edge of the published map of Sidney & Neff, Appendix VI, A, No. 12.

36. Compare the Merrimack plant with the series of dormitories in the northwest corner of the Yard—Massachusetts, Harvard, Hollis, Stoughton, Holworthy, etc.

37. The mills were started in that year. The drawing was published in 1849 in the *New England Offering*.

38. The Bay State Mills and the Hamilton Company have been rebuilt long since, but an idea of the style they represented can be gained at Holyoke, Massachusetts, where a great textile establishment has survived as the municipal power plant. Here, as in Lowell, there is a long line of buildings beside the canal, with an emphasized central unit carrying until recently a cupola. A single bridge spans the stream continuing the line of the axial street. Opposite, on the shore, the housing and secondary industrial buildings are ingeniously arranged either parallel or at right angles to the river. As one looks down the main avenue, in the foreground the view is hemmed in by two long files of boarding houses, rather small in scale. Further on the ends of a series of larger buildings project at right angles to the street, creating a feeling of recession. The view terminates in the arresting central block of the mill.

39. It appears on a print published in 1836. The road was only opened in 1835, so that the station must date from the early 30's. See Drake, *op. cit.*, p. 191.

40. Mr. Lewis Mumford suggests a comparison with Euston Station, London.

41. See Drake, *op. cit.*, II, 108.

42. See E. M. Upjohn, *Richard Upjohn, Architect and Churchman*, Fig. 10.

43. *Ibid.*, p. 44.

44. See *The Lowell Book*, p. 15.

VII: FULLY ROMANTIC ARCHITECTURE, THE PRIVATE HOUSES

1. An interesting example of this is the publication of James Montgomery's *A Practical Detail of the Cotton Manufacture of the United States of America and the State of the Cotton Manufacture of That Country Contrasted and Compared with That of Great Britain, with Comparative Estimates of the Cost of Manufacturing in Both Countries* (Glasgow, John Niven, 1840). This important book is significant because it reveals a new interest in

the purely technical aspects of manufacturing. It aroused immediate criticism in America, and an anonymous answer to it was
published, entitled *Strictures on Montgomery on the Cotton
Manufactures of Great Britain and America, also a Practical Comparison of the Cost of Steam and Water Power in America* (by
the Author, Newburyport, Morss & Brewster, 1841). As the
leading proponent of steam mills in and about Newburyport at
this time was General Charles James, he was probably the author.

James (?) writes: "Proprietors of water mills, generally, in
the interior, are under the necessity of purchasing land, and
erecting dwellings, for the accommodation of their operatives.
. . . In seaports, this necessity does not exist. Dwellings are generally found in abundance, already erected and any deficiency
is readily supplied by the owners of real estate themselves. Added
to this, there is another consideration. There is, in general, to be
found in the maritime places, an abundance of help, of nearly
all descriptions wanted in the mill. A vast proportion of these
persons either cannot or will not leave their homes to labor in
distant establishments without the inducement of high wages;
and many not even for that inducement. But they readily and
gladly go into mills in their immediate vicinity, will work for
less wages than would command their services abroad, and in
fact can well afford to do so, as they can live as well with their
own families and friends, at much less expense." *Ibid.*, p. 17.
What he is really saying is that owing to the gradual decline of
the smaller New England seaports, there was a large supply of
nearly destitute labor on the market of which the enterprising
employer could avail himself at sweat shop wages. This was
something new, and the desire to take advantage of it shows a
complete change in the attitude of the executives towards labor
from that which Appleton, Jackson, and Lowell professed. The
last words along this new line were spoken by A. N. Gulliver,
before the New England and Cotton Manufacturers Association.
(See *Transactions*, April 22, 1903.) He stated, "The most satisfactory way in which to handle any class of labor is to have its
sole connection with the mill one of work—well performed, it will
mean continuous employment, poorly done, immediate discharge."

2. H. J. H. Robinson, in *Loom and Spindle*, on p. 86 makes the statement: "After a time, as the wages became more and more reduced, the best portion of the girls left and went to their homes,
or to the other employments that were fast opening to women,

until there were very few of the old guard left; and thus the status of the factory population of New England gradually became what we know it to be today." Quoted by permission of Thomas Y. Crowell & Company. Although the cities of the Lowell group had very little influence on American industry generally, sporadic imitations occurred. For example, the Waltham Watch Company, being a new industry, was able to maintain high paternalistic standards until quite late. See John Swinton, *A Model Factory in a Model City.*

3. Norman Ware has admirably characterized the spirit of the forties. "It is customary for later and perhaps more sophisticated generations to regard with complacency the 'hot-air' period of American history. And certainly there were enough freaks abroad to warrant some derision. Phrenology flourished, alongside the 'Water-Cure.' The Millerites waited on God. The Grahamites had a vision that was later to make famous Bernard Shaw, Upton Sinclair, and whole-wheat bread. The 'Disciples of the Newness' left Boston for a played-out farm. Robert Owen flitted back and forth across the Atlantic and about the cities of the New World catechizing the prince and the pauper in the true laws of life. The Land Reformers saw New York as a desert but for a few storage warehouses and docks, and every man under his own vine and fig tree on a ten-acre lot or a quarter-section farm. There was the ever-recurrent 'new woman'—at that time in bloomers —to worry the prurient. Temperance reform, the wrongs of Hungarian liberals, Association, capital punishment, and slavery, all gave birth to 'movements.' It was an era of lost causes." See *The Industrial Workers, 1840-1860,* p. 18. Quoted by permission of Houghton Mifflin.

4. The tradition of town vs. corporation hostility was founded in 1832 when Edson led the city fathers to vote to erect two brick grammar schools, against the opposition of Boott and all the clever lawyers he could muster. The corporations as the chief taxpayers had to foot the bill, and Boott never entered Edson's church again. The community continued spending money fast, and there remained a sharp conflict of interests between the large taxpayers and the majority of the citizens who owned little or no real or personal estates. The first strike in Lowell occurred in 1836, an abortive spree in which the mill girls marched around for the day and listened to speeches. Nothing was gained, and

the executives took pains to punish the culprits. See H. J. H. Robinson, *op. cit.*, p. 83.

5. Significantly the *Vox Populi*, the Lowell newspaper opposed to "the Interests," was founded in 1841, one year after the first issue of the *Lowell Offering* appeared. This last was one of several magazines written and edited entirely by the mill girls, under the wing of the church. Their "propagandist value was readily seen by the corporations, and they were saved from an early grave, the usual destiny of the press of the period, by the intervention of the unofficial representatives of the corporations, the *Lowell Courier*." They were thus "a part of a rather elaborate defense of the factory system, propagandist in its nature, and elicited by attacks from various quarters upon the corporations." N. Ware, *op. cit.*, pp. 79, 89. I personally feel these statements as to the character of the *Lowell Offering* are a little too strong, though its general satisfaction with existing conditions cannot be denied.

6. See above, p. 60.

7. F. W. Coburn, *History of Lowell and Its People*.

8. See the *Records of Resolutions with Regard to Streets*. Manuscript in the Office of the City Engineer at Lowell, being a transcript of the proceedings of the City Council.

9. By 1845 most of the Lowell companies were anxious to expand their plants. More water power was available, but only by constructing a new canal. The Locks and Canals Company over a period of years had advanced money to the various manufacturing concerns which they could not repay. It was accordingly in no position to undertake the task of building the new waterway. So it sold the machineshop to a new independent concern for some $200,000, and disposed of most of the remaining real estate for $300,000, and bought in its own shares at a cost of $583 per share of $500 par value. It then sold itself outright to the manufacturing companies for $600,000. As reorganized, the Locks and Canals Company, now the subsidiary of the textile corporations collectively, proceeded to build a new canal. This enlarged the power from some 5,500 H.P. to about 8,500 H.P. Later improvements were added and the power was 3,000 H.P. more. These improvements consisted chiefly in the substitution of turbine wheels, for the old overshot wheels.

10. It is probably for this reason that the highly desirable land around the South Common should have been developed comparatively

late—after the map of 1850 was published; and that it should have been given over to public buildings, and the residences of those who could afford to drive to town in their own carriages.

11. See Appendix VI, A, Nos. 7 and 12.

12. See Coburn, *op. cit.*

13. See Appendix V.

14. Between 1831 and 1860 the number of spindles more than quadrupled, the number of operatives less than doubled. See M. T. Copeland, *The Cotton Manufacturing Industry of the United States,* p. 11.

15. See above, p. 142.

16. It would be hard to find a more passionate condemnation of the Greek Revival than the review of *Rural Architecture* in the *North American Review,* Vol. LVIII (Boston, Otis Broaders, 1844), which the index of the magazine attributes to Arthur Gilman. On p. 438 he states, "The elevation of the Parthenon, Erectheum or The Illissus is the Procrustes bed, on which the relentless measure of all our public and private wants and uses is taken, and we are seldom allowed any alternative. Because a *façade* is beautiful in one situation, it is without hesitation adopted in all. A leaf cut out of Stuart's 'Athens,' that inexhaustible quarry of bad taste, supplies our architect with his design and his detail; he duplicates the columns of the Choragic monument under the crowded portico of the suburban citizen's abode; and sacrifices in every situation, all discrimination and all distinctive character to his imaginary Moloch of classical chasteness. We are almost tempted to suppose, that whenever he sits down to his drawing-board, an attendant stands close at his elbow, to whisper in his ear the dismal motto which as Montaigne relates, was every day repeated by the pages of Darius; 'Sir, remember the Athenians.' So effectually does he remember them, that he finds room in his memory for nothing else. Without columns, he cannot compose any thing; and with them, he seems to think he cannot fail of being fine. Thus, market-house, cottage, bank, town-hall, law-school, church, brewery and theater, with him are all the same. It matters not how widely different their character, how exactly opposite their purpose. His blind admiration for the Grecian colonnade seems to obtrude the object of its bigotry into every situation where its inappropriateness becomes most evident and most ridiculous."

17. The great theoretical expression of the need for such an architecture are the essays of Horatio Greenough. See his essay "Amer-

ican Architecture" in *A Memorial of Horatio Greenough* by Henry
T. Tuckerman.

18. An interesting reflection of the current trend of taste away from
Gothic cottages is the review of *A Treatise on the Theory and
Practice of Landscape Gardening,* in the *North American Review,*
Vol. LVI, 1843. This is given to W. B. O. Peabody in the index of
the magazine. On page 10 there is the statement: "The Gothic,
too, so far as cottages are concerned has nearly had its day. The
sight of the well-fed, portly citizen in chivalrous armor would
not be more unsuited to our present habits of thought than the
application of that style to the comfortable villa and the homely
cottage, which always seem uneasy and out of place in such
masquerades."

19. See A. J. Downing, *The Architecture of Country Houses,* p. 262.

20. See Appendix VI, A, No. 12.

21. See the review of *Rural Architecture,* in the *North American
Review,* LVIII (1844), p. 455. The review is anonymous, but the
index of the Magazine gives Arthur Gilman as the author.

22. It is impossible to date accurately the examples discussed. But
the chronological relationship of the most important types is
clear, and it is perfectly easy to relate the others to them, so as
to form a comprehensive picture.

23. See Downing, *op. cit., Architecture of Country Houses,* p. 262.

24. The present form of the windows and perhaps that of the door
may be the result of a later rebuilding.

25. William Livingstone's career is so typical of the first generation of
the bourgeoisie that it is worth repeating here. In 1823 he arrived
at Chelmsford at the age of twenty with only the clothes on his
back. By dint of odd jobs he amassed enough money to purchase
a horse and a cart, and by 1827 he was well enough established to
get the contract for a canal from Sebago Lake to the Sebago
River. He then did more work on rivers in central Massachusetts,
and before 1831 he was back again in Lowell, setting himself up
as a wholesaler, dealing in grain, flour, lumber, coal, lime, brick,
and cement. He bought land, some of which he rented out for
stores, living on the rest. In 1831, with one Sidney Spaulding, he
bought 120 acres of land which was immediately laid out in streets
and sold off shortly. Thereafter, in addition to his trade, he con-
tracted for the building of new mills, and soon went into the manufacture of boxes as well. He chartered and built the Lowell and
Lawrence, and the Salem and Lowell Railroads, fighting the

opposition of the Boston and Lowell Railroad in the House of Representatives. He owned a newspaper, was a director of several local banks, and in his spare time held political offices both in the city and in the state. He died shortly after retiring to his new mansion. See *Illustrated History of Lowell and Vicinity, Massachusetts,* pp. 172 ff.

26. The fact that this was built in imitation of the Livingstone House was much more obvious a few years ago than it is now. Originally the house had a cupola, and before its recent coat of paint, it was almost identical in color effect with its larger neighbor.

27. This in itself is a significant index of the rise of a new point of view towards the history of architecture. As long as revivalism remained in its decorative stage, only details were necessary in books. Once it passed into its archaeological stage, it became necessary to teach builders how to organize the whole of a structure properly.

28. Henry-Russell Hitchcock, Jr., in his *American Architectural Books,* on p. B. 18, refers to a certain William Brown of Lowell. I regret that I have found no mention of this man.

29. The layout of the residential districts of the Federalist seaports derived from English real-estate development practice. See John Summerson's article, "The Great Landowners' Contribution to Architecture," for an early instance.

VIII: FULLY ROMANTIC ARCHITECTURE, PUBLIC BUILDINGS

1. See F. P. Hill, *Lowell Illustrated.*

2. See Charles Cowley, *Illustrated History of Lowell,* pp. 94, 100.

3. See S. A. Drake, *History of Middlesex County, Massachusetts,* II, 112.

4. See E. M. Upjohn, *Richard Upjohn, Architect and Churchman,* Fig. 57.

5. See *Illustrated History of Lowell and Vicinity, Massachusetts,* p. 413.

6. This may hardly seem like a scientific procedure, but the uniformity between the buildings of the various towns is really amazing. Thus all the city halls are more or less alike, being built before the romantic period. All the towns have Episcopal churches put up in the fifties or sixties, of almost identical form. All built their first highschool in the forties, rebuilt in the seventies, again in the nineties, and put up a great addition to the rebuilding in the twentieth century. The motive for building was therefore

not so much necessity as the desire to keep up with the Joneses. It seems fair, accordingly, to assume that in the middle forties Lowell would have reacted as Manchester did to the need for a new city hall.

7. This and the following quotation are from C. E. Potter, *The History of Manchester, formerly Derryfield, New Hampshire.* Well might the author find the town hall peculiar, for certainly it must be one of the earliest civic buildings in the Gothic style, with the exception of Haviland's Eastern States Penitentiary, and the curious early series of masonic halls.

8. Mr. Lewis Mumford points out that the Manchester Town Hall is remarkable because, while most Gothic Revival buildings tended to reduce the window area, this enlarges it to sixteenth-century proportions.

9. See Cowley, *op. cit.,* p. 141.

10. This fact is masked at the present time by the fact that a new courthouse replaces the original façade. Undue emphasis is given therefore to the unimportant broad rear view. This is characteristically slurred over in contemporary drawings.

11. See Cowley, *op. cit.,* p. 153.

12. Gothic was by way of being a traditional style for jails, thanks perhaps to the fame of Haviland's Eastern States Penitentiary. There is also a Gothic jail in Lawrence, Mass.

13. See S. Latham, "The Architectural Significance of the Rice Mills of Charleston, S. C." in *The Architectural Record,* LVI, (1924) p. 179.

14. *Ibid.,* pp. 180, 181.

15. The situation in England is pretty well characterized by W. Fairbairn, in *Mills and Millwork,* Section V, on mill architecture. He says: "At first these mills were square brick buildings without any pretensions to architectural form, as shown in Fig. 248. [Shows a large barnlike mill, perfectly plain.] This description of building with bare walls was for many years the distinguishing features of a cotton mill, and for many years they continued to be of the same form and character throughout all parts of the country. About the year 1827 I made the designs for a new mill of a different class, and persuaded the proprietor to allow some deviation from the monotonous forms then in general use. This alteration had no pretensions to architectural design; it consisted chiefly in forming the corners of the building into pilasters, and a slight cornice round the building . . . It was speedily copied

in all directions with exceedingly slight modifications, but always with effect, as it generally improved the appearance of the buildings, and produced in the minds of the mill owners and the public a higher standard of taste."

16. Nothing in New England can compare to the Harmony Mills at Cohoes, New York, however. This was a complete brick Louvre. For an illustration, see A. S. Bolles, *Industrial History of the United States*, p. 409.

17. See J. B. Clarke and M. D. Clarke, *Manchester; a Brief Record of Its Past and a Picture of Its Present*, p. 200.

18. *Ibid.*, p. 290.

19. *Ibid.*, pp. 279, 290, 298.

20. See W. R. Bagnall, *Contributions to American Economic History.*

21. The general form and location of the Merrimack dressing mill were imitated in an addition built to the Boott mills in 1867. The Merrimack mill has been recently torn down. The Boott mill still survives.

22. Mr. Lewis Mumford maintains that this is too sweeping a statement. Of course such buildings as Richardson's Ames Building on Harrison Avenue in Boston, and Babb, Cook, and Willard's De Vinne Press Building in New York display a splendid sense of form. But I know of no parallel to these in strictly industrial architecture. It is very interesting that there should be such a great aesthetic difference between these metropolitan warehouses and the manufacturing establishments of the factory towns when the aesthetic possibilities were nearly the same in both cases.

IX: CONCLUSION

1. The executives were under the mistaken impression that they could not operate profitably without cheap raw materials. Accordingly, foreseeing a rise in the price of cotton, they sold off their unused cotton, notably to the mills in Lawrence, which realized enormous profits from wartime operations. See Charles Cowley, *Illustrated History of Lowell*, p. 60.

2. See the Hon. Benjamin Butler's oration in the *Proceedings in the City of Lowell at the Semi-Centennial Celebration of the Incorporation of the Town of Lowell, March 1st, 1876*, pp. 41, 42. "Another cause which retarded our prosperity, quite frequently overlooked, came in the years 1848-9, and was the discovery of gold in California. . . . During that fever we lost nearly fifteen hundred young and middle-aged men, who left us for the golden

state, and they were among the best, most energetic and most enterprising of our citizens, or they would not have had the energy to go. . . . In addition to the loss of the labor and enterprise of these men to our growing city, and the diminution of the population by the absence of their families, there was an actual withdrawal from us of some million and a quarter of capital actually here."

3. See Appendix V.

4. See C. D. Long, *Building Cycles and the Theory of Investment.*

5. See J. C. Ayer, *Some of the Usages and Abuses in the Management of Our Manufacturing Corporations.*

6. The selling agents were paid a commission on the basis of total sales, not on the basis of profits, so that it was obviously to their advantage to sell, even at a loss to the company.

7. The attitude of these subordinates is reflected in Cowley, *op. cit.,* p. 61: "During the last forty years, a great variety of mechanical talent has been developed by the corporations of Lowell. But, strange to say, no method has been devised to retain in the service of these companies the talent thus developed by opening to its possessors a wider field of action. Accordingly, when an overseer or employee of any grade, has so mastered his business as to be fitted for the highest positions—so often filled by men wholly ignorant of the manufacturing process—his almost only hope of advancement lies in quitting the company's employ." It was a matter of deliberate policy that the chief executives were "men, wholly ignorant of the manufacturing process." This is explained in W. R. Bagnall, *Contributions to American Economic History.* On pp. 2121 and 2202 Bagnall states: "The Agents or Superintendents of all the corporations . . . were gentlemen selected for their offices, not on account of any mechanical knowledge or experience in manufacturing, their training before their appointments having been wholly mercantile or professional, but for their executive ability, their knowledge of human nature, their ability to control large numbers of operatives and their social standing. The latter consideration was an important one, especially in the early years of the enterprise at Lowell, in the estimate of the principal promoters, as it was their desire to give an elevated tone and character to the community." "It seemed to be the theory of administration of most of the companies at Lowell, that, while a knowledge of all the processes of manufacture might be a valuable qualification for the office of superintendent, there might

result from even a minute knowledge, and an experience in machinery going back to childhood, too great conservatism, narrow prejudice in favor of old machinery and methods and a tenacious clinging to them, which would impede real progress and the introduction of valuable improvements; while a fresh mind, however inexperienced, but with mechanical tastes and aptitude, aided by the suggestions of competent subordinates and overseers, would soon come to an accurate and thorough appreciation of methods, processes, and devices, and would more rapidly and surely advance the mills in the path of improvement and progress."

8. See S. A. Drake, *History of Middlesex County, Massachusetts*, II, 67.

9. See Chapter II, note 13.

10. See Chapter I, note 8.

11. See Chapter VII, note 1.

12. Cowley, *op. cit.*, p. 200, tells how Prince Jerome Napoleon visited Lowell in 1861, on the recommendation of Chevalier. "More than a quarter of a century had elapsed since Chevalier's visit; the New England girls on whom he then gazed so admiringly had passed away; and their places were now filled by a motley crowd of Americans, English, Scotch, Irish, Dutch, and French Canadians, who were hardly likely to arouse that exquisite poetic sentiment which Chevalier felt for the factory girls of 1834." Chevalier's opinions are quoted at length above, Chapter II, note 31.

13. This is not overstatement. Dickens visited Lowell and wrote a chapter about it in his book on America. Chevalier was sent there on a special mission by Louis Philippe. The London *Times* and the *Edinburgh Review* reviewed the *Lowell Offering*, and a copy of it was carried into the French Chamber of Deputies as an argument in favor of Industrialism. As for the histrionic behavior of people in Lowell, one need only recall the hullabaloo in Lowell when Senator Clemens made the allegation in the Senate that "the Southern slaves were better off than the northern operatives." See H. J. H. Robinson, *Loom and Spindle*, p. 193. This is but one instance out of many which might be cited.

14. The fundamental reason for these changes was the decline in the quality of the men who made up the citizenry. There can be no question that the first residents of Lowell were a remarkable group of people. Even contemporaries recognized this fact; see

the letter from the Hon. Josiah G. Abbott, published in the *Semi-Centennial Proceedings,* p. 83: "I think all who lived there at that time (1834) and for the next twenty years will agree with me in saying that no city of its size, ever contained a more remarkable people, or a pleasanter or more cultivated city. I doubt if any place of as large a population, ever had within its borders a larger number of very able men, who would be marked and remarkable in any community. The reason of it was, I think, that for some years our state had not been especially progressive or prosperous, but on the contrary, quiet and even languishing. Our lands, for agriculture, could not compete with the abundant fertility of the West. Our commerce had been paralyzed by the war with England, and was slow in recovering. Lowell was the real beginning of a new epoch for our state. Here was an opening for men of energy, power and activity, who have been waiting for an opportunity—and it was improved."

After the Civil War the inhabitants of Lowell were not so distinguished. The citizens who attained prominence were men like James Cook Ayer and Benjamin Butler, men who were brought up in the ante-bellum city. It is not until our own day that Lowell has again produced any people of comparable eminence.

15. Of course the most obvious reason for the break in architectural continuity is the architectural revolution that took place everywhere in America between 1857 and 1865. Lowell reflects this change very vividly. Hints of the coming High Victorian style are always hard to find in the buildings of the fifties. Examples are even rarer in the architecture of the textile cities of central New England than in most places. The most striking instance that I have discovered is a polychromed Gothic tower added to the Manchester Mills in Manchester, New Hampshire, in 1850.

16. See Chapter VII, note 2.

17. See Appendix IV.

18. The best discussion of the problem of southern competition and the New England textile industry is in the first chapter of E. G. Keith, *The Financial History of Two Textile Cities*; a study of the effects of industrial growth and decline upon the financial policies and practices of Lowell and Fall River, Massachusetts. On p. 29 Keith makes the statement: "Broadus Mitchell has estimated that a southern mill, running 55 hours a week, has a manufacturing cost nearly 17 per cent less than that of a Massachusetts mill running 48 hours."

19. This process was already in full swing in the 90's. Robinson, *op. cit.,* p. 209, remarks: "Nor are the houses kept clean and in repair as they used to be. In Lowell, when I last walked among the 'blocks' where I lived as a child, I found them in a most dilapidated condition—houses going to decay, broken sidewalks, and filthy streets; and contrasting their appearance with that of the 'Corporation' as I remember it, I felt as if I were revisiting the ruins of an industry once clean and prosperous." Quoted by permission of the publisher, Thomas Y. Crowell and Co., New York.

20. It cannot be denied that at other times and in other places the results would have been far different. The collapse of the Fugger family in the sixteenth century did not entail the destruction of the Fuggerei of Augsburg.

21. The framework proposed represented essentially the planning practices of the great baroque parks and fiat settlements, modified in matters of design by the new romantic classicism. See S. Giedion, *Spätbarocker und romantischer Klassizismus,* Part III, section II, "Raumfolge der Aussenräume."

22. The most useful source for this material is Werner Hegemann and Elbert Peets, *The American Vitruvius: an Architect's Handbook of Civic Art.* Chapter VII is devoted to Washington, and on p. 248 appears a reproduction of the plan of Detroit. The Paterson problem is complicated. The best source here is J. S. Davis, *Essays in the Earlier History of American Corporations,* Essay III. The "S.U.M.": The First New Jersey Business Corporation. Paterson, N. J., was founded as an industrial town in 1791 by the Society for the Establishment of Useful Manufactures. Hamilton recommended Major L'Enfant to the directors, and he was hired apparently as a sort of general manager of all the building enterprises. It was expected that he would plan the town which was projected, and he seems to have been interested in doing so. But there is some doubt whether he actually ever drew a plan. Certainly contemporary sources (quoted in Davis) refer to his having done so. But so far as I know the plan does not exist, moreover "in his large correspondence he denied ever having made such plans and no such requirement was in his contract." See C. E. Dietz, *A History of Paterson and Passaic County* [p. 12].

23. The immediate results were wholly negative, chaotic. Yet in architecture just this chaos permitted, as no plan could, the evolution of building types completely adapted to the material desiderata

of modern life. And it is not the traditional forms of buildings that are the essential ingredients of our cities today, but these newer types—department stores, office buildings, apartment houses, school complexes, residential suburbs, public parks, all of them creations of the nineteenth century.

24. Furthermore, the whole conception, as applied to industrial towns, was "in the air" throughout the nineteenth century, as contemporary European utopias prove. It was, moreover, peculiarly sympathetic to New England at this time, witness the colonies founded by the Transcendentalists, etc.

25. The most notable case was that quadrant of land between the Lawrence Company and the Western Canal, which remained undeveloped even as late as 1868.

26. See above, p. 17.

27. At Lowell in 1826 almost the whole population of 2,500 were employees of the corporations, see above Chapter V, note 17. According to Josiah Curtis, "Hygiene in Lowell," II, 511, the population in 1849 was about 33,000, of whom half were directly connected with manufacturing, and four fifths of these (40 percent of the total), with the great corporations. According to M. T. Parker, *Lowell, a Study of Industrial Development*, pp. 2 and 33, the number of persons engaged in manufacturing in Lowell in 1938 was something over 12,000, of whom only 2,250 were employed by what remained of the "great corporations" (that is, the great corporations employed some 250 less people in 1938 than they had in 1826, when the town was founded). Meanwhile the population dependent on these workers was just over 100,000 in 1940, *Hotel Red Book,* 1941, p. 343. Lowell therefore provides an excellent example of the point under discussion. Parker, *op. cit.,* p. 173, shows that the maximum number of persons employed in the cotton industry in Lowell was 15,074 in 1890. The population of the city continued to increase long after this date. In 1895 it was 84,367 (*ibid.,* p. 89) and in 1920 it rose to 112,759. Only then did it decline. The number of people engaged in cotton manufacturing has decreased by 97½ percent since the peak. The population has decreased only 12 percent since its peak. Its resiliency cannot be attributed to the growth of new industries in Lowell, except to a very slight extent. What it really reflects is the inertia of population in a large center.

28. There is a third type of housing project that may best be called the metropolitan type. In some ways this is transitional between

the other two, in others it is unique. The outstanding examples of this type are in London. This housing differs from the princely type in two respects. It was not designed for courtiers and executed under the eye of an absolute monarch. It was planned for members of a ruling oligarchy. It was not built as a state enterprise; rather it was put up by private persons as a speculation. Socially considered, this housing did not differ substantially from the princely type. In both cases what was achieved was a thin crust of dwellings masking a chaos—more or less crowded—of slums. In England, "The formation of an aristocratic nucleus was conceived to be the cardinal gambit in the speculative game. Once your aristocrats were installed in the square, your social climbers and professional men flocked to the neighboring streets; your shopkeepers to whatever markets and back lanes you cared to provide." (John Summerson, "The Great Landowners' Contribution to Architecture," p. 435, quoted by permission of the publisher.) Thomas Sharp in *English Panorama*, pp. 55 ff., has well described the class consciousness of these English housing developments. Elsewhere he states that "while the English town was not in any sense the instrument of a personal absolutism, many of its chief benefits were enjoyed only by one powerful section of the community." (Sharp, *Town Planning*, p. 22. Quoted by permission of Penguin Books.) Architecturally considered, dwelling for dwelling, this housing was closer to the paternal type. "The English town was built for no other purpose than to house free citizens as comfortably and pleasantly as was possible according to the standards of the time, and with as much outward order and seemliness as could be achieved without the exercise of tyrannical compulsion." *Ibid.*, p. 18. Quoted by permission of the publisher, Penguin Books, Harmondsworth, England. It was thus in the vernacular architecture. The housing has the virtues and defects of the paternal type. Building in the accepted way, without thought of display, in the best cases "produced a district which for its human treatment remains unsurpassed to this day." (S. Giedion, *Space, Time and Architecture, the Growth of a New Tradition*, p. 451.) On the other hand the building was merely housing, and lacked the integration with the community as a whole which characterized the best continental examples.

29. In an article, "Low-Cost Housing, the New England Tradition," published in the *New England Quarterly*, Vol. XIV, No. 1, March, 1941, p. 21, I made the statement. "Incidentally, of course, the

houses sheltered the retainers of the court. But the buildings were not planned so as to be convenient places to live, any more than the park was laid out so as to be a convenient place to grow vegetables." This is putting the matter much too strongly, and I am greatly obliged to Professor Henry-Russell Hitchcock, Jr., for calling my attention to this inaccuracy. Actually the houses were suitable places in which to live, in terms of a life characterized by innumerable servants. But they were not convenient, in our sense, even then. The living quarters and working conditions of the servants were abominable. Nor did any architect think of planning a house, even their part of a house, from their point of view. This is proved by the fact that John Wood feels that he has to apologize for "feeling as the cottager himself" when designing a cottage. See above, Chapter IV, note 40, p. 185.

30. The earliest instance I know is the Fuggerei of Augsburg, erected in 1519. This consists of a special colony of more than fifty cottages with its own church and water supply surrounded by a wall. In the article in the *New England Quarterly* referred to in note 29 I have suggested that such paternalistic housing was accepted as a more or less normal responsibility of aristocrats, at least under certain conditions, and that the conception of housing as a philanthropy is a Victorian notion. Apparently this is not entirely true; there was always a philanthropic aspect to such developments. This is proved in the case of the Fuggerei by the inscription over the entrance. "Ulrich, George and Jacob Fugger of Augsburg, blood brothers, being firmly convinced that they were born for the good of the city, and that for their great property they have to thank chiefly an all-powerful and benevolent God, have out of piety and as an example of special generosity founded, given, and dedicated 106 dwellings, both buildings and furnishings, to those of their fellow citizens who live righteously, but are beset by poverty." (J. Strieder, *Jacob Fugger the Rich, Merchant and Banker of Augsburg, 1459-1525*, p. 176. Quoted by permission of the Adelphi Company.) One wonders if possibly such an urban development did not represent an evolution of the late medieval "hospital" and similar charitable foundations, rather than an outgrowth of the feudal system.

31. The greatest series of these housing developments is in England, see Sharp, *English Panorama*, pp. 51 ff. Most of the English developments represented rural "slum-clearance." In a few cases whole villages were built, or rebuilt. Significantly, in the examples

he cites, the motives for complete rebuilding were anything but philanthropic. The old villages were located too close to the manor house. In either event the houses erected were simple and traditional in style.

APPENDIX I: ECONOMIC BACKGROUND

1. See R. M. Tryon, *Household Manufactures in the United States, 1640-1860,* p. 45.
2. *Ibid.,* p. 269.
3. *Ibid.,* pp. 14, 15.
4. *Ibid.,* p. 17, quoted by permission of the publishers, University of Chicago Press.
5. G. L. Beer, *The Commercial Policy of England toward the American Colonies,* p. 75.
6. Tryon, *op. cit.,* p. 36.
7. *Ibid.,* p. 16.
8. *Ibid.,* p. 43.
9. *Ibid.,* p. 89.
10. *Ibid.,* p. 55.
11. *Ibid.,* p. 5.
12. *Ibid.,* p. 124.
13. *Ibid.,* p. 127.
14. *Ibid.,* p. 142.
15. *Ibid.,* p. 132.
16. *Ibid.,* p. 143.

APPENDIX III: THE SITE OF LOWELL

1. See H. A. Miles, *Lowell, as It Was and as It Is,* p. 193.
2. See H. J. H. Robinson, *Loom and Spindle or Life among the Early Mill Girls,* p. 66. Quoted by permission of the Thomas Y. Crowell Company.
3. See C. F. Ware, *The Early New England Cotton Manufacture,* p. 217. Quoted by permission of Houghton Mifflin.
4. Robinson, *op. cit.,* p. 77, quoted by permission of the Thomas Y. Crowell Company.
5. C. F. Ware, *op. cit.,* p. 214.
6. Miles, *op. cit.,* p. 112.
7. *Ibid.,* p. 113.
8. C. F. Ware, *op. cit.,* p. 241.

9. See *The Lowell Offering and Magazine,* written and edited by factory operatives, V, 188.

10. Miles, *op. cit.,* p. 113.

11. *Ibid.,* pp. 114-15.

12. C. F. Ware, *op. cit.,* p. 249.

13. *Ibid.,* p. 250. Quoted by permission of the publishers, Houghton Mifflin Company.

14. Robinson, *op. cit.*

15. *Proceedings in the City of Lowell at the semi-centennial celebration of the incorporation of the town of Lowell, March 1, 1876,* p. 129.

16. Robinson, *op. cit.,* p. 91, quoted by permission of the Thomas Y. Crowell Company.

17. *Ibid.,* p. 91, quoted by permission of the Thomas Y. Crowell Company.

18. *Ibid.,* p. 105, quoted by permission of the Thomas Y. Crowell Company. Miles, *op. cit.,* p. 73.

19. See Norman Ware, *The Industrial Worker: 1840-1860,* p. 120, quoted by permission of Houghton Mifflin.

20. See Lucy Larcom, *A New England Girlhood, Outlined from Memory,* p. 209.

21. *Ibid.,* p. 222. Quoted by permission of Houghton Mifflin.

22. Robinson, *op. cit.,* pp. 46, 91 ff.

23. *Ibid.,* p. 92.

24. *Ibid.,* p. 93. Quoted by permission of the Thomas Y. Crowell Company.

25. Miles, *op. cit.,* p. 194.

26. Larcom, *op. cit.,* p. 223. Quoted by permission of Houghton Mifflin.

27. Robinson, *op. cit.,* Chapters VII, VIII.

28. Michel Chevalier, *Lettres sur l'Amerique du Nord,* note 33, p. 394.

29. Larcom, *op. cit.,* p. 163.

30. Whittier, "The City of a Day," *Prose Works,* II, 294.

31. Robinson, *op. cit.,* p. 13.

32. Larcom, *op. cit.,* p. 252.

33. *Ibid.,* p. 165, quoted by permission of Houghton Mifflin.

34. Robinson, *op. cit.,* p. 17, footnote.

35. Quoted in N. Ware, *op. cit.,* p. xiv.

36. *Ibid.,* p. 102, quoted from Benjamin F. Butler, *Butler's Book, Autobiography and Personal Reminiscences,* p. 95.

37. *Ibid.,* p. 107.

38. Miles, *op. cit.*, pp. 133 ff.

39. *Ibid.*, pp. 131 ff.

40. Robinson, *op. cit.*, pp. 57, 72.

41. *Ibid.*, p. 72.

42. *Ibid.*, p. 72, quoted by permission of the Thomas Y. Crowell Company.

43. Larcom, *op. cit.*, p. 233, quoted by permission of Houghton Mifflin.

44. Robinson, *op. cit.*, p. 71, quoted by permission of the Thomas Y. Crowell Company.

45. *Ibid.*, pp. 71 ff., quoted by permission of the Thomas Y. Crowell Company.

46. *Ibid.*, p. 89.

47. Larcom, *op. cit.*, p. 152.

48. John Swinton, *A Model Factory in a Model City*, p. 11. Quoted by permission of the American Waltham Watch Company.

49. Miles, *op. cit.*, p. 67.

50. *Ibid.*, p. 68.

51. Robinson, *op. cit.*, p. 91.

BIBLIOGRAPHY

As this book touches on engineering, economics, sociology, and local history, the number of books that one might legitimately have read in the preparation of it is extremely large. Fortunately, however, most of that material has been dealt with in secondary sources. As this is primarily a study of nineteenth-century architecture, the author, when dealing with non-architectural material, relied principally upon those secondary sources, and read only such of the primary sources as seemed necessary and were easily available. There is no need to include in this bibliography anything except those books which the author found useful. Comprehensive bibliographies of other phases of the subject can be found elsewhere. For engineering, see C. J. N. Woodbury, *Bibliography of the Cotton Manufacture;* for economics see Caroline F. Ware, *The Early New England Cotton Manufacture,* and E. G. Keith, *The Financial History of the Textile Cities;* for living conditions and working conditions, see Norman R. Ware, *The Industrial Worker;* for the history of the city, see F. W. Coburn, *History of Lowell and Its People.* There is so little written material on American nineteenth-century architecture that I have not included here any of the general books on the subject. The main source of the information on the nineteenth-century architectural background has been the courses, conversations, and correspondence I have had with Professors Hitchcock of Wesleyan, Talbot Hamlin of Columbia, Dmitri Tselos of New York University, and with Mr. Lewis Mumford.

Addison, Agnes. Early American Gothic, in *Romanticism in America,* ed. by George Boas, Baltimore, Johns Hopkins Press, 1940.

Appleton, Nathan. Introduction of the Power Loom and Origin of Lowell. Lowell, Printed for the Proprietors of the Locks and Canals on Merrimack River, H. Penhallow, 1858.

Atkinson, E. Report on English Cotton Mills and Methods. Transactions of the New England Cotton Manufacturers' Association, Oct. 31, 1863.

Ayer, James Cook. Some of the Usages and Abuses in the Management of Our Manufacturing Generations. Lowell, C. M. Langley, 1863.

Bagnall, William R. Contributions to American Economic History: Sketches of the Manufacturing Establishments in New York City and of Textile Establishments in the Eastern States. Ed. by Victor S. Clark. Manuscript in the Baker Library School of Business Administration, Harvard University.

——— Samuel Slater and the Early Development of the Cotton Manufacture of the United States. Middletown, Conn., 1890.

Baird, R. H. The American Cotton Spinner, Boston, Phillips, Sampson & Co., 1856.

Barnard, Henry. School Architecture or Contributions to the Improvement of School Houses in the United States. New York, A. S. Barnes, 1849.

Batchelder, Samuel. Introduction and Early Progress of the Cotton Manufacture in The United States. Boston, 1836.

Bayles, J. Lowell, Past, Present and Prospective. Lowell, Citizen Newspaper Company, 1891.

Beer, G. L. The Commercial Policy of England toward the American Colonies. New York, Columbia University Press, 1893. "Columbia University Studies in History, Economics, and Public Law," Vol. VII, No. 2.

Behrendt, Walter Curt. Modern Building, Its Nature, Problems, and Forms. New York, Harcourt, Brace and Company, 1937.

Bishop, J. Leander. A History of American Manufactures. Philadelphia, Edw. Young & Company, 1861.

Bolles, A. S. Industrial History of the United States from the Earliest Settlement to the Present Times, Being a Complete Survey of American Industries, Embracing Agriculture, etc. Norwich, Conn., Henry Bill Publishing Co., 1889.

Browne, G. W. The Amoskeag Manufacturing Company. Printed and Bound in the Mills of the Amoskeag Manufacturing Company, Manchester, N. H., 1915.

Buckingham, J. S. National Evils and Practical Remedies. London, 1849.

Burgy, J. H. The New England Cotton Textile Industry. Baltimore, 1932.

Byrne, W. History of the Catholic Church in the New England States. Boston, Hurd & Everts Co., 1899.

Cary, T. G. Profits on the Manufactures at Lowell. Boston, 1845.

Cawley, James. Historic New Jersey in Pictures. Princeton, Princeton University Press, 1939.

Chambré, A. St. John. Historical Sermon, March 15, 1853. Boston, Weeks, Jordan and Co., 1859.

Chevalier, Michel. Lettres sur l'Amerique du Nord. 3d ed. Paris, Librairie de Charles Gosselin et Cie., 1837.

———— Society, Manners, and Politics in the United States: Being a Series of Letters on North America. Tr. from the 3d Paris ed. Boston, Weeks, Jordan and Company, 1839.

Chronicle of Textile Machinery, 1824-1924, A. Issued to Commemorate the One Hundredth Anniversary of the Saco-Lowell Shops. Boston, Privately Printed, Saco-Lowell Shops, 1924.

Clarke, John B. Manchester: a Brief Record of Its Past and a Picture of Its Present. Written by Maurice G. Clarke under the direction of John B. Clarke. Manchester, John B. Clarke, 1875.

Coburn, Frederick W. History of Lowell and Its People. New York, Lewis Historical Publishing Company, 1920.

Coolidge, John. "American Gothic Churches, 1823-1893." Harvard University Honors Thesis, 1935. Copies in Harvard University Library and in Avery Library, Columbia University.

———— "Low-Cost Housing, the New England Tradition," in the *New England Quarterly*, XIV (Spring, 1941).

Copeland, Melvin Thomas. The Cotton Manufacturing Industry of the United States. Cambridge, Harvard University, 1912.

Cowley, Charles. Illustrated History of Lowell. Revised ed. Boston, Lee & Shepard, 1868.

Curtis, Josiah. "Public Hygiene of Massachusetts." Part of the "First Report of the Committee on Public Hygiene of the American Medical Association," Published in *Transactions of the American Medical Association*, Vol. II. Philadelphia, Printed for the Association, 1849.

Davis, Joseph Stancliffe. Essays in the Earlier History of American Corporations. Cambridge, Harvard University Press, 1917.

Dickens, Charles. American Notes for General Circulation. Boston, Ticknor and Fields, 1867.

Dietz, Charles E. A History of Paterson and Passaic County. Printed in the Paterson Public Schools by the Printing Classes, n. d.

Downing, Andrew Jackson. The Architecture of Country Houses. New York, D. Appleton, 1851.

Drake, Samuel Adams. History of Middlesex County, Massachusetts. Boston, Estes & Lauriat, 1880.

Edson, Theodore. An Address Delivered at the Opening of the Colburn Grammar School, Dec. 13, 1848. Lowell, Jos. Atkinson, 1849.

—— Historical Discourse on the Occasion of the Fiftieth Anniversary of the 1st Introduction of Stated Public Working, etc. Lowell, Marden and Rowell, 1874.

Fairbairn, William T. Treatise on Mills and Millwork, Part II. London, Longmans, Green, 1863.

Federal Writers Project. Rhode Island: a Guide to the Smallest State. Boston, Houghton Mifflin Company, 1937.

Fergusson, James. History of the Modern Styles of Architecture. 2d ed. London, John Murray, 1873.

Field, Edward. State of Rhode Island and Providence Plantations at the End of the Century: a History. Boston and Syracuse, Mason Publishing Company, 1902.

Forbes, A., and J. W. Greene. The Rich Men of Massachusetts. Boston, W. V. Spencer, 1851.

Gandy, J. Designs for Cottages. London, John Harding, 1805.

Giedion, S. Space, Time, and Architecture. Cambridge, Harvard University Press, 1941.

—— Spätbarocker und romantischer Klassisismus. München, F. Bruckmann, 1922.

Gilman, A. Review of *Rural Architecture* in the *North American Review*, LVIII (Boston, Otis Broaders, 1844).

Goodale, A. M. Some Points in the History of the Boston Manufacturing Company. Papers Read before the Citizens' Club of Waltham, Season of 1891-92. Waltham, Mass., 1891.

Greene, Stephen. Modifications in Mill Design Resulting from Changes in Motive Power, *Transactions of the New England Cotton Manufacturers' Association*, No. 65, Oct. 27, 1897. Waltham, Mass., Press of E. L. Barry, 1898.

Gulliver, Arthur H. Factory Tenements, *Transactions of the New England Cotton Manufacturers' Association*, No. 74, Ap. 22-23, 1903. Waltham, Mass., Press of E. L. Barry, 1903.

Hall, Basil. Travels in North America in the Years 1827-8. Philadelphia, Corey, Lee & Corey, 1829.

Hegemann, Werner, and Elbert Peets. The American Vitruvius: an Architect's Handbook of Civic Art. New York, Architectural Book Publishing Company, 1922.

Hill, Frank P. Lowell Illustrated: a Chronological Record of Events and Historical Sketches of the Large Manufacturing Corporations. Comp. and ed. by Frank P. Hill. Lowell, Mass., 1884.

Hitchcock, Henry-Russell, Jr. American Architectural Books: a List of Books, Portfolios, and Pamphlets Published in America before 1895. Middletown, Connecticut, 1938-39.

—— The Architecture of H. H. Richardson and His Times. New York, Museum of Modern Art, 1936.

—— Rhode Island Architecture. Providence, Rhode Island Museum Press, 1939.

Howe, O. H. "Early Town Planning, New England," *American Architect*, Oct. 13, 1920.

Hunt, G. W. ed. Historical Sketch of the First Baptist Church, Lowell, Mass. Lowell, Courier-Citizen Co., 1926.

Hurd, Richard. Principles of City Land Values. New York, Record and Guide, 1903.

"Justitia." Strictures on Montgomery on the Cotton Manufactures of Great Britain and America; also a Practical Comparison of the Cost of Steam and Water Power in America. By the Author, Newburyport, Morse & Brewster, 1841.

Keir, M. Industries of America—Manufacturing. New York, Ronald Press Co., 1928.

Keith, E. G. The Financial History of Two Textile Cities: a Study of the Effects of Industrial Growth and Decline upon the Financial Policies and Practices of Lowell and Fall River, Massachusetts. Thesis, Ph. D., Harvard University, 1937. Typewritten copy in the Harvard University Library.

Kenngott, George F. The Record of a City: a Social Survey of Lowell, Massachusetts. New York, the Macmillan Company, 1912.

Larcom, Lucy. A New England Girlhood, Outlined from Memory. Boston, Houghton & Mifflin, 1889.

Latham, S. "The Architectural Significance of the Rice Mills of Charleston, S. C.," *Architectural Record*, LVI (1924).

Long, Clarence D. Building Cycles and the Theory of Investment. Princeton, Princeton University Press, 1940.

Lowell, Mass. Annual Reports of the Receipts and Expenditures of the City of Lowell, 1838, et seq.

────── Annual Reports of the School Committee.

────── Lowell Board of Trade. City of Lowell, Massachusetts, Its Manufacturing Interests and Business Advantages. Lowell, 1902.

────── Contributions of the Old Residents' Historical Association, 1879-1904. Lowell, Stone, Bacheller & Livingstone, Vols. 1-6.

────── Contributions of the Lowell Historical Society. Lowell, Butterfield Printing Company, Vols. 1-2, 1913-1926.

────── Exercises at the 75th Anniversary of the Incorporation of the Town. Lowell, Courier-Citizen, 1901.

────── Illustrated History of Lowell and Vicinity. Lowell, Courier-Citizen, 1897.

────── Trades and Labor Council, Lowell, Mass. Lowell, a City of Spindles. Lowell, Lawler & Co., 1900.

────── The Lowell Book. Edited by a Committee from the First Unitarian Church. Boston, Geo. H. Ellis, Printer, 1899.

────── Proceedings in the City of Lowell. At the semi-centennial celebration of the incorporation of the town of Lowell, March 1, 1876. Lowell, H. Penhallow, 1876.

────── Record of Resolutions with Regard to Streets, 1840, et seq. Manuscript in the City Engineer's Office at Lowell, transcript of the proceedings of the City Council.

The Lowell Offering, written exclusively by females employed in the mills. Lowell, Powers & Bagley, Vols. 1-5 (1840-45).

Lynd, Robert S., and Helen M. Middletown: a Study in American Culture. New York, Harcourt, Brace & Company, 1929.

────── Middletown in Transition: a Study in Cultural Conflicts. New York, Harcourt, Brace & Company, 1937.

McKenzie, R. D. The Metropolitan Community. McGraw-Hill Book Company, New York, 1933. Monograph prepared under the Direction of the President's Research Committee on Social Trends.

Main, Charles T. Notes on Mill Construction, *Proceedings of the New England Cotton Manufacturers Association*, Nos. 41-45, 1868-88.

Meserve, H. G. Lowell: an Industrial Dream Come True. Boston, National Association of Cotton Manufacturers, 1923.

Miles, H. A. Lowell, as It Was, and as It Is. Lowell, Powers & Bagley, and N. L. Dayton, 1845.

Montgomery, James. A Practical Detail of the Cotton Manufacture of the United States of America and the State of the Cotton Manufacture of That Country Contrasted and Compared with That of Great Britain, with Comparative Estimates of the Cost of Manufacturing in Both Countries. Glasgow, John Niven, 1840.

Mumford, Lewis. The Culture of Cities. New York, Harcourt, Brace & Company, 1938.

Nelson, Charles A. Waltham Past and Present, and Its Industries. Cambridge, Thomas Lewis, 1879.

O'Dwyer, George. The Irish Catholic Genesis of Lowell. Rev. ed. Lowell, Mass., printed by Sullivan Brothers, 1920.

Owen, Robert. The Life of Robert Owen by Himself. London, G. Bell, 1920.

—— New View of Society. London, 1818.

Parker, Margaret Terrell. Lowell: a Study of Industrial Development. New York, the Macmillan Company, 1940.

Peabody, W. B. O. Review of *A Treatise on the Theory and Practice of Landscape Gardening*, in *North American Review*, LVI (1843).

Pease, John C., and John M. Niles. Gazetteer of the States of Connecticut and Rhode Island, Written with Care and Impartiality from Original and Authentic Materials. Hartford, Printed and Published by Wm. S. Marsh, 1819.

Place, Charles A. Charles Bulfinch, Architect and Citizen. Boston, Houghton Mifflin Company, 1925.

—— "From Meeting-House to Church in New England," in *Old-Time New England*, 1922-23.

Potter, Chandler E. The History of Manchester, formerly Derryfield, New Hampshire. Manchester, C. E. Potter, 1856.

Proceedings . . . at the semi-centennial celebration, etc. *See* Lowell, Proceedings, etc.

Ranlett, W. H. The Architect: a Series of Original Designs for Domestic and Ornamental Villas Connected with Landscape Gardening, Adapted to the United States. New York, William H. Graham, 1847-49.

Rasmussen, Steen E. London, the Unique City. New York, the Macmillan Company, 1937.

Richards, J. M. An Introduction to Modern Architecture. Harmondsworth, Penguin Books, Ltd., 1940.

Robinson, Harriet Jane Hanson. Early Factory Labor in New England. (From the Fourteenth Annual Report of the Mass. Bureau of Statistics of Labor, 1883.) Boston, Wright & Porter Printing Co., 1889.

———— Loom and Spindle; or, Life among the Early Mill Girls. New York, Thomas Y. Crowell & Company [1898].

Scoresby, W. American Factories and Their Female Operatives. London, Longmans, Green, 1845.

Sharp, Thomas. English Panorama. London, J. M. Dent & Sons, 1938.

———— Town Planning. Harmondsworth, Penguin Books, Ltd., 1940.

Shaw, E. The Modern Architect. Boston, Dayton & Wentworth, 1855.

Shlakman, V. Economic History of a Factory Town, Chicopee, Mass. "Smith College Studies in History," Vol. XX, Nos. 1-4, Oct. 1934-July 1935. Northampton, Mass., Department of History, Smith College.

Staub, H. H. & Cie. Cité Ouvrière de H. M. Staub & Cie, près Cisslingen. Stuttgart, Bode, 1867.

Strieder, J. Jacob Fugger the Rich, Merchant and Banker of Augsburg, 1459-1525. Tr. by M. L. Harsough and ed. by N. S. B. Gras. New York, the Adelphi Company, 1931.

Summerson, John. "The Great Landowners' Contribution to Architecture," in the Journal of the Royal Institute of British Architects, Vol. XLVI, 3d series (1939).

Swinton, John. A Model Factory in a Model City: a Social Study, 1887. Published by the American Waltham Watch Co., Jan., 1888.

Tryon, Rollin Milton. Household Manufacture in the United States, 1640-1860. Chicago, University of Chicago Press, 1917.

Tuckerman, Henry T. A Memorial of Horatio Greenough. New York, G. P. Putnam, 1853.

Upjohn, Everard M. Richard Upjohn, Architect and Churchman. New York, Columbia University Press, 1939.

Vagts, Alfred. "The German Army of the Second Reich as a Cultural

Institution," in *The Cultural Approach to History*, C. F. Ware, ed. New York, Columbia University Press, 1940.

Ware, Caroline F. The Early New England Cotton Manufacture. Boston, Houghton Mifflin Company, 1931.

Ware, Norman R. The Industrial Worker, 1840-1860: the Reaction of American Industrial Society to the Advance of the Industrial Revolution. Boston, Houghton Mifflin Company, 1924.

Waters, W. History of Chelmsford, Massachusetts. Lowell, printed for the town by the Courier-Citizen Company, 1917.

Webber, S. Manual of Power for Machines, Shafts and Belts, with the History of Cotton Manufacture in the United States. New York, D. Appleton and Company, 1879.

Weber, A. F. The Growth of Cities in the Nineteenth Century: a Study in Statistics. Submitted in partial fulfillment of the requirements for the degree of Doctor of Philosophy in the Faculty of Political Science, Columbia University. New York, 1899.

White, G. S. Memoir of Samuel Slater. Philadelphia, 1836.

Whittier, John Greenleaf. The Prose Works of John Greenleaf Whittier, Vol. II. Sketches contributed to *The Stranger in Lowell*, 1843. Boston, Houghton Mifflin Company, 1866.

Wolfe, A. B. The Lodging House Problem in Boston. Boston and New York, Houghton Mifflin Company, 1906. "Harvard Economic Studies," No. II.

Wood, John. A Series of Plans for Cottages or Habitations of the Labourer Either in Husbandry or the Mechanic Arts. London, J. Taylor, 1806. (There was an earlier edition.)

Woodbury, C. J. H. Bibliography of the Cotton Manufacture. Waltham, E. L. Barry, 1909.

CATALOGUE OF THE
ILLUSTRATIONS

Figures 4, 6, 9, 10, 11, 13-16, 18-20, 22-26, 28, 29, 32, 35-37, 39, 41, 43-45, 50-52, 54-64, 66-73, and 78-88 are from photographs taken by Margaret Noyes of Intervale, New Hampshire. Figure 1, portions of the title page, Figures 3, 5, 42, 89, and 90 are from drawings made by Mr. Edward Moulthrop of Princeton, New Jersey. The frontispiece is from a photograph published by permission of the New York Public Library, and Figure 76 is from a photostat of an illustration published in the *Illustrated History of Lowell and Vicinity, Massachusetts*, reproduced by permission of the publishers, the Courier-Citizen Company of Lowell. Figures 12, 17, 21, 27, 38, 74, 75, 77, 91, and 92 are from photographs taken by the author. The remaining figures are reproductions of illustrations previously published in books or on the borders of maps, etc.

Wherever possible the exact date of buildings is given. In these instances the source of the date will be found at the appropriate place in the footnotes. When this is not possible an approximate date is given. In many cases these approximate dates are based upon the presence or absence of the building in question on one of several maps. There are many maps of Lowell, some of them listed in Appendix VI, A. Not all of these maps are accessible, and not all of those which can be studied are trustworthy. In dating a building the author has therefore used only Maps 3, 7, 8, 14, and 15. When it is not possible to date a building on the evidence of the maps, then the date of the building is guessed, on the basis of its style.

FRONTISPIECE

Lowell, ca. 1833, as Seen from across the Merrimack. From a photograph of a print entitled "Lowell, from the House of Elisha Fuller, esq., Dracut, by E. A. Farrar, Pendleton Lithograph, entered 1834." I am obliged to the New York Public Library for permission to publish a reproduction of the copy of this lithograph now in the Phelps Stokes Collection.

On the left is seen the mouth of the Concord River, and the Pawtucket Canal leading into it. The large mill with a cupola on the extreme left belongs to the Middlesex Company. Just to the right are five mills on the further bank of the Pawtucket Canal, the mills of the Hamilton and Appleton Companies. Their boarding houses appear as a regular series of roofs, directly over the mouth of the Concord. In front of these mills is a large plot of land stretching down to the Merrimack River. Here, very soon the Boott and Massachusetts Mills were to be built. The large L-shaped structure, with a cupola, is Wyman's exchange, Lowell's first big business block. Just to the right in the background may be seen the row of houses built for the employees of the Machine Shop. The tower of St. Anne's rises over the bridge across the Merrimack. Beside it, the line of the Merrimack Canal is clearly visible. The canal is fringed by a row of elms, which partly screen Boott's string of boarding houses. Just to the right of these are the five mills of the Merrimack Company, the cupola of the central mill rising just to the left of a tree in the foreground. Beyond the last mill, a single brick block with a projecting stair tower is all that is visible of the plant of the Suffolk Company. Beyond it there are four boarding houses (rising above two pyramidal industrial buildings) belonging to the Lawrence Company. Compare with Figure 19. Finally, on the extreme right, there are the four Lawrence Mills.

TITLE PAGE

Adapted by Edward Moulthrop from the title page of the *New England Offering*, Harriet Farley, Editor and Publisher, Published at Lowell, 23 Central Street, 1849.

FIGURES

1. *Site of Lowell, ca. 1820, Later Developments Shown.* Drawn by Edward Moulthrop, the topographical outlines being taken from a reproduction of Map 15 (see Appendix VI, A), the roads from a photostat of Map 2, to which certain information had been added by the Locks and Canals Company, and the indications of property from a photostat of Map 4.

    The map shows East Chelmsford as it existed before the arrival of the Merrimack Manufacturing Company. It shows the location of the chief streets of the city in relation to the original country roads. It shows the property purchased by the Merrimack Manufacturing Company, and the area reserved for the cotton mills and their housing.

2. *The Plant of the Merrimack Manufacturing Company, ca. 1850.* Bird's-eye view, from a photostat of the lithograph on the border of Map 14 (Appendix VI, A).

The view shows in the extreme foreground the counting house or office of the Company. This is surrounded on three sides by the Canal. In the center of the picture are the five original mills built during the 1820's. Three are parallel to the course of the river, two are at right angles to it. The central mill is crowned by a cupola. In the background is the large new mill built in 1847-48, see Chapter V, note 13. On the extreme left is a portion of the plant of the Print Works associated with the Merrimack Manufacturing Company. See Figure 3, for a plan of the site.

3. *A Map of Part of Lowell, ca. 1852, Showing the Plant and Housing of the Merrimack Manufacturing Company and Adjacent Property.* Drawn by Edward Moulthrop from Map 14 (Appendix VI, A).

This Map shows the juncture of the Merrimack Canal with the river, and the surrounding buildings. On the bank of the river (just under the second letter "R") is the large mill of 1847-48. Below it are the five original mills, rectangular buildings with projecting stair turrets in the center, and attached picker houses on either side. To the left of this group are the innumerable buildings of the Print Works; below it is the Counting House. The housing development lies between the Counting House, the Plant of the Print Works and Merrimack Street, which is marked "Chief Street of City." On the right-hand portion of the housing development there are three rows of the original series of small boarding houses, but half of the row nearest the canal had already been torn down and replaced by the New Block (just opposite the words "Unskilled Labor"). In the middle of this same row is the smaller brick block built by Kirk Boott, ca. 1825. On the left of the housing development are the large brick rows built for the skilled labor. At the lower end of the housing area are the dwellings of the executives, facing the main street. The property owned by the Merrimack Manufacturing Company is surrounded by a heavy dotted line. The area corresponds to that section of the mill property which forms the cross piece of the F-shaped, crosshatched area on Figure 1. On either side, next to the river, is property which belongs to other manufacturing corporations. Otherwise the Merrimack Manufacturing Company is surrounded by property used for public buildings and the houses of the bourgeoisie.

No less than eighteen of the illustrations of this book depict buildings situated in this portion of Lowell. The numbers of these illustrations are placed in circles which are located on this map at the approximate point where the artist stood when making the pictures. Arrows indicate the direction he was facing. Thus, Figure 2 was made from a point just below the letter "i" in "Counting House." Figures 4 and 5 illustrate a boarding house facing the Merrimack Canal, the second one below the central brick block. Figure 8 shows the front row of boarding houses facing the canal, Figure 9 the central brick block in this row. Figure 10 shows one of the boarding houses in the middle row, the third from the upper end, while Figure 11 is a view showing the back of the middle row and the front of the third row taken between the second and third houses from the bottom. Figure 16 is a view of a church to the right of the Merrimack property. Figure 18 is a view of one of the blocks in the left hand part of the housing development. It was taken from the middle of the street just over the letters "ti" of "executives." Figure 25 is a view of the rectory to the right of the church in Figure 16. Figures 42, 43 and 44 are views of the New Block at the upper end of the row of boarding houses facing the Canal. Figure 48 is a view of the original railroad station, long since destroyed, which stood on Merrimack Street just where it crossed the Canal. Figure 68 is a view of one of the later blocks of boarding houses in the upper left hand corner of the housing development. Figure 74 is a view of the second row of boarding houses looking towards the Counting House. Figure 91 is a view of the Dressing Mill which had not yet been built in 1852 and consequently does not appear on this map, but which was parallel to the counting house and nearly in line with it, just to the right. Figure 92 is a view of the Dressing Mill seen from the rear.

4. *View of Dutton Street Looking Northeast.* From a photograph by Margaret Noyes. It shows No. 22 in the foreground, a second identical wooden house, the brick block in the middle of the row,

and in the background the New Block. The house in the foreground is one of the original group of boarding houses, built from the designs of Kirk Boott, ca. 1825. The chimneys have been rebuilt, and the front porch was added after a remodeling in the 1890's. Originally the house had green blinds beside the windows; cf. Figure 8. For the location, see Figure 3.

5. *Plan of 22 Dutton Street.* This plan was redrawn by Edward Moulthrop from a plan of the house made at the time it was remodeled at the very end of the century, a plan, now in the possession of the Merrimack Manufacturing Company. Presumably it represents the disposition of the house as it was built ca. 1825 from the designs of Kirk Boott. The two halves of the house were identical, and were used for boarding houses. The plan is described at some length in Chapter IV, note 45.

6. *Houses Built for the Chelmsford Glass Works, ca. 1802.* From a photograph by Margaret Noyes. For the dating of these houses see Chapter IV, note 41.

7. *Model Cottages.* From photostats of plates III and XI of John Wood, *A Series of Plans for Cottages or Habitations of the Laborer,* etc. Plates made in 1781. Note the remarkable similarity to the blocks of houses in Figures 6 and 9.

8. *View of Dutton Street in 1849.* Photostat after an engraving published as the frontispiece to the *New England Offering,* Vol. 1, 1849. The view shows on the left one of the original boarding houses and next to it the brick block in the center of the row (this is very poorly drawn) and beyond the New Block of ca. 1845. On the right are the elm trees that line the Merrimack Canal, while in the background is the great mill which had only just been completed and which stood on the bank of the river. Compare this with Figure 4 which shows the same street, taken from much the same point of view, as it appears today. Also compare it with Figures 2, 3, 9, and 44.

9. *Brick Block, Dutton Street, Built from the Designs of Kirk Boott, ca. 1825.* From a photograph by Margaret Noyes. This brick block originally formed the central unit of a long row of wooden boarding houses. In the Inventory of Polls and Taxable Property for 1826 the Merrimack Manufacturing Company is listed as owning several brick blocks of tenements. That fact suggests that

this block was originally intended to provide apartments for the families of the skilled workmen. Compare the design to the larger cottage shown in Figure 7. Other views of this same building appear in Figures 4 and 8. For the location, see Figure 3.

10. *Boarding Houses, Worthen Street, Built from the Designs of Kirk Boott, ca. 1825.* From a photograph by Margaret Noyes. Double boarding houses. For the location, see Figure 3.

11. *Rear View of Worthen Street Boarding Houses, Built ca. 1825.* From a photograph by Margaret Noyes. For the location, see Figure 3.

12. *Boarding Houses, Broad Street, Somersworth, New Hampshire.* From a photograph by the author. Built for the Great Falls Manufacturing Company. Unlike most later industrial housing, Boott's scheme of isolated double units is retained. These houses are as well proportioned as any in Lowell, while the greater distance both between the individual units and between the opposite rows and the splendid planting make this the finest housing development in central New England. Somersworth can rival the best work in Rhode Island.

13. *Paul Moody House, Built from the Designs of Kirk Boott, ca. 1825.* From a photograph by Margaret Noyes. This house was made for Paul Moody, the agent of the Locks and Canals Company's Machine Shop. It is an example of the type of house which was erected for important executives at this time.

14. *Kirk Boott House, Lowell, Built ca. 1825.* From a photograph by Margaret Noyes. This is the mansion which Boott, as one of the major stockholders in the manufacturing enterprises, built for himself. It clearly shows how conservative was his taste.

15. *W. B. Moody House, Haverhill, Mass., Built ca. 1821 from the Designs of John Haviland of Philadelphia.* From a photograph by Margaret Noyes. This house is to be compared with Figure 14. It shows the type of residence a progressive architect would design at this period. For the plan of this house see the reference Chapter IV, note 57.

16. *St. Anne's Church, Lowell, Finished in 1826, Built from the Designs of Kirk Boott.* From a photograph by Margaret Noyes. The church was planned to be three bays long, but as originally built it was only two bays long. The additional bay was completed in

the middle of the century, together with a projecting chancel. Until recently there were pinnacles at the corners of the tower. St. Anne's is typical of the Gothic Churches which the less well educated gentlemen amateurs were designing during the 1820's and 1830's. For the location, see Figure 3.

17. *Stone Mill, Newmarket Manufacturing Company, Newmarket, New Hampshire.* From a photograph by the author. Identical with many of the mills that were being built in Lowell and elsewhere during the late thirties and early forties.

18. *"John Bull's Row," Lowell, Built ca. 1827.* From a photograph by Margaret Noyes. As originally built it was a story and a half high. Later, another story was added. This housing development was erected to accommodate the families of the skilled workmen who were brought over from England to establish the Merrimack Print Works. Cf. Figure 9. For the location, see Figure 3.

19. *Housing for the Lawrence Manufacturing Company, Lowell, Built in the Early 1830's.* From a photograph by Margaret Noyes. This housing is a good example of the type of arrangement which became standard throughout central New England in the 1830's and 1840's. The boarding houses and tenements are arranged in a series of long parallel blocks, three and a half stories high. One end of each block is adjacent to the mill yard. The other faces on a street. Next to the blocks at this outer end is the house of the agent, which here is visible in the background. Compare with Figures 21, 44 and 47.

20. *Agent's House, the Lawrence Manufacturing Company, Lowell, Built in the Early 1830's.* From a photograph by Margaret Noyes. Compare with Figures 19 and 13. In the 1820's the house of the agent was almost identical with the houses of the workers (cf. Figures 13 and 10). In the 1830's when the boarding house blocks were enlarged, the executive mansion grew proportionately.

21. *Housing of the Amoskeag Manufacturing Company, Manchester, New Hampshire.* From a photograph by the author. Compare with Figures 19, 44 and 47. The housing in Manchester is remarkable because of the great space between the blocks, allowing for ample back yards, and because of the straightforward way it is adjusted to the sloping ground.

22. *House, Middlesex Street at School Street, Lowell, Built ca. 1833.*

From a photograph by Margaret Noyes. First appears on Map 6 (Appendix, VI, A). A good example of the uniformity of style which prevailed in the industrial and private architecture of Lowell before the advent of Romanticism. The continuous dormer suggests the monitor on a factory roof; the gable ends recall some of the housing blocks.

23. *House on Market Street at Cabot Street, Lowell, Built ca. 1839.* From a photograph by Margaret Noyes. First shown on Map 7 (Appendix VI, A). A fine example of the large bourgeois house of the period; cf. the houses in Figure 76. In the built-up portions of the town multiple dwellings such as these were usual.

24. *House on Pawtucket Street at Fletcher Street, Lowell, Built ca. 1833.* From a photograph by Margaret Noyes. First shown on Map 6 (Appendix VI, A). A late example of the type of free-standing private house which had been common in this vicinity since the middle of the eighteenth century.

25. *Rectory, St. Anne's Church, Lowell, Built from the Designs of Kirk Boott ca. 1826.* From a photograph by Margaret Noyes. Almost finished in 1826. Nearly identical with the house in Figure 24, except for the self-consciously Greek porch which may, however, be a later addition. For the location, see Figure 3.

26. *House on North Side of William Street, Lowell, Built ca. 1839.* From a photograph by Margaret Noyes. First shown on Map 7 (Appendix VI, A). A typical petty bourgeois house of the period. A house such as this vividly illustrates how high the quality of the industrial housing was.

27. *Shops, Corner of Market Street and Lewis Street, Lowell, Built ca. 1839.* From a photograph by the author. First shown on Map 7 (Appendix VI, A). Recently destroyed. Early descriptions of Lowell mention many small wooden shops which must have looked much like this. They were very soon replaced by brick structures.

28. *Shops, Corner of Merrimack Street and John Street, Lowell, Built ca. 1833.* From a photograph by Margaret Noyes. First appears on Map 6 (Appendix VI, A). A typical brick business building of the period. Note how similar it is to Figure 27, and how much more mechanical its design is than the somewhat earlier shops shown in Figure 29.

29. *Shops, Newmarket, New Hampshire.* From a photograph by Margaret Noyes. The relatively small windows, the heavy proportions, the projecting eaves and the free and original treatment of the gable head and the corner suggest a date not later than 1825. Compare with Figures 9 and 13. Notice that the orthodox arrangement of the ground floor with granite posts carrying granite lintels over very wide spans has not yet been perfected.

30. *Corner of Gorham and Central Streets, Lowell.* From an old photograph. In the center is Tower's Drug Store, which gave its name to the corner. At the left is the Washington House, a typical large hotel of the 1830's. Both buildings appear first on Map 6 (Appendix VI, A).

31. *Newmarket House, Newmarket, New Hampshire.* From a photograph by the author. A typical hotel of the 1830's.

32. *Ayer Home, Lowell, Built ca. 1825 from the Designs of Kirk Boott.* From a photograph by Margaret Noyes. This was built by the Merrimack Manufacturing Company as a hotel. Notice the porch and compare it to Figure 25. Notice also the balcony at the back which was famous for its view of the falls of the Merrimack.

33. *St. Patrick's Church, Lowell, Built in 1831.* From a photostat of an engraving published in the *Lowell Offering*, I, 210. A Gothic church which is typical of those designed by builders during the 1820's and 1830's.

34. *First Baptist Church, Lowell, Built in 1826.* From a photostat of an engraving published in the *Lowell Offering*, I, 145. A typical meeting house of this period. It is significant that a well-established denomination such as the Baptists should erect a church that was so conservative in its design.

35. *City Market House, Market Street, Lowell, Built in 1837.* From a photograph by Margaret Noyes. All the public buildings erected in Lowell at this period were just such plain rectangular structures as this. The pilasters at the corners and the deep plain band they carry are a timid recognition of the Greek Revival. A cupola was added to this building at a later date, but except for the base, it has since been removed.

36. *Grammar School, Belvidere, Built in 1840.* From a photograph by Margaret Noyes. The type of building erected for the Grammar

Schools in Lowell remained practically uniform from 1833 until 1857. Note the similarity to the Market House.

37. *Grammar School, Centralville, Built in 1857.* From a photograph by Margaret Noyes. The location of the building at a street intersection, the crowning of the main façade with a cupola, and the somewhat lighter proportions of the details are the only significant differences between this and the preceding public buildings. These features are not an indication of the comparatively late date. All of them may be found on conservative buildings erected twenty years earlier, for example, Figure 39.

38. *Town Hall, Nashua, New Hampshire.* From a photograph by the author. Recently destroyed. This structure alone presents the trim appearance that all the pseudo-Greek public buildings must have shown in the days when they were properly maintained.

39. *St. Paul's Methodist Church, Hurd Street, Lowell, Built in 1839.* From a photograph by Margaret Noyes. A typical church of the classic type.

40. *First Freewill Baptist Church, Lowell, Built in 1837.* From a photostat of an engraving published in the *Lowell Offering*, I, 263. Built on the most expensive and dramatic site in town as a speculation. The attempt to combine features from the Classic and the Gothic Revivals is characteristic of the point of view of the unsophisticated enthusiasts at this time. Compare with Figure 78.

41. *House on Tyler Sreet, Lowell, Built ca. 1839.* From a photograph by Margaret Noyes. First appears on Map 8 (Appendix VI, A). Shows the attempt to adapt the Greek Revival to the typical middle-class double house of the type shown in Figure 23, by running the axis of the roof at right angles to the street, and adding Greek detail. The house retains the traditional narrow rectangular proportions, with the long side on the street. A compromise type of building that was soon abandoned.

42. *Plan of the "New Block" of Boarding Houses Built in Lowell by the Merrimack Manufacturing Corporation ca. 1845.* Plan drawn by Edward Moulthrop on the basis of a contemporary ground plan in the possession of the Merrimack Manufacturing Company. For date, see Chapter VI, note 32. The original plan of the ground floor has disappeared. The upper floors are the same in principle as those of the boarding houses designed by Boott,

twenty years earlier (Figure 5), but they are much larger and the design is modified because the building has only two free exposures.

43. *Alley behind the New Block, Lowell.* From a photograph by Margaret Noyes. The great objection to Boott's planning of the housing development of the Merrimack Manufacturing Corporation (Figure 3) was the fact that the rows of houses were too close together. When one row of the original small boarding houses was torn down and replaced by the much larger New Block, there was very serious overcrowding. Compare the narrow space shown here with the ample back yards between the blocks of boarding houses which are found at Manchester, New Hampshire (Figure 21). For the location, see Figure 3.

44. *Façade of New Block, Lowell.* From a photograph by Margaret Noyes. In its main lines the New Block follows the usual scheme (cf. Figure 19). The frieze and cornice, however, reflect the influence of the Greek Revival, and the staccato accents of the lintels and dormers are typical of the style of the 1840's.

45. *Middlesex Mills, Lowell, Built ca. 1845.* From a photograph by Margaret Noyes. First shown on Map 14 (Appendix VI, A). Shows the addition of Greek detail to the type of mill shown in Figure 17.

46. *Hamilton Mills, Lowell, Rebuilt in 1846.* From a photostat of the lithograph on the border of Map 14 (Appendix VI, A). The two portions right and left were built in the late twenties. The central portion was added in 1846. It shows the desire for display characteristic of this period when the mills were at the height of their prosperity, and when the influence of romanticism was beginning to be felt. But this expansion and self-advertisement is at the expense of comfort, witness the loss of light and air in the linking of these two buildings.

47. *Bay State Mills, Lawrence, Mass. Built in 1846.* From a photostat of an engraving published in the *New England Offering*, for November, 1849 (p. 241). The accompanying description is so interesting that it is reproduced in full. "We have given an isometrical view of the 'Bay State Mills,' engraved from a daguerreotype kindly furnished by the politeness of Mr. D. Roes, esq., superintendent of those mills, and the adjoining boarding houses.

Our girls will readily see that this is a supposed view from a height like looking down from a balloon, and our far-off subscribers, who have never seen a picture of any New England mills and boarding houses, may rest assured, that from this they can form a correct idea of one of the finely laid out and well-proportioned 'corporations' of New England. A slight description will suffice to illustrate this place. The buildings to the right and left of the entrance to the 'yard' are, the one a counting-room with other offices, and the other a cloth-room, with other necessary apartments of that nature. Then there are mills nos. 1, 2 and 3 and 'the River Mill' where one roof covers 1,500 feet in length of building. The boarding-houses without the 'yard' will be readily distinguished from the mills. They are very handsomely finished buildings and more convenient, probably, than any others of the kind in our country. Our manufacturing companies seem to spare no pains to improve upon each other, when erecting new buildings, and the operatives reap great benefit from this rivalry. The fine finish of the wood-work and plaster, in doors and ceilings within; the conveniences of clothes yards, pumps, wood-sheds &c. without, will with difficulty be improved upon when another 'new city' is made to order. Let us describe one house very superficially. At the left, as you enter, is a cosy little room exclusively belonging to the mistress of the house. At the right are two dining rooms connected by folding doors, the front room rather the larger of the two, and each forming a pleasant sitting room at other than meal times. Passing through the entry, you enter the kitchen, with all necessary conveniences 'and appointments' for the elaborate preparation of 'Thanksgiving dinner' or the serving of a hasty 'plate of soup.' Then there is the back kitchen with its gigantic boiler or caldron, for the washing-day service and conveniences for diverse other important household exercises. On the second floor is the parlor and the sick room, a small chamber with a fireplace assigned to the invalid who may need seclusion and extra warmth. Then there are the sleeping apartments for the boarders, some calculated for two, some for four, and the larger will accommodate six, and give every advantage of room, air, &c. with the smaller bed-rooms—every advantage but their privacy.

"We think we have written enough to convince our readers who have had no opportunity for personal observation that our factory boarding houses will well compare with other houses for public accommodation. They are inferior to none but our first-class hotels, and the residences of very wealthy citizens. And while the mill owners thus provide for the physical well-being of the Operatives in their employ, we are happy to see a genuine effort for their mental and moral welfare. We trust that the exertions made to exclude from the town all fomenters and *nuclei* of crime and iniquity will be crowned with success, and that 'the new city' so beautifully encircled with Nature's still-fresh charms, will also be girt about with the more glorious circlets of purity and intelligence." Page 241.

48. *First Railroad Depot, Lowell, Built ca. 1835.* Photostat from a cut published in the *Contributions of the Lowell Historical Society* I, 410. The railroad station is significant as an indication of the fact that in America in the 1830's the desire to build an impressive and monumental building entailed the use of Greek forms. It is an amusing attempt to use them functionally. On the right is the Merrimack House, the business hotel, built by the Locks and Canals Company. Compare it with the shops in Figure 28 and the Washington House in Figure 30. For the location, see Figure 3.

49. *The Second Universalist Church, Lowell, Built in 1838 from the Designs of Dr. Duesbury.* From a photostat of an engraving published in the *Lowell Offering*, I, 256. A quaint Gothic building, but advanced in the way that the Gothic detail is organized. Perhaps a provincial reflection of Richard Upjohn's contemporary St. John's Church, Bangor.

50. *House on Park Street, Belvidere, Built ca. 1845.* From a photograph by Margaret Noyes. First appears on Map 14 (Appendix VI, A). The form of the pseudo-Greek public building with its pilaster strips, ironwork and flaring eaves (Figures 35, 36, 38) is here adapted to a house.

51. *Double House, Chapel Hill District, Lowell, Built ca. 1855.* From a photograph by Margaret Noyes. A lower-middle-class adaptation of the Gothic House of the type popularized by Andrew Jackson Downing.

52. *"The Manse," Andover Street, Belvidere, Built ca. 1845.* From a

photograph by Margaret Noyes. A typical romantic cottage, unusual only in its lack of jigsaw work.

53. *J. H. Rand House, Belvidere, Built in the Late 1840's*. From a photostat of the lithograph on the border of Map 14 (Appendix VI, A). An unusually elaborate Italian villa. It is significant that the largest and oldest manufacturing company in Lowell should have purchased this house for their chief executive.

54. *John Nesmith House, Belvidere, Built ca. 1841*. From a photograph by Margaret Noyes. This is shown faintly on Map 7 (Appendix VI, A). Perhaps the building was projected but not yet executed. It appears on Map 14. The handsomest house in Lowell, it derives from English regency models. Originally it had a curving balustrade around the semicircular terrace.

55. *Butler House, Belvidere, Built ca. 1843*. From a photograph by Margaret Noyes. First appears on Map 14 (Appendix VI, A), but obviously it is only a few years later than the Nesmith House. Built by a wealthy mill executive. Like the Nesmith House this derives ultimately from Regency models.

56 and 57. *Details of the John Nesmith House, Belvidere, Built ca. 1841*. From photographs by Margaret Noyes.

58. *House on Centre Street, Lowell, Built ca. 1839*. From a photograph by Margaret Noyes. First appears on Map 7 (Appendix VI, A). The portico house was the first type of romantic building which was taken up by the lower middle class. A portico was indubitably grand, and it could be added to the usual three-bay type of small house, without changing the plan.

59. *Gothic House, Thorndike Street near Gorham Street, Lowell, Built in the Early 1850's*. From a photograph by Margaret Noyes. Does not appear on Map 14 (Appendix VI, A). This is the most elaborate Gothic House in Lowell. It represents an adaptation of the type of house popularized by Andrew Jackson Downing. This particular example is very close to several designs published in William H. Ranlett's *The Architect*, notably design No. 16.

60. *Fletcher House, Facing North Common, Lowell, Built ca. 1845*. From a photograph by Margaret Noyes. Illustrated in a lithograph on the border of Map 14 (Appendix VI, A). A middle-class

adaptation and elaboration of the great Belvidere mansions, the Nesmith house and the Butler house.

61. *House on Mount Vernon Street at Bowers Street, Lowell, Built ca. 1853.* From a photograph by Margaret Noyes. Not shown on Map 14 (Appendix VI, A). A later and simplified version of the Fletcher House. Cf. Figure 65.

62. *House on Andover Street, Belvidere, Built ca. 1850.* From a photograph by Margaret Noyes. (Dated on basis of style.) It is possible that this house was remodeled, the windows and perhaps the doorway being changed at a later date.

63. *House on Highland Street, Lowell, Built in the Mid Fifties.* From a photograph by Margaret Noyes. The Renaissance revival at its height.

64. *Christian Science Church, Nashua, New Hampshire.* From a photograph by Margaret Noyes. A very beautiful Italian villa. Compare it with Figure 53.

65. *Drawing for an Italian Villa.* From a photostat of Plate 64 of Edward Show's *The Modern Architect.* Note the general similarity to Figures 61, 66, and 67. These houses represented original compositions on the basis of some such drawing as this, rather than copies of drawings.

66. *William Livingstone House, Thorndike Street at Chelmsford Street, Lowell, Built in 1852.* From a photograph by Margaret Noyes. The masterpiece of the bracketed style in Lowell.

67. *House on Highland Street, Lowell, Built in the Late Fifties.* From a photograph by Margaret Noyes. Originally this house had a turret in the center of the roof. It is obviously an imitation of the Livingstone house, built a few years earlier. The crowded composition and the use of more solid forms indicate a more advanced style.

68. *Housing for Skilled Workmen, Tilden Street, Lowell, Built ca. 1850.* From a photograph by Margaret Noyes. All domestic quality is lost, but elaborate consoles are added under the eaves, as if to compensate for the grimness of these barracks. A good illustration of what romantic architecture generally meant for industrial housing.

69. *House, Chapel Hill District, Lowell, Built in the Mid Fifties.* From a photograph by Margaret Noyes. The typical three-bay petty

bourgeois house is decked out with all the fixings of the bracketed style. Notice how the building has sprouted bay windows, and the crowding together of forms on the facade.

70. *Early Bracket, Lowell.* From a photograph by Margaret Noyes. Still completely two-dimensional in conception, but the naturalistic acorn and the very complex curves of the strut announce the second stage in the evolution of the bracket.

71. *Detail of the William Livingstone House, Lowell, Built in 1852.* From a photograph by Margaret Noyes. The height of the second stage. The brackets on the right are similar in shape to that in Figure 70, but the pendant is much more elaborate, and the bracket is ornamented on its lower and lateral faces. The brackets on the right are given naturalistic forms.

72. *Detail of House in Figure 69, Lowell.* From a photograph by Margaret Noyes. Another example of the second stage at its climax. Notice the delicate petals of the pendant, and the introduction of an acorn in relief above it, also the elaborate rosettes. But the third stage is foreshadowed in the tiny brackets above. They have already abandoned the canonical shape, and the relatively large size of the pendants makes for a feeling of solid forms crowded together, a feeling that is typical of the late 1850's. Notice how all the forms are conceived in terms of three dimensions.

73. *Late Bracket, Lowell.* From a photograph by Margaret Noyes. The earlier form of the bracket has been abandoned. The shape now approaches a solid triangle. Note the prominence of the great circular form. Although the decoration is elaborate, it is no longer naturalistic in character.

74. *Worthen Street, Lowell, Houses Built ca. 1825 from the Designs of Kirk Boott.* From a photograph by the author. This view shows the typical eighteenth-century conception of the street as a corridor lined with buildings. Despite the isolation of the individual units, the collective effect is more significant than the design of each one singly. For the location, see Figure 3.

75. *Dane Street, Lowell, Houses Built ca. 1853.* From a photograph by the author. The buildings do not appear on Map 14 (Appendix VI, A), but they may be dated in the 1850's on the basis of their style. This view illustrates the typical nineteenth-century con-

ception of the street as a group of separate buildings, placed side by side. Despite the fact that the houses are identical in design, the sawtooth effect of the gables destroys any unity in the appearance of the group as a whole. One is expected to examine each house as if it were a unique and isolated building.

76. *Appleton Street, Lowell, the Eastern End. Built up ca. 1835.* From a photograph reproduced from p. 776 of the *Illustrated History of Lowell and Vicinity*, by permission of the publishers (Lowell, Courier-Citizen Company, 1898). Almost all the buildings shown were erected ca. 1835, since they first appear on Map 6 (Appendix VI, A). The effect of a single unified composition is strongly marked, even though the buildings are not identical and were built without much consideration for one another.

77. *Appleton Street, Lowell, the Western End. Built up ca. 1848.* From a photograph by the author. This portion of the street was only opened after 1845, but all the houses were built very shortly, as they appear on no. 12 (Appendix VI, A). The absence of any unity of effect is emphasized by the conscious individualization of the separate houses.

78. *House, Howard Street near Thorndike Street, Lowell, Built ca. 1839.* From a photograph by Margaret Noyes. First appears on Map 7 (Appendix VI, A). Unusually elaborate for a petty bourgeois house of this period. The attempt to combine Classic and Gothic styles is quite characteristic of the enthusiasm and naïveté of the lower middle class. Cf. Figure 40.

79. *St. Patrick's Church, Lowell, Built in 1854.* From a photograph by Margaret Noyes. A typical example of the dull and scholarly reproductions of medieval monuments which were being built at this time.

80. *Housing, Nashua, New Hampshire.* From a photograph by Margaret Noyes. The buildings may be dated ca. 1848 on the basis of their style. The small-scale and domestic quality of the best of the earlier housing developments is retained, but the influence of the romantic movement is evident in the design of the units. A most unusual and attractive group. Contrast with Figure 68 which is much more typical.

81. *Store, John Street near Merrimack Street, Lowell, Built ca. 1850.* From a photograph by Margaret Noyes. The building may be

dated on the basis of its style. A characteristic attempt to treat decoratively what was still accepted as a purely utilitarian type of building. Notice that the facade is treated as a unit by itself and aesthetically is independent of the rest of the building.

82 and 83. *The Town Hall, Manchester, New Hampshire, Built in 1845 from the Designs of Edward Shaw.* From photographs by Margaret Noyes. A type of Gothic structure which was originally developed for churches is here successfully adapted to secular use. It is most unusual among Gothic structures of this period thanks to the large size and simple form of the windows.

84 and 85. *The Court House, Lowell, Built in 1850.* From photographs by Margaret Noyes. The original facade has been swallowed up by a later addition. A well-proportioned building with beautifully designed detail. The architect effectively contrasts the wood and the brick.

86. *Massachusetts Mills, Lowell, as Rebuilt in 1853.* From a photograph by Margaret Noyes. In 1853 two older mills were rebuilt, an extra story being added (notice the change in the brickwork over the fifth story windows) and they were joined together into a single long unit. A typical instance of the desire to take advantage of necessary expansion in order to make mill architecture more monumental. Compare with Figure 46.

87. *The Jail, Lowell, Built in 1856 from the Designs of J. H. Rand.* From a photograph by Margaret Noyes. A clumsy building in conception, proportions, and details, it illustrates the stagnation of monumental architecture during the late 1850's.

88. *Print Works, Manchester, New Hampshire, Built in 1853.* From a photograph by Margaret Noyes. An attempt to treat the whole of an industrial building in one of the historical styles, the "Italian style" in this instance. This building is exceptional. Generally only one conspicuous portion of the mill buildings was decorated, as in Figure 86.

89 and 90. *Map of Lowell showing the Development of the City from 1820 to 1850.* Drawn by Edward Moulthrop. The topographic outlines are taken from Map 15 (Appendix VI, A). The indications of roads which existed before 1825 are from no. 2, of roads and land developed between 1820 and 1825 are from no. 3, of roads and land developed between 1825 and 1840 are from no. 7,

and of roads and land developed between 1840 and 1850 are from no. 12.

91. *Tower of the Merrimack Manufacturing Company's Dressing Mill, Built in 1863.* From a photograph by the author. Recently destroyed. The masterpiece of romantic mill architecture in Lowell. For the location, see Figure 3.

92. *Rear View of the Merrimack Manufacturing Company's Dressing Mill.* From a photograph by the author. This illustrates the loss of light and air which resulted from the crowding of large structures such as the Dressing Mill into the small yards which were provided in the 1820's for the manufacturing companies. Contrast with Figure 2. For the location, see Figure 3.

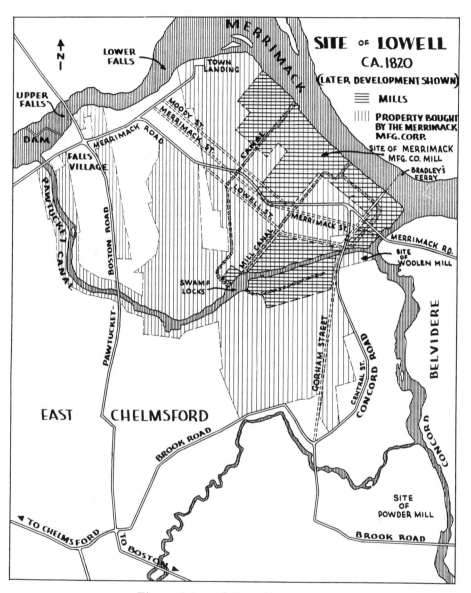

Fig. 1. Map of Lowell, 1820-25

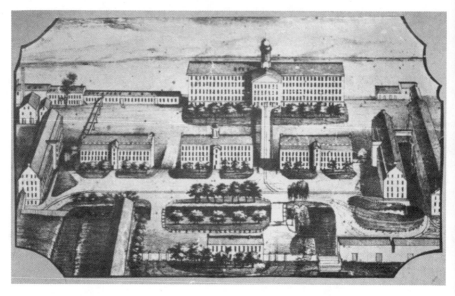

Fig. 2. The Plant of the Merrimack Manufacturing
Company ca. 1850

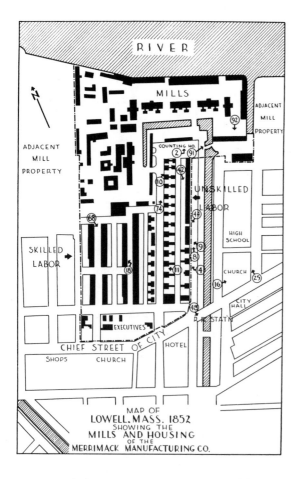

Fig. 3.

A Map of Part of
Lowell ca. 1852,
Showing the Plant
and Housing of the
Merrimack Manufac-
turing Company and
Adjacent Property
(Moulthrop)

Fig. 4. View of Dutton Street Looking Northeast (Noyes)

Fig. 5. Plan of 22 Dutton Street (Moulthrop)

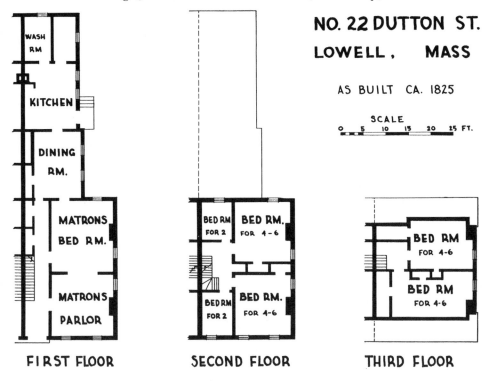

WASH RM

KITCHEN

DINING RM.

MATRONS BED RM.

MATRONS PARLOR

FIRST FLOOR

BED RM FOR 2

BED RM. FOR 4-6

BEDRM FOR 2

BED RM. FOR 4-6

SECOND FLOOR

BED RM FOR 4-6

BED RM FOR 4-6

THIRD FLOOR

**NO. 22 DUTTON ST.
LOWELL, MASS**

AS BUILT CA. 1825

SCALE

0 5 10 15 20 25 FT.

Fig. 6.
Houses Built for the Chelmsford Glass Works, ca. 1802. (Noyes)

COTTAGES WITH ONE ROOM

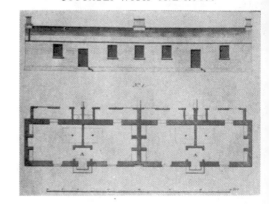

COTTAGES WITH TWO ROOMS

Fig. 7.
Model Cottages Designed by John Wood, 1781

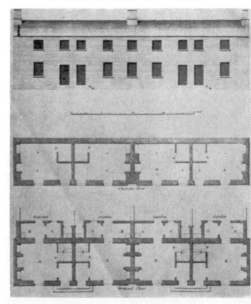

Fig. 8. View of Dutton Street in 1849

Fig. 9. Brick Block, Dutton Street, Built ca. 1825 (Noyes)

Fig. *10*. Boarding Houses, Worthen Street, Built ca. 1825
(Noyes)

Fig. *11*. Rear View of Worthen Street Boarding Houses, Built ca. 1825
(Noyes)

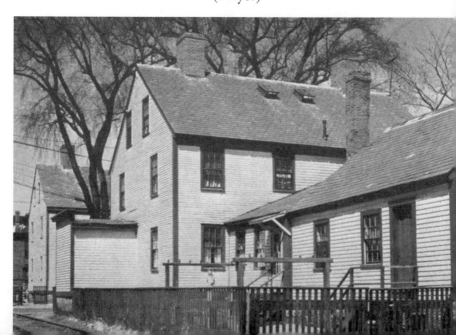

Fig. 12. Boarding Houses, Broad Street, Somersworth,
New Hampshire

Fig 13. Paul Moody House, Built ca. 1825 (Noyes)

Fig. 14. Kirk Boott House, Built ca. 1825 (Noyes)

Fig. 15. W. B. Moody House, Haverhill, Mass., Built ca. 1821 (Noyes)

Fig. 16. St. Anne's Church, Lowell, Finished in 1826 (Noyes)

Fig. 17. Stone Mill, Newmarket Manufacturing Company, Newmarket, New Hampshire

Fig. 18. "John Bull's Row," Lowell, Built ca. 1827
(Noyes)

Fig. 19. Housing for the Lawrence Manufacturing Company, Lowell,
Built in the Early 1830's (Noyes)

Fig. 20. Agent's House, the Lawrence Manufacturing Company, Built in the Early 1830's (Noyes)

Fig. 21. Housing of the Amoskeag Manufacturing Company, Manchester, New Hampshire

Fig. 22. House, Middlesex Street at School Street, Lowell,
Built ca. 1833 (Noyes)

Fig. 23. House on Market Street at Cabot Street, Lowell,
Built ca. 1839 (Noyes)

Fig. 24. House on Pawtucket Street at Fletcher Street, Lowell,
Built ca. 1833 (Noyes)

Fig. 25. Rectory St. Anne's Church, Lowell, Built ca. 1826
(Noyes)

Fig. 26. House on the North Side of William Street, Lowell, Built ca. 1839
(Noyes)

Fig. 27. Shops, Corner of Market Street and Lewis Street,
Lowell, Built ca. 1839

Fig. 28. Shops, Corner of Merrimack Street and John Street, Lowell,
Built ca. 1833 (Noyes)

Fig. 29. Shops, Newmarket, New Hampshire (Noyes)

Fig. 30. Corner of Gorham and Central Streets, Lowell

Fig. 31. Newmarket House, Newmarket, New Hampshire

Fig. 32.
Ayer Home, Lowell,
Built ca. 1825 (Noyes)

Fig. 33.
St. Patrick's Church,
Lowell, Built in 1831

Fig. 34.
First Baptist Church,
Lowell, Built in 1826

Fig. 35.
City Market House,
Market Street, Low-
ell, Built in 1837
(Noyes)

Fig. 36.
Grammar School, Belvidere, Built in 1840 (Noyes)

Fig. 37.
Grammar School, Centralville, Built in 1857 (Noyes)

Fig. 38.
Town Hall, Nashua,
New Hampshire

Fig. 39.
St. Paul's Methodist
Church, Lowell, Built
in 1839 (Noyes)

Fig. 40.
First Freewill Bap-
tist Church, Lowell,
Built in 1837

Fig. 41.
House on Tyler
Street, Lowell, Built
ca. 1837 (Noyes)

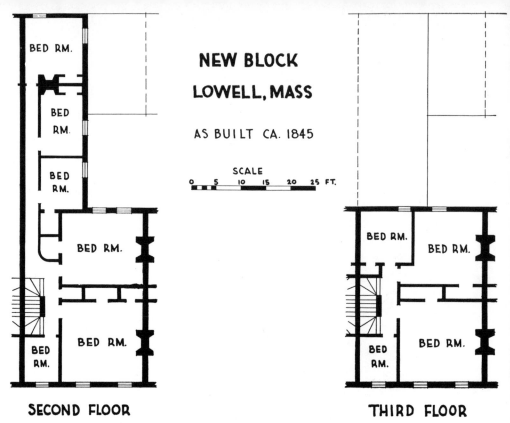

NEW BLOCK
LOWELL, MASS

AS BUILT CA. 1845

SCALE

0   5   10   15   20   25 FT.

BED RM.

BED RM.

BED RM.

BED RM.

BED RM.

BED RM.

SECOND FLOOR

BED RM.

BED RM.

BED RM.

BED RM.

BED RM.

THIRD FLOOR

Fig. 42. Plan of the "New Block" of Boarding Houses
Built in Lowell ca. 1845 (Moulthrop)

Fig. 43. Alley behind the New Block, Lowell (Noyes)

Fig. 44. Façade of the New Block, Lowell (Noyes)

Fig. 45. Middlesex Mills, Lowell, Built ca. 1845 (Noyes)

Fig. 46. Hamilton Mills, Lowell, Rebuilt in 1846

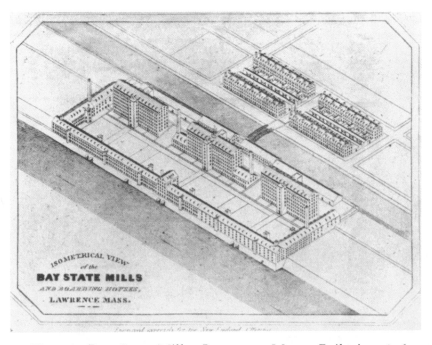

ISOMETRICAL VIEW
of the
BAY STATE MILLS
AND BOARDING HOUSES,
LAWRENCE MASS.

Fig. 47. Bay State Mills, Lawrence, Mass., Built in 1846

Fig. 48. First Railroad Depot, Lowell, Built ca. 1835

Fig. 49. Second Universalist Church, Lowell,
Built in 1838

Fig. 50. House on Park Street, Belvidere, Built ca. 1845 (Noyes)

Fig. 51. Double House, Chapel Hill District, Lowell, Built ca. 1855 (Noyes)

Fig. 52. "The Manse," Andover Street, Belvidere, Built ca. 1845 (Noyes)

Fig. 53. J. H. Rand House, Belvidere, Built in the late 1840's

Fig. 54.
John Nesmith
House, Belvidere,
Built ca. 1841
(Noyes)

Fig. 55.
Butler House,
Belvidere, Built ca.
1843 (Noyes)

Fig. 57. Detail of the John Nesmith House, Belvidere, Built ca. 1841 (Noyes)

Fig. 56. Detail of the John Nesmith House, Belvidere, Built ca. 1841 (Noyes)

Fig. 59. Gothic House, Thorndike Street near Gorham Street, Lowell, Built in the Early 1850's (Noyes)

Fig. 58. House on Centre Street, Lowell, Built ca. 1839 (Noyes)

Fig. 60. Fletcher House, Facing North Common, Lowell,
Built ca. 1845 (Noyes)

Fig. 61. House on Mount Vernon Street at Bowers Street, Lowell,
Built ca. 1853 (Noyes)

Fig. 62. House on Andover Street, Belvidere, Built ca. 1850 (Noyes)

Fig. 63. House on Highland Street, Lowell, Built in the Mid Fifties (Noyes)

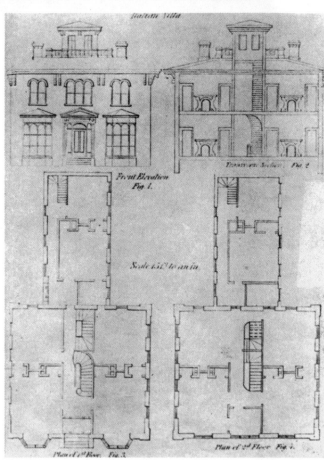

Fig. 64.
Christian Science Church, Nashua, New Hampshire (Noyes)

Fig. 65.
Drawing for an Italian Villa

Fig. 66. William Livingstone House, Thorndike Street at Chelmsford Street, Lowell, Built in 1852 (Noyes)

Fig. 67. House on Highland Street, Lowell, Built in the Late Fifties (Noyes)

Fig. 68. Housing for Skilled Workmen, Tilden Street, Lowell, Built ca. 1850 (Noyes)

Fig. 69. House, Chapel Hill District, Lowell, Built in Mid Fifties (Noyes)

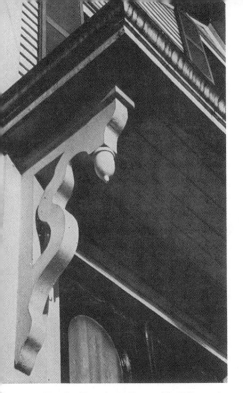

Fig. 71. Detail of the William Livingstone House, Lowell, Built in 1852 (Noyes)

Fig. 70. Early Bracket, Lowell (Noyes)

Fig. 73. Late Bracket, Lowell (Noyes)

Fig. 72. Detail of House in Figure 69, Lowell (Noyes)

Fig. 74. Worthen Street, Lowell, Houses Built ca. 1825

Fig. 75. Dane Street, Lowell, Houses Built ca. 1853

Fig. 76. Appleton Street, Lowell, the Eastern End, Houses Built ca. 1835

Fig. 77. Appleton Street, Lowell, the Western End, Houses Built ca. 1848

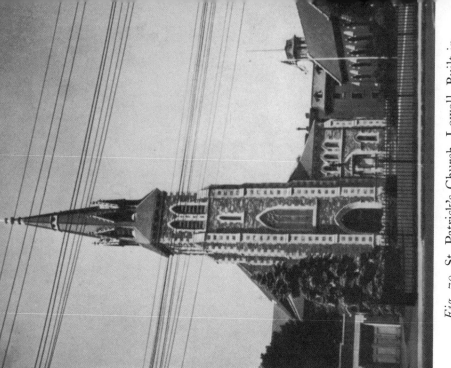

Fig. 79. St. Patrick's Church, Lowell, Built in
1854 (Noyes)

Fig. 78. House, Howard Street near Thorndike Street,
Lowell, Built ca. 1839 (Noyes)

Fig. 80. Housing, Nashua, New Hampshire (Noyes)

Fig. 81. Store, John Street near Merrimack Street, Lowell (Noyes)

Fig. 83. Detail of the Town Hall, Manchester, New Hampshire (Noyes)

Fig. 82. Town Hall, Manchester, New Hampshire, Built in 1845 from the Designs of Edward Shaw (Noyes)

Fig. 84. Court House, Lowell, Built in 1850 (Noyes)

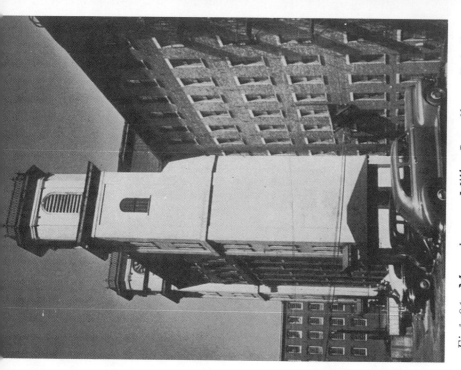

Fig. 86. Massachusetts Mills, Lowell, as Rebuilt in 1853 (Noyes)

Fig. 85. Detail of the Court House, Lowell (Noyes)

Fig. 87. The Jail, Lowell, Built in 1856 (Noyes)

Fig. 88. Print Works, Manchester, New Hampshire, Built in 1853 (Noyes)

Figs. 89 and 90. Map of Lowell Showing the Development

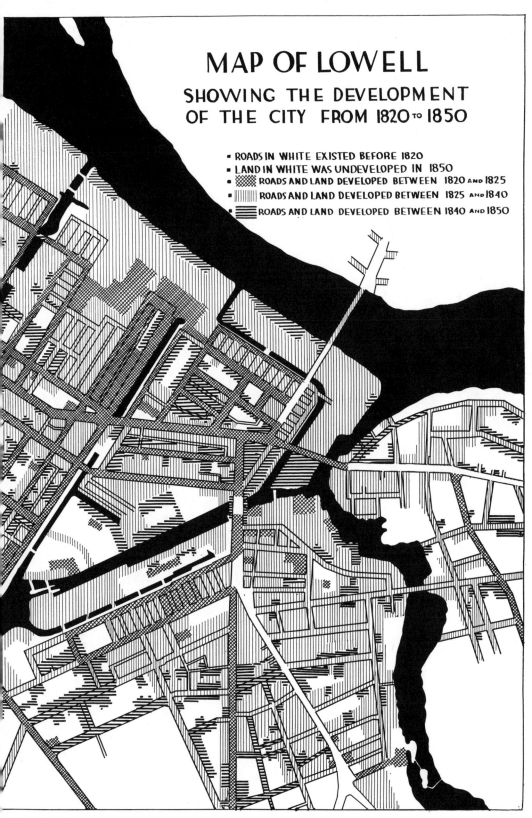

MAP OF LOWELL

SHOWING THE DEVELOPMENT
OF THE CITY FROM 1820 TO 1850

- ROADS IN WHITE EXISTED BEFORE 1820
- LAND IN WHITE WAS UNDEVELOPED IN 1850
- ROADS AND LAND DEVELOPED BETWEEN 1820 AND 1825
- ROADS AND LAND DEVELOPED BETWEEN 1825 AND 1840
- ROADS AND LAND DEVELOPED BETWEEN 1840 AND 1850

of the City from 1820 to 1850 (Moulthrop)

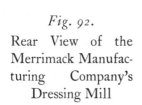

Fig. 91.
Tower of the Merrimack Manufacturing Company's Dressing Mill, Built in 1863

Fig. 92.
Rear View of the Merrimack Manufacturing Company's Dressing Mill

INDEX

Abbott, Josiah G., quoted, 214

Agent, functions defined, 167; *see also* Executives

Almy, Brown & Slater, 179, 180

Almy and Brown, spinning mill, 10, 157, 178; profits, 11; capital, 162

Amesbury, mill at, 47, 182

Amory, William, 173

Amoskeag Manufacturing Company housing, 239; *illus.:* pl. 21

Amoskeag, mill at, 101

Appleton Manufacturing Company, 46, 77, 202

Appleton, Nathan, 19, 21, 27, 28, 45, 160, 165, 169, 175, 176, 204; quoted, 13, 20, 165, 166, 174, 176, 180, 191

Appleton Street Congregational Church, 65

Appleton, William, 160, 162

Architects, a rarity in America, 190

Architectural books, 35, 42, 90, 97, 209

Architecture, *see* Nineteenth-century American architecture, *and under styles*, *e.g.*, Classic style, Gothic, etc.

Ayer, Daniel, 78

Ayer Home, 241; *illus.:* pl. 32

Ayer, James Cook, 106, 214

Bagnall, W. R., 176, 193; quoted, 177, 190, 212

Baird, R. H., quoted, 193

Baroque period housing, 114

Barristers' Hall, 62, 199

Batchelder, Samuel, 166; quoted, 174

Bavarian bronze foundry, 99

Bay State Mills, Lawrence, 70, 203; description of, 243–45 (*illus.:* pl. 47); boarding houses, 244

Behrendt, W. C., quoted, 152

Belvidere, 123, 173; opened up, 50, 62, 75; houses, 79, 82, 84, 88, 89; Livermore estate, 77; map, 145

Benjamin, Asher, 56

Bennett's Mill, Charleston, S. C., 99

Beverly, spinning mill, 29, 178

Bibliography, 223–31

Black list, 133

Boarding houses, life in, 133 f., 136, 244; decline of system, 135–38; *see also* Housing, of unskilled labor

Bond, Phineas, quoted, 122

Books, architectural, 35, 42, 90, 97, 209

Boott, John W., 174, 189

Boott, Kirk, 20, 28, 60, 62, 100, 110, 164, 167, 174, 175, 176, 183, 191, 201; put in executive control, 21; his carrying out of Lowell's ideal project, 23–27, 35; at top of leading class, 32; residence, 33, 40, 50, 88, 189, 238 (*illus.:* pl. 14); organization of yard, layout of houses, 35 ff., 68; taste in building, 37, 40, 45; his church and rectory, 42, 53; death, 73; position in relation to founders, 165; land purchases, 168; responsible for layout of town? 170; salary, 170, 189; diary, 176; wealth, 40, 189; as architect, 190; opposition to public spending, 200, 205; designs by, 237, 238, 240, 241, 248; *illus.:* pl. 9, 10, 13, 14, 16, 25, 32, 74

Boott Mills, 46, 77, 101, 149, 211

Boston capitalists, 160, 162

Boston, churches, 43

Boston Manufacturing Company, 12, 30, 159, 160, 168, 170, 180; capital, 14; established, 18 f., 21; finances, 18, 45 f.;